"Through *Calming the Storm*, Fr. Gerald Murray, in an extraordinary and excellent manner, manifests his priestly character and exercises the pastoral charity which is the form of priestly spirituality. In the context of the history of his own lifelong relationship with Christ, which began at the moment of his baptism, Fr. Murray shows us the way to navigate, with Christ, the exceedingly troubled waters in which the world and the Church find themselves today. From his conversations with Diane Montagna, it is clear that Christ is the center of his life and that he desires only to put his considerable talents, especially for profound, clear, and concise reflection and communication, at the service of Christ and His Mystical Body, the Church. In the same way, with true fatherly affection and firmness, Fr. Murray unequivocally urges us to keep Christ at the center of our lives. He reassures us that Christ is with us, above all in the Barque of St. Peter, and that, if we remain faithful in love of Him, He will calm the stormy waters which would otherwise envelope and drown us. We owe a debt of deepest gratitude to Fr. Murray and Diane Montagna for the labor of their love of Christ and of His Church, which has brought into our hands the great gift of *Calming the Storm*."

—**Raymond Leo Cardinal Burke,
Former Prefect of the Apostolic Signatura**

"Fr. Gerald Murray, in a theologically profound and spiritually rich dialogue with Vatican journalist Diane Montagna, speaks his mind freely on the crises in the Church and the world that shake the faith of many people. He sets forth the fundamental teachings of the Church with clarity and precision, as he does so well on EWTN's *The World Over*.

He points us back to the need for complete fidelity to the Lord, who alone calms the storms. For the Son of God Himself assures us that His Church, built upon rock, cannot be overpowered by anyone, even till the end of the world."
—*Gerhard Cardinal Müller, Former Prefect of the Congregation for the Doctrine of the Faith*

"Fr. Gerald E. Murray, parish priest, canon lawyer, and frequent media commentator on religious topics, addresses the difficulties and challenges facing the Catholic Church today in *Calming the Storm*. He encourages us to look to Christ, as did the Apostles when they feared that their boat would be swamped by the stormy winds and waves on the Sea of Galilee. His clearly reasoned defense of Catholic teaching and his encouragement to pursue greater holiness in our daily lives guide us in finding and following the sure path of fidelity to the Lord in his Church."
—*Robert Cardinal Sarah, Former Prefect of the Congregation for Divine Worship and the Discipline of the Sacraments, Archbishop Emeritus of Conakry (Guinea)*

"With precision and candor, Fr. Gerald Murray lays bare the challenges facing the Church at this turning point in her history. He faces into the storm with bold Christian confidence, knowing that Our Lord will never permit His beleaguered vessel to be overthrown, and he invites and inspires the same confidence in us."
—*Bishop Athanasius Schneider, Auxiliary Bishop of the Archdiocese of Saint Mary in Astana, Kazakhstan*

"Straight answers to difficult questions in the Catholic Church are in short supply these days. Fortunately, we have my fellow 'Papal Posse' member, Fr. Gerald Murray, and his new book to lead us through the confusion and bickering to the eternal truths. If you want to know what the Church truly teaches, look no further."

—*Raymond Arroyo,* **New York Times Bestselling Author, Fox News Analyst, Host of EWTN's The World Over**

"This interview with Fr. Murray provides a glimpse into the complex simplicity of what Catholic clerics call a 'priest's priest.' The passages about his formation—from early years in the family, through schooling, and then into the priesthood—explain how, based on the foundation of his native intellect, Fr. Murray is so able to speak to thorny current issues in the Church and the world with clarity of thought informed by charity in truth. In our volatile and shifting times, this volume could provide young men with inspiration to make good life choices and to develop a rule of life for their vocations as well as strengthening anyone who has become disoriented and discouraged by news of current events."

—*Fr. John Zuhlsdorf,* **Columnist and Blogger**

"Fr. Gerald Murray is a clear trumpet during a time of cacophony and confusion, a herald courageously crying out in the desert to make straight the Lord's way. This book is the fruit of forty years of prayerful reflection on modern challenges through the eyes of faith and the heart of an incisive and experienced pastor. *Calming the Storm* will inspire you, help you see more clearly, motivate you to action, and equip you, like Fr. Murray, to be able always, even in the storm, to give a reason for the hope Christians bear within."

—*Fr. Roger J. Landry, Author of*
**Plan of Life: Habits to Help You Grow Closer to God**

"Fr. Murray takes on the tough Catholic and cultural questions of the day with his typical New York clarity—but always with charity. A must-read for every committed Catholic and those who would like to be one."

—*Doug Keck, President and Chief Operating Officer of EWTN, Host of* **EWTN Bookmark**

"Fr. Gerald Murray's words arrive like manna from heaven: Grace-filled nourishment for Catholics starving for the truth!"

—*Maria M. Maffucci, Editor in Chief of the* **Human Life Review**

# CALMING *the* STORM

# CALMING
# *the* STORM

**Navigating the Crises Facing the
Catholic Church and Society**

FR. GERALD E. MURRAY
*in conversation with* DIANE MONTAGNA

Steubenville, Ohio
www.emmausroad.org

Emmaus Road Publishing
1468 Parkview Circle
Steubenville, Ohio 43952

©2022 Gerald E. Murray and Diane Montagna
All rights reserved. Published 2022
Printed in the United States of America

Library of Congress Control Number 2021950421
ISBN 978-1-64585-192-9 (hardcover)
978-1-64585-194-3 (ebook)

Unless otherwise noted, Scripture quotations are taken from The Revised Standard Version Second Catholic Edition (Ignatius Edition) Copyright © 2006 by the Division of Christian Education of the National Council of the Churches of Christ in the United States of America. Used by permission. All rights reserved.

Excerpts from the Catechism of the Catholic Church, second edition, copyright © 2000, Libreria Editrice Vaticana—United States Conference of Catholic Bishops, Washington, DC. Noted as "CCC" in the text.

Cover design and layout by Allison Merrick
Cover image by Simon Hurry

*To the memory of my father*

I HAVE SAID THIS TO YOU, THAT IN ME
YOU MAY HAVE PEACE. IN THE WORLD
YOU HAVE TRIBULATION; BUT BE OF GOOD CHEER,
I HAVE OVERCOME THE WORLD.
JOHN 16:33

# CONTENTS

| | |
|---|---:|
| INTRODUCTION | 1 |
| *Chapter 1*: CHAMPION OF THE GOSPEL | 9 |
| *Chapter 2*: AGE OF CONFUSION | 79 |
| *Chapter 3*: CROOKS AND HIRELINGS | 147 |
| *Chapter 4*: WINDS OF REVOLUTION | 229 |
| *Chapter 5*: STANDING UP FOR TRUTH IN A HOSTILE CULTURE | 315 |
| *Chapter 6*: TRUST AMID THE TUMULT | 393 |
| *Chapter 7*: AWAKENING CHRIST | 423 |

# INTRODUCTION

Fr. Gerald Murray has become a familiar and reassuring voice for many Catholics amid the tumult and confusion of the present age, both within and without the frontiers of the Church. Now, for the first time, he has provided us with a book-length reflection on these turbulent times, taking as his starting point the Lord's calming of the storm on the Sea of Galilee.

Fr. Murray was born into a devout Irish-American family in New York City in 1959, on the feast of St. Philip Neri. His parents were both lawyers and met in law school. Fr. Murray's mother, who put her legal career on hold to raise their three children, made sure the Catholic Faith was lived and explained at home, and she taught her children to strive for excellence in all they did. His late father, a missal-carrying Catholic and conservative in the mold of the *National Review,* had a pivotal influence on Fr. Murray's religious and intellectual formation, introducing him to the works of literary giants such as G. K. Chesterton and St. John Henry Cardinal Newman. Educated at Regis High School, a private Jesuit boys academy on the Upper East Side of Manhattan, and then at Dartmouth College, Fr. Murray entered St. Joseph's Seminary (Dunwoodie) in 1980 and was ordained at St. Patrick's Cathedral in New York City on December 1, 1984. After serving at a Spanish-speaking parish in the South Bronx, a Hispanic parish in northern Manhattan, and then at St. Patrick's Cathedral, he was sent to Rome where he earned a doctorate in canon law at the Pontifical Gregorian University.

Returning to New York after his studies in Rome, Fr. Murray spent only a few months as a canonist on the Archdiocesan marriage tribunal, as he was unwilling to compromise and rubber stamp annulments. The Archbishop of New York at that time, John Cardinal O'Connor, nevertheless made full use of his new canonist's extensive language abilities (Spanish, French, Italian, Portuguese, and Latin), assigning him to a predominantly African French-speaking parish on Manhattan's West Side. In 2012 Timothy Cardinal Dolan assigned him to the United Nations Parish, the Church of the Holy Family, on the East Side of Manhattan, where he continues to serve today.

Turbulence and transformation have characterized key moments in Fr. Murray's life. Raised in the shadow of the Vietnam War, he entered seminary at the dawn of Pope St. John Paul II's renewal of the post-Conciliar Church and began his priestly ministry as the assistant of a refugee priest from Communist Cuba. His doctoral studies took place at the apogee of the pontificate of the Polish Pope in the wake of the new *Code of Canon Law*.

Fr. Murray's purpose in undertaking these interviews is to help the reader navigate the uncharted and increasingly stormy waters, both in the Church and in society, by keeping the eye of the soul fixed serenely on Christ.

# INTRODUCTION

The text of the present work is drawn from several interviews. The first took place at the Church of the Holy Family in Manhattan over several days in early September 2020 amid the COVID-19 crisis. The remainder were conducted via video calls between New York and Rome. Fr. Murray then carefully reviewed the manuscript and refined and amended his responses.

The present work is divided into seven chapters. In Chapter 1, I discuss with Fr. Murray his life and vocation. In Chapter 2, we explore why we are in an age of confusion, and what is at the core of the disunity not only between the Church and the world but between different factions in the Church as well. In Chapter 3, we discuss what to do when prominent pastors or those in authority are making headlines by teaching against the Faith. In Chapter 4, we consider the right response when there is pressure from within to change Church Tradition. In Chapter 5, we consider how best to stand up for truth in a hostile culture. In Chapter 6, we ask how the laity can follow Christ and trust that the Church is his instrument when there seems to be so much in-fighting within the Church. Finally, in Chapter 7, we look at what the laity specifically can do to assist the Church in a time of crisis.

It is hard not to be struck by Fr. Murray's single-minded devotion to the Lord, his knowledge of the Faith, his concern for souls, his wholesome demeanor, his frankness, and his realism. He personifies so much of the best of Catholic priestly life. He also has a great appreciation for the military through serving as a US Navy chaplain, and so it is especially appropriate that the title of this book is inspired by the Gospel account of the "Calming of the Storm" taken from St. Matthew's Gospel (8:23–27).

Fr. Murray has served as a frequent guest on Fox News since the pontificate of John Paul II. In 2013, during the conclave that elected Pope Francis, Fr. Murray became a member of EWTN's "Conclave Crew" and then of the "Papal Posse" on *The World Over with Raymond Arroyo*. Since then, he has become known as a solid, reliable, and authoritative commentator on Church affairs and has distinguished himself for his courage and calm in providing commentary and criticism for all those perplexed by the disturbing upheavals that have become routine in recent years.

The citizens of New York City are famously distinguished by their directness in sharing views solicited and unsolicited, but also by their kindness and solidarity in the face of adversity. The reader will agree that these characteristics are present in abundance in the insight, counsel and comfort afforded by an outstanding pastor and scholar in the pages that follow.

There are several people whose invaluable assistance I wish to acknowledge. First, I want to thank Edward Pentin, without whose help, journalistic expertise, and tireless work covering the Vatican this book would not have been possible. Secondly, I wish to thank Scott Hahn and all the team at Emmaus Road Publishing for their professionalism and commitment to publishing *Calming the Storm*. And last but not least, I wish to express my gratitude to several friends for their advice and plentiful insights, including Roger McCaffrey, Fr. Ezra Sullivan, OP, and Alan Fimister.

*Diane Montagna*
August 14, 2021
Feast of St. Maximilian Kolbe
Vigil of the Assumption of the Blessed Virgin Mary

And when he got into the boat,
his disciples followed him.
And behold, there arose a great storm on the sea,
so that the boat was being swamped by the waves;
but he was asleep.
And they went and woke him, saying,
"Save us, Lord; we are perishing."
And he said to them,
"Why are you afraid, O men of little faith?"
Then he rose and rebuked the winds and the sea;
and there was a great calm.
And the men marveled, saying,
"What sort of man is this,
that even the winds and sea obey him?"
Matthew 8:23–27

*Chapter 1*

# CHAMPION OF THE GOSPEL

"And when he got into the boat, his disciples followed him." (Matt 8:23)

**Fr. Murray, as a Catholic priest whose discipleship has been forged through the turbulence of the past fifty-five years in both the Church and society, you've become regarded as a "champion of the Gospel"—as St. John Chrysostom called the disciples in his commentary on St. Matthew's account of the calming of the storm.[1] How did it all start? Where and when were you born?**

I was born in Brooklyn, New York, on May 26, 1959.

---

[1] St. John Chrysostom, *Homilies on Matthew*, Homily 28 on Matthew 8:23–24, in *Ancient Christian Commentary on Scripture, New Testament,* ed. Manlio Simonetti, vol. 1a, *Matthew 1–13* (Downers Grove, IL: InterVarsity Press, 2001), 168.

> He took the disciples with him, not for nothing and not merely to face an absurd hazard but in order to permit them to witness the miracle that was to take place on the sea. For like a superb trainer, he was gradually coaching and fitting them for endurance. He had two objectives in mind. He wanted

***The Feast of St. Philip Neri.***
Yes, a happy saint to have as your patron. My mom, Mary Jane Moyles, is from Brooklyn; my dad, Gerald E. Murray, was from Hoboken, New Jersey. They met in law school, and after they married in 1958, they moved to Brooklyn, and that's where I was born.

***Can you say a little bit more about how your parents met?***
My dad was awarded a scholarship to Regis High School, which is one of the top Jesuit high schools—and top high schools—in the country. It's located on the Upper East Side of Manhattan. After four years at Regis, he won a scholarship to St. Peter's College in Jersey City, New Jersey, another Jesuit school.

***Did he receive a traditional Jesuit education?***
Yes, and he said that in college they received the same education that Jesuit scholastics received, so they studied philosophy and theology. I've seen his textbooks and it was all very serious and Thomistically-oriented. It was a very good education. He graduated from high school in 1949 and college in 1953.

***A decade before the Second Vatican Council . . .***
It was a decade before, and a different time in the life of the

> to teach them to remain undismayed amid dangers and modest in honors. So, to prevent them from thinking too much of themselves, having sent away the multitude, he kept them near him but permitted them to be tossed with a tempest. By doing so he disciplined them to bear trials patiently. His former miracles were indeed great, but this one contained a unique kind of discipline of exceptional importance. For it was a sign akin to that of old. To do this, he took his disciples with him by himself. He permitted others to see his other miracles, but when trials and terrors were rising, he took with him none but those he was training to be champions of the gospel.

Church and in the Society of Jesus, certainly. My dad was drafted into the US Army and served a year and a half in Korea following the truce being declared. He was part of the American contingent in South Korea and was not involved in combat. But while he was in Korea, he went to Japan where he took the Law School Admissions Test (LSAT)—the exam to get into law school—and then he enrolled in Fordham Law School. In 1955 he started at Fordham Law.

**Also a Jesuit school.**
Yes, and it was there that he met my mom. She was born in Brooklyn, New York and went to parochial school. Then she went to the Convent of the Sacred Heart in Greenwich, Connecticut. Then she went to Newton College of the Sacred Heart in Newton, Massachusetts. Upon graduation, she went to Fordham Law.

**A woman ahead of her time.**
Well, the interesting thing was that her mother was a lawyer. My mom's family is very interesting. My grandfather, whom I never knew because he died in 1942, had been a seminarian at the North American College in Rome in the early 1920s. He did one year there and decided he didn't have a priestly vocation. So, he came back to America, completed his college education, then went to Brooklyn Law School, as did my grandmother. They married, but my grandmother did not practice law at first but raised the family. My mother has four brothers, so my grandmother raised five kids.

**Four boys and one girl . . .**
Yes, Mom could hold her own. Sadly, her father died of cancer when she was eight years old. My grandmother told my mom, "You need to have a career in case one day something happens to your husband." So, she went to Fordham Law.

**How many women were enrolled at the time?**
She was one of two women to graduate in her class. The other was Geraldine Ferraro, the eventual 1984 vice-presidential candidate of the Democratic Party. She and my mother were in different sections, so they didn't see one another much. Back in the old days, students were seated alphabetically. Mom's maiden name was "Moyles"; Dad's was "Murray," so Dad was the lucky one to be sitting next to the only female in that section. Jesuits were traditionally great educators, and, in this case, they were great matchmakers.

**Did they strike up a friendship right away?**
Yes, pretty much so. My dad was very enthralled with my mom. He was a high school basketball player. He played on the 1948 undefeated Regis High School team. He then worked as a high school coach while attending college, and then he did various jobs as a law student to make some money. They became very close, and then he proposed, and they got married.

**And both of your parents came from devout Catholic families?**
They both came from devout, practicing families. On my dad's side, two of his cousins became diocesan priests, a third cousin was a Jesuit. My mother also had two cousins who became priests. Those were the days when there was a united purpose

in the Church, the idea being that we're going to educate young Catholic men and women to be contributors to society and to the life of the Church. They very much had a formation in which love for the Church and being well-educated compelled them to live their faith in the proper sense. They realized that faith is not just an attachment to a lifestyle; it was the motivating factor of all that they did. On Sundays we always got dressed up and went to Mass and sat together as a family. I went to Catholic grammar school, as did my two sisters.

*How many siblings do you have?*
I have two sisters. I am the first, then comes my sister Margot who sadly died in 1993 following unsuccessful brain surgery. She and her husband Chris had one daughter, my niece Mary Kate. My other sister Mary Jane, who is four years younger, lives in New England. She and her husband Glenn have four children: Andrew, Tyler, Margot, and Teddy.

*Are you 100 percent Irish?*
I'm 98 percent Irish according to Ancestry.com. My grandparents' surnames were McGrath, Murray, Moyles and Keenan: all Irish-Americans. The Murrays go way back and left Ireland for America sometime in the 1840–1850s.

*You've said that Catholicism was the heart of your parents' life, and elsewhere talked about the first time as a boy you realized your father went to daily Mass. Can you say more about that?*
Yes, we lived in an apartment in Brooklyn Heights until I finished second grade. I must have been in first or second grade,

and I remember Dad coming home one night—he worked as a lawyer on Wall Street—and he mentioned that, before going to work that day, he'd been to daily Mass. I was stunned. I said, "Dad, you only have to go on Sunday." Typical kid attitude: "If I'm told to do it once, why would I do it twice?" And he said, "Well, I like to go to Mass." That opened my eyes to see that religion is not simply a matter of obligation and goes beyond a sense of fulfilling a duty; it involves putting love into doing more—more prayer and receiving Communion more frequently. That inspired me and, as I grew up, I realized that one of the great things that these Jesuit and other Catholic colleges did was to inspire a commitment to daily Mass among the students.

My dad was one of those missal-carrying Catholics before the Council, and the pages and cover of his missal were very worn. It was a lesson for me. His life of piety and devotion was serious.

**What do you remember about your First Holy Communion?**
I made my First Holy Communion when I was in first grade, so that would have been May 1966. The practice of the school I attended, St. Angela Hall, was for students to receive their First Communion in first rather than second grade. It was a source of joy. In the picture I have, the altar was facing East. As any kid would, I remember what I was wearing: a white suit with Bermuda shorts and long white socks and white shoes. I remember my mom taking me to the store to buy this special clothing.

That day made a great impression on me. We had wonderful Ursuline Sisters teaching us.

***Does any sister stand out in your memory?***
My second-grade teacher was a young sister. She inspired me. She always told us, "Children, you can do much more than you think. You can go beyond limits and accomplish a lot." There was an annual school fair that included athletic competitions, like a three-legged race and other things. Sister said, "We're going to practice for this race so that you kids can win!" And it worked: we did much better than the others. She was an inspiration because of her positive reinforcement combined with her insistence on practice. She didn't just say, "You guys are great and here's your trophy." No, she said, "You've got to work hard and practice, and we're going to help you practice." I remember her, and I also remember the sisters explaining the Mass and Holy Communion and Heaven to us. They made it easy for us to understand the joy and happiness of Heaven.

***Would the Mass at your First Holy Communion have been the Old Mass or the New Mass?***
That I don't remember. It was 1966, so I think they already had what we would now call the "transitional" vernacular Mass, that is, the Roman Missal with some parts in English and some changes made. I do know that, when I became an altar boy in third grade, we still had the old "Prayers at the Foot of the Altar," but in English. It was the old Missal but in English.

***Interesting . . . they should have stopped there.***
Yes, that's what the German liturgist Msgr. Klaus Gamber said, that the reform implemented in the immediate aftermath of the Council was sufficient to satisfy the will of the Council Fathers. But then it changed, the New Mass was implemented, and they

dropped the Prayers at the Foot of the Altar. The altar boys had less to do; I remember that.

**Is it true that your father had a great influence on developing the way you think about the challenges both in the Church and in society?**
Yes, my dad was very well-trained by the Jesuits in high school and college. He was a clear thinker who believed in the Aristotelian-Thomistic understanding of creation and the world. He firmly believed in the intelligibility of the universe. He was a *National Review* conservative from the 1950s, so he was very aware of the challenge that Communism posed, not simply militarily but ideologically. He inspired me—and all of us, my sisters too—to be independent thinkers, not to simply go along with what was happening. He displayed that in the way he analyzed things, and as Mom was also a lawyer, at the dinner table if we got into a debate, you had to really defend your position. But it had to be based not simply on, "Well, that's what I think" or "I want it to be that way." You had to show why it was logically consistent, or reasonable, or necessary.

**Not your typical family dinner conversation. What is your earliest recollection of this?**
I grew up during the Vietnam War, and I do remember as a little child—maybe at six or seven years old—my parents watching the news, and there were pictures of the fighting in Vietnam, and the casualty figures would come up. Unfortunately, part of the American government's view on promoting morale among civilians was to say that we always killed more of the North Vietnamese and the Viet Cong than they killed of our soldiers.

As a little kid, you say, "Oh good, the Americans are winning." But then I remember thinking, "My goodness, there are a lot of problems in the world."

I also remember going to visit my grandfather, my dad's father, and one or two of my uncles were still living with him—they hadn't married. There was a *Time Life*-style book on the Second World War there, and I remember looking through the pictures, so as a kid, I was formed to think realistically about the world, that there is evil in the world, that evil has to be met and can't be appeased, and about the value of courage and bravery. My dad served in the Army; my mom and dad's brothers also served. In those days there was a draft, so everyone served. We were very conscious of the value of the American military and of the necessity of fighting Communism.

In addition to reading *National Review*, my dad was a subscriber to the Conservative Book Club founded by Neil McCaffrey, who was part of *National Review* in the early days of the magazine. The Conservative Book Club was founded along with something called Arlington House, which was a publishing arm because not all conservative writers could find publishers. Post-Reagan, it's hard to understand this. The American conservative movement before the election of Ronald Reagan was an insurgency that couldn't count on the ability to circulate its ideas in a wide fashion through existing institutions. *The Wall Street Journal* was always conservative, but most of the other press was hostile to conservative views.

**This is likely surprising for younger people today . . .**
It was not as easy as it is now. Arlington House published a lot of authors, some of whom remain well-known in the conservative

world. In the world of media, William F. Buckley, Jr. had *Firing Line* on Channel 13 (PBS), and you occasionally had some conservative commentators on other networks, but there was no Fox News. It was nothing like what we have now; it was a different world.

**So, your father was very much a part of this movement . . .**
Yes, he was. Dad was very much a realist, but he had confidence that the Aristotelean-Thomistic view of the world was not simply an interpretation but was, in fact, an understanding of reality, the truth of which is confirmed when you go against it. When you don't respect the nature of man or creation, you produce chaos. He understood that birth control is a perfect example of this, and that it has led to the reduction of the number of children, and an increase in unhappiness, infidelity, abortion, sex-selective abortion (because people only want "designer babies"), promiscuity, the homosexual lifestyle (because sex is no longer connected to its natural purpose), and cohabitation (because sex is not about commitment and progeny, committed fruitful love between a man and woman). And where does this absurdity go? Anywhere you want.

**Can you say a bit more about your father's particular love for the law?**
Yes, that's interesting because lawyers—as I learned from my dad—spend a lot of time reading and writing. He would frequently take work home, so on Saturday afternoons he would be listening to the weekly broadcast of the Metropolitan Opera and correct either things he had written, or documents other lawyers had written for him. He became a very good

editor and he used to edit my high school assignments; he was very happy to do it.

Once I asked him, "Dad, do you really like being a lawyer?" He said, "I've never had a bad day in the practice of the law." He loved it, and of course part of this was his basic confidence that the American legal system is just; that it is not arbitrary. That's an inheritance we received from English Common Law.

Then there is the experience in America that justice is administered according to rules that were set previously, so it's not adapted in order to accomplish an end. Legislators can change laws, but that should be a serious process which is based on deliberation.

**Law can become a vehicle for injustice . . .**
My dad would make the distinction between law and justice. If you said to him, "We want to fight for justice," he'd say, "You want to fight to uphold just laws, because the definition of justice is debatable while just laws are set forth plainly in writing." The goal is to say, "We enact just laws based on deliberation by our elected representatives, and they are obviously subject to US Constitutional constraints. They have to be in agreement with, and not in denial of, the founding document of the country. And they must always be in harmony with the natural law, given by God."

Law is an inheritance over time, so certain valuable inherited legal principles and maxims or ways of doing things have an origin or reasoning that may not be immediately evident to the people at the time.

*Can you give an example?*

One example would be statutes of limitation, which now have been set aside in the case of the sexual abuse of minors. The statute of limitations is a convention; it's not a natural law principle. After ten years, say, a crime cannot be prosecuted. There's no principle of natural law that says that, but there are principles that include reliability of witnesses, questions on why they were waiting to make the accusation against the person, the ability to recollect past events, possible destruction of physical evidence, and all the rest. People who are offended and have crimes committed against them deserve a hearing, but when it comes to civil matters, you don't have an endless time frame in which to bring somebody to court, according to the way statutes of limitations are written. They can be exempted, and I think it's a good thing they were exempted with sex abuse cases because the fact of the matter is, when figures of parental authority like priests or coaches committed these crimes upon minors, they often did it with the knowledge that they had scared the victims into silence, and the victims felt helpless and were told, "Tell no one. No one is going to believe you. I'll destroy you. Bad things will happen to you or your family." Remember that the victims were children or minors. It's not very generous to have a statute of limitations that says once you get to the age of eighteen you have only five years to file a criminal complaint or a lawsuit.

Those are the kinds of things you can debate. But this is one example of saying, "The law is one thing, but what's just? Let's debate it, and then let's write a new law if we think we should."

***What is the relation of law both to divine law and to human law?***
Laws are rules governing behavior, external actions, so as to uphold a just social order. The reason laws are necessary is because of the fallen state of man. In the Garden of Eden, before the Fall, there was no need for law . . .

***Except "Do not eat of the fruit of the tree . . ." (Gen 3:3).***
Yes, God issued the command to Adam and Eve not to do wrong. They failed the test.

There is a natural inclination in man, because of original sin, to do wrong. How do we constrain that? One of the ways is to establish clear rules for behavior and rules for sanctioning misbehavior. Law exists as a reflection of divine law. God's purpose and order, as communicated to man through the natural order, is then distilled into written laws that are then promulgated, made known to the community, and then people have to abide by them. They are based on the natural order that is in creation. That natural order is discernible, but it takes wisdom and reflection to properly discern and understand what it means.

The example of laws against incest is a perfect example. What is the purpose of the human sexual-reproductive faculty? What is the nature of kinship? What is the scientific understanding of disease and where does that come from? These things are discoverable, and the conscience is naturally inclined to make judgments about these things. Conscience, when it's not deformed, will rejoice in seeing good laws obeyed and will be horrified in seeing good laws disobeyed and the results that follow.

Regarding the relationship between divine law and

human law: human law has to be subject to divine law in the sense that it has to be in conformity with it. But not everything that derives from divine law become a subject or matter of positive human law, in the sense that it's not really a matter for the State to write a law saying you have to worship God by going to Mass on Sunday or face legal sanctions. The competence of the State is not the salvation of souls directly. On the other hand, society does owe to God a debt of obedience. Everything created is subject to the Creator, but it's not been given to the State to directly administer certain things that are given to the Church. And this is why, in our country, it is good that we have freedom of religion, so that the Church can teach and govern herself according to its mandate from God. It's not a mandate given to it by the State; the State has no role in that. When the State arrogates to itself things that are the subject of the Church's authority, it's an injustice, and we fight it.

The Ten Commandments don't become obligatory only when you're baptized. They are obligatory on all mankind (see Rom. 2:14–16). They are not necessarily recognized by people before they embrace the Faith, but they are generally known. And that's actually the role of culture: to form people in a mindset in which the obligations of the creature are understood and the fulfillment of those obligations is fostered. That's why it's good that society attempt to organize itself in a way that allows people to discharge religious duties with the greatest amount of freedom. Now, that freedom is constrained by the fact that those religious duties have to be fulfilled properly—so we don't permit child sacrifice, even if someone claimed, "My religion tells me that I can kill children to please God."

*Or Satanism . . .*

Yes, by definition Satanism is not a religion because it doesn't involve the worship of the deity. It's a spiritual deformation. The calming of the storm is an apt symbolism that God exercises authority over his world independently of our even recognizing it. The Apostles cried out, and the Lord calmed the storm. It was a sign of his divine power and authority. But also, it shows that where God's intervention is sought, there is social harmony and peace. These are fostered much better where God's will is recognized and obeyed.

*Returning to your upbringing, I understand that your father had an extensive library and was a great lover of G. K. Chesterton and St. John Henry Cardinal Newman. Did he guide your reading growing up, and what specific books were formative?*

Yes, he did, particularly during my high school years. As a kid, I read the *Hardy Boys* and Jules Verne novels and things like that, but I particularly liked history. It was my major in college. I liked literature and languages, which my parents encouraged by sending me to France one summer as a high school student to learn French. Then in college I learned Spanish, and Italian when I went to Rome to study canon law, and I had learned Latin with the Jesuits.

*And Portuguese . . .*

Yes, I learned it in high school. I did the three years of Latin, and in the fourth year I could do whatever I wanted. Our Spanish teacher was married to a Brazilian woman, and he taught a course in introductory Portuguese. That was great, and when

I was in seminary, I spent two months in Fatima, Portugal, working at the information office to practice Portuguese.

**You have a real love of languages . . .**
I do. I only regret not having learned German.

I always liked history, and my dad encouraged me to read *Witness* by Whittaker Chambers. He said it was the greatest autobiography of the twentieth century. I read it and agreed with him.

**Can you say a bit more about it?**
Whittaker Chambers (1901–1961) was an interesting man. He was raised on Long Island, New York. His father was a literary man who was also a designer for magazines. His mother raised him and his brother, Richard, in Lynbrook. Their father was largely absent from the mother—it was not a very happy marriage. Chambers was very smart and enrolled in Columbia University. He came under the influence of Communists and joined the Communist Party. He went to work for *The Daily Worker* newspaper and was recruited to become a Communist spy and spied on the United States. The Stalinist "purges" were underway, and he was not happy with the way the Communists were acting. He married Esther Shemitz, a woman he'd met through the Communist Party, and they had two children. He left the Communist Party and fled from New York to Florida. It was a dramatic scene. He knew that he was likely to be subject to assassination by a Communist spy, so he fled from his house in the middle of the night, went undercover for a time, and eventually remerged and worked as an editor and writer at *Time Magazine*. Chambers played a great part in helping America to understand the true nature of Communism because he did so

not simply from a strategic or military perspective, but from his knowledge of the ideology of Communism and what it meant as a threat to American society.

### Did he ever convert to Christianity?

Yes, he was baptized as an Episcopalian and was influenced by Quakerism and was friendly with one or more priests but never became a Catholic. Chambers was very close to William F. Buckley, Jr. and members of the *National Review* circle. He became an editor at *National Review* for a short time, but his health was not good, and he died at the age of sixty.

Chambers' greatest claim to fame, which is the centerpiece of the book, is that he had kept evidence of his spying activity, and one of the spies he had worked with was Alger Hiss (1904–1996), who was assisted by his wife, Priscilla. Hiss, a federal employee, would purloin government documents, copy them, and pass them onto the Soviets; Chambers was involved in all of this. Alger Hiss rose to prominence in the Roosevelt and Truman administrations. Whittaker Chambers accused him publicly of being a Soviet spy. Hiss denied it, but the drama of what transpired, including hearings before the House Un-American Activities Committee (HUAC), gripped the nation. Chambers was summoned as a witness. Hiss was summoned. They confronted each other. In the book, Chambers described in great detail the nature of their working relationship. Hiss tried to deny they knew each other and lied about what they did.

It's a great book. The opening chapter is titled, "A letter to my children." Chambers takes a pessimistic view of the West in its confrontation with Communism. Even though we beat the Soviet Union in the Cold War, on a cultural level the Left's view of the world is largely triumphant, and the Antifa-Black Lives Matter ideology that we're facing is pure Communism: there is no objective truth; lying and stealing on behalf of the ideology and the Party are good; Western civilization has to be torn down; man must be remade in the image of "X," whatever they determine that to be.

Chambers is a heroic figure, and the book *Witness* is great. I recommend it. It's an American story because this involved people working for an evil Soviet government yet trying to pretend to be living as normal American citizens—Alger and Priscilla Hiss, Whittaker and Esther Chambers—and Chambers said, "No. I'm not going to do this anymore." There's a famous line in the book, when Chambers was questioned about informing, and he said: "It is an obligation to inform," meaning it's an obligation to bring to the attention of the government subversives who are working for the government. In the history of the Communist Party in the United States, Chambers is one of the most fascinating figures.

**What other books did your father have you read?**
I remember reading G. K. Chesterton's *Orthodoxy* and the *Father Brown* novels—those were great. Chesterton said that in order to make a point you don't always have to hit people over the head with it. In other words, you could teach about morality and order and human foibles and divine solutions through characters such as the detective Fr. Brown. I read a lot of Chesterton. I also read a lot of William F. Buckley's books. My father also had a book in his library called *Our Vietnam Nightmare*, by Marguerite Higgins. She was a female journalist in the Second World War, the Korean War, and the Vietnam

War, and there were very few female war correspondents then. She was among the first journalists to enter the Nazi concentration camp Dachau upon its liberation by the American Army. She was a pioneer female journalist and was a good person. She had been in Communist circles in California as a young college student but rejected Communism. In college, I started reading Cardinal Newman.

**Before we move on to your university years, can you say a word about the life lessons you learned growing up in the Murray home?**
Here's one you'll like: "Eat at your home dining room table as if you were a guest so that when you go to someone's house, you'll know exactly what to do." So, manners and politeness were important in our home. My family was also big on working for your own money, through babysitting or having a newspaper route or caddying at a golf club. When I was in college, I worked summers as a clerk in a law office to learn about the law but also to earn spending money. We learned to save money, and not to spend it all once we earned it.

**What other life lessons did you learn at home?**
Respect girls and be polite. My father was very much a gentleman. He knew how to smile and not get into an argument when it wasn't worth it. He knew how to tell a joke and used to say that timing was everything. He was an athlete and encouraged sports for us kids. And he liked to read.

*How did your family spend Sundays?*
On Sunday, we would get dressed up and go to Mass together. After Mass, Dad often stopped at the bakery to buy doughnuts, and then we'd have a big brunch with bacon and eggs. That was considered a big deal—and it was. It was a way to keep holy the Lord's Day in the family.

One of the people I'd see at Mass on Sundays was the philosopher Dietrich von Hildebrand. He and his wife Alice were members of our parish. At the time, of course, I didn't know who Dietrich von Hildebrand was. He had long white hair and was very much an artist. Lyman and Madeleine Stebbins also belonged to our parish. He founded Catholics United for the Faith (CUF), a lay apostolate to support, defend, and advance the efforts of the teaching Church, and he became a big influence on me in college.

*And your parents had a good marriage?*
They had a wonderful marriage. They were married in 1958 at St. Patrick's Cathedral. I was ordained a priest at the Cathedral, so St. Patrick's has special meaning for my family. When my parents married, my mother decided to forgo practicing as an attorney in order to raise the children. She had gotten her law degree and passed the bar exam but did not then seek a job as a lawyer and raised us three kids.

*Had she planned on that before she and your father married?*
Yes. My mother was a serious Catholic, she went to schools run by the Religious of the Sacred Heart of Jesus, of course before the Second Vatican Council. At the time, the order was thriving, and had many vocations. The Society had been founded in France at the time of the French Revolution by St. Madeleine

Sophie Barat (1779–1865). They were very good educators of women. Their education was grounded in forming future wives and mothers who would be capable of explaining the Faith and would also be knowledgeable leaders within their families and communities. My mother met wonderful women in high school and college who were lifelong friends.

Catholicism was well-explained and lived in our home. She was not happy after the Council that many of the Sacred Heart Sisters abandoned teaching, and the order is unfortunately in complete free-fall.

Part of the crisis that the Council and its implementation precipitated in the life of the Church was the questioning of past practice and belief. When you say "getting up to date"—*aggiornamento*—is a principle of operation, it really means, "You've got to get with it." And the measure of "getting with it" is set by the standards of the popular culture. In the religious world, it became the standard of Christianity acceptable to the world, which in the United States was liberal Protestantism, and that remains to this day the standard by which the German hierarchy, for example, is trying to steer the Church in a way that has nothing to do with Catholicism but is an imitation of liberal Protestant ideas.

So, in one sense, the sisters were victims of the dynamic the Council set in motion, which is this questioning of the past coupled with a naïve confidence that innovation and change were going to produce true Christian holiness and Christian flourishing. In fact, the changing of the rules turned into a rejection of all rules, and the questioning of tradition became an embrace of fads. The Sacred Heart Sisters left behind their religious habit. They found it to be too old-fashioned and constraining. But then they became indistinguishable and unrecognizable as an organization working together under the inspiration of St. Madeleine Sophie. The next thing was getting out of the classroom.

**They lost their identity . . .**
They lost their identity and began pursuing a new set of ideas of where they thought the Church is going. So it became social work and things of that sort, which are valuable—we need social workers and we need people to help immigrants and all the rest—but the sisters forgot that by training young Catholic women in the Faith and knowledge and science, they (not the sisters) could go out and do that work. They could become the hands of the Church in dealing with the poor and the immigrant and the needy.

**Teaching is also an enduring charism. There are always going to be young women who will become wives and mothers . . .**
Yes. Chesterton loved paradoxes. He once said that the most confining experiences can be the most liberating. So, the contemplative nun in her cell has the greatest freedom in the world interiorly, and her presence there inspires lay people and others, including priests, to do their jobs well, knowing that someone is praying for them and someone is reminding them of the primacy of God and prayer. The sister in the classroom is a reminder that there's more to life than simply learning how to earn money and get ahead. We learn how to earn money in order to raise a family, serve a community, promote the mission of the Church. I saw that my mother's friends, my godmother and her sisters—who were serious, devout Catholics—became

involved in the pro-life movement, were CCD teachers, helped pregnant women—all kinds of things.

**Did you mother ever take up practicing law?**
Yes, my mom began practicing law when my youngest sister was in high school, and she developed a home-office practice in areas that she enjoyed: wills and estate planning and real estate contracts.

**What was your father's area of expertise?**
My dad, as a young lawyer, worked in a large Wall Street firm, Cleary Gottlieb, and then worked for the New York Telephone Company, so he became a specialist in utility law. He was involved in the breakup of AT&T and other cases. One of the things he taught me was the value of economics. I didn't like economics in college. I wanted to know philosophy and history and religion. He told me, "In order to do my job in the field of utility law, I have to know economics because I have to know how you make money in the world of selling telephone service, pricing, and all the rest." So, through him I realized its importance. When you look at economics, you realize that it's not simply about calculating numbers. It's about analyzing human behavior, how you incentivize behavior, and how you make money.

**I'm sure it has served you well at the parish!**
Yes! It's very good for priests, oh my goodness! And that's a whole other topic. I remember reading George Gilder's book *Wealth and Poverty* in college—I recommend it to everyone.

**Getting back to your Mom . . .**
Yes, she only retired in her early 80s, she loved it so much. When you have your own practice, you develop bonds with your clients that then extend to their friends and children who become your clients. She is smart. She's demanding. She's precise. And people like that.

**Was she demanding with you and your sisters?**
Oh yes, absolutely!

**Can you share an example?**
Oh my gosh, let's see. Well, for one thing, when we were little kids, she said we had to get As. She said, "I don't want to see any of these Bs and Cs." She said, "You're smart enough to do it." She taught my sisters and me to read before we went to school, so when we arrived in first grade we already knew how to read. Her mother, in addition to being a lawyer, became a public school teacher, so we had textbooks from my grandmother. My mother sat us down on the couch and we read sentence by sentence the introductory books to reading.

**So, you were homeschooled in your early years?**
Yes, in that regard, and I can see why homeschoolers win spelling bees. Parents can also be more demanding because they are working with their own kids: they're not going to take any sass!

**And how was your relationship with your sisters?**
I had a good relationship with my sisters growing up, but I took unfair advantage of male chauvinism to say, "I'm the lead dog here." My parents were absolutely insistent on respecting and

loving my sisters, looking out for them. Once I went to college, the relationships entered a new and more respectful phase on my part. But it was a happy home. It was definitely united. It sounds strict, but it was not terrorizing at all. My dad had a good sense of humor; he was a natural actor. In many ways, he reminded me of Pope St. John Paul II because he knew how to speak in public in a convincing way. Part of it was his high school acting background. With my mom, the Faith was everything. She is a very serious Catholic.

**Did you pray the Rosary as a family?**
No, we didn't have that practice. My mom was an old-style Catholic. She learned before the Council to pray the Rosary during Mass. I don't know if you've seen that.

**I do it sometimes. Some see it as a way to remain close to Our Lady during Mass or to remain recollected.**
And in the Old Mass you can understand why. When I started to offer the Old Mass, I understood why people would say the Rosary, because the priest was saying the prayers up at the altar and they were united with it, but they're not necessarily going to follow everything word by word, and the Rosary helps you to meditate.

One of the Jesuits at Regis, where I went to high school, once said, "Knowledge makes a bloody entrance." What he meant by this is that studying is hard, and learning is not easy. For instance, when I read colloquially written English these days, I say to myself, "These poor people were never taught the difference between colloquial speaking and how you write for publication." That's a great loss because there's a discipline to learning how to organize your thoughts on paper. When you're a lawyer, one of the things you have to do is write with concision and precision, so my dad taught me to get rid of extraneous and repetitive phrases.

My parents were demanding, and I'm grateful for it because it taught me a lesson. When I became a Navy chaplain and saw the demands we make on young Sailors and Marines, I said to myself, "This is so wise." If you're going to accomplish difficult tasks in life, you have to be trained, and the training has to become second nature. Between getting up in the morning, keeping an orderly room, keeping your focus on finishing the reading you have to do, taking the time to write well when you are asked, fulfilling your social duties and obligations, eating right, exercising, and of course prayer and being God-centered: that's something the post-World War II generation understood that we don't really understand now. For me, it's very distressing to see the detachment of most Americans from the military in the sense of not appreciating the sacrifices they make or trying to imitate in a certain way their discipline. There are arguments for and against the draft—my dad was against the draft because he thought his period on active duty was a loss of valuable time. On the other hand, if all the males go through the draft, at least they are familiar with answering to authority for more than simply earning a paycheck. They learn to maintain order and cohesion and learn necessary military skills, and that can translate into life.

**Let's turn to your vocation.**

Yes, that is a beautiful gift from God. I had no idea of becoming a priest in high school. As I said, I went to a Jesuit school, and five or six of my classmates joined the Jesuits out of high school.

***Did you want to be married?***
I wanted to be married, certainly. And I was thinking of becoming a lawyer in imitation of my parents. But one of my teachers, I think he was a lay teacher, said to us: "You'll be surprised who in your class becomes a priest." And I'm the only one in my class who became a priest. All the guys who joined the Jesuits did not persevere to ordination. From Regis High School, I went to a secular school, Dartmouth, and graduated in 1980.

***An Ivy League school.***
Yes, it was the best school I got into. I'm an ice hockey player and I like the north; I like the cold weather. I went for a visit, and it was beautiful. I had a great experience there and was blessed and can see divine providence at work. Dartmouth has a wonderful Catholic Newman Center, The Aquinas House at Dartmouth, known simply as "AQ." A priest named Fr. William Nolan had been sent to Dartmouth as a young Redemptorist and he started the Catholic Newman Center and eventually built a Catholic center with a chapel, library, study rooms, and a rectory. He eventually left the Redemptorists, and became a priest of the Diocese of Manchester and stayed at the Newman Center for thirty-five years. He was a wonderful man. He was a traditional man of the Church. He believed in the doctrine and defended it.

Fr. Nolan, who was still at Dartmouth when I was there, inspired many young men to join the priesthood. He maintained the traditions of the Church, he had weekly Benediction, a nightly Rosary, and an annual retreat for students who wanted to attend. He would do one-day retreats periodically and provided Catholic literature in the library to read. He sold Image Books, which was the great Catholic imprint at the time.

***Did you go to daily Mass as a college student?***
I remember my mom said to me when I was a kid, "Go to Mass every day during Lent; it's a good practice." In grammar school, the Church was joined to the school, so I could do that. In high school, I fell out of that custom, but during the second half of my senior year, during Lent, I was working as an intern in a law office because during the second semester of senior year, you could do something different if you wanted to. On the way to work, I would stop at a chapel on 43rd Street and go to the 8:00 a.m. Mass. When I got to Dartmouth, I went to daily Mass during Lent the first year and never stopped.

They also had the nightly Rosary at 10:00 p.m. in the chapel. I remember the nuns teaching us to pray the Rosary in grammar school, so I said: "Let me start that again." I went back to Confession, which I had not completely neglected, but the Catholic student center at Dartmouth made it easy to go. And I met all these wonderful Catholic men and women. Some of the men entered seminary; a couple of the girls became nuns. Fr. Nolan was the avuncular-type priest, happy and smiling. He gave long sermons that were well-developed and explained the nature of the Faith, so he inspired a lot of us. I remember one day during my sophomore year, he said to me, "You never know, Gerry, maybe you're going to be a priest. The Lord may be calling you." So, I started thinking, and by my junior year, decided I wanted to become a priest.

***Were there other priests who inspired your vocation?***
Yes, one was an Opus Dei priest named Fr. Sal Ferigle from Cambridge, Massachusetts. Opus Dei has a house near Harvard. I used to go down occasionally to Boston with a

buddy of mine who was friends with Opus Dei. I really got to like Fr. Sal and talked to him about the priesthood.

Opus Dei provided great formation and spiritual direction. They have an association for priests, called the Priestly Society of the Holy Cross. Once I was ordained, I joined, but when it came time a few years later to make a final commitment I said, "No." I didn't want to continue; it didn't feel right for me, but I've remained close to Opus Dei. Some of the other Opus Dei priests were influential in my vocation, including Fr. Arne Panula (1946–2017), who died before his time in Washington, DC, after a battle with cancer, and Msgr. William Stetson, who has also gone to the Lord.

I was also friendly with Lyman Stebbins of Catholics United for the Faith (CUF). Reading the CUF newsletter was a great source of information and strength. I read *The Wanderer* newspaper and learned a lot from it. I started reading the *National Catholic Register*. I became familiar with Dietrich von Hildebrand's ideas. I read Hilaire Belloc and other Catholic authors. I read Newman. At Dartmouth, one could propose seminars to teachers. An English professor, who was a Newman scholar from the point of view of Newman as a literary figure, offered a seminar on Newman. There were five or six of us in the class. Of that number, one became a nun, I became a priest, another fellow converted to Catholicism, and another became a permanent deacon.

***It sounds like you were blessed with excellent intellectual formation at that time. At a certain point, the decision to pursue a vocation to the priesthood has to come from the will. How did that happen? And was it a struggle to let go of the desire to be married?***

No, not really. Concerning marriage, I basically said, "This is a good sacrifice to make to become a priest." I remember discussing with one of my Dartmouth friends that I wanted to dedicate my life to promoting the Church. This was before deciding to become a priest, but it was part of the process leading that way. By my junior year I had made the decision and said, "This is what I'm going to do." Then, in my senior year, I told my parents I wasn't going to take the LSAT—the entrance exam for law school—and I wrote to the rector of the seminary in the Archdiocese of New York requesting to enter. I entered seminary the following year, in 1980.

***How did your parents respond when you told them?***

My dad was happy. My mom was a little concerned that I'd made a decision I'd be unhappy with later, because she knew a number of women who had left the convent.

***A very natural response at the time given her own experience.***

Yes, that was an understandable caution at the time. But then, later on, she was very happy and very proud. I was very happy because I'd been well-informed that the seminary at Dunwoodie in New York was orthodox.

*You entered seminary in 1980 at a time that, for many seminaries, marked the height of the madness. What was your experience at Dunwoodie like?*

At Dunwoodie, doctrine and moral theology and canon law were all taught from a serious, orthodox Catholic point of view. There was no contradicting the Church's teaching in any of those areas. Terrence Cardinal Cooke was the archbishop at the time, then came Cardinal O'Connor. The outstanding figures at the seminary at the time were the moral theology professor, Msgr. William B. Smith, and the dogma teacher, Fr. James T. O'Connor. Both men were solid, devout Catholic priests who were good communicators of the Catholic tradition. The canon law professor was excellent, Fr. Joseph Penna.

The Scripture department was more problematic because they were of the form criticism school. I spent a lot of time studying Raymond Brown and other writers whom I did not find good at all, and I read critiques of their works, including that by Msgr. George Kelly. One of the joys in my later years as a priest has been reading Scott Hahn and his associates' (such as Brant Pitre, John Bergsma, Curtis Mitch) books and listening to their lectures because they talk about Scripture from the point of view of the Jewish roots of Catholic teaching, the patristic understanding, and the dogmatic and liturgical truths communicated in Scripture and embodied in the life of the Church. The form criticism style of teaching was basically literary studies based on unproven and often unstated presuppositions.

*That sounds very boring . . .*
Boring, and it undermines some doctrines because it contains anti-supernatural presuppositions. For instance, when considering the Scripture passage of the miracle of the coin in the fish's mouth (Matt 17:24–27), I remember asking one priest if he believed that happened, and he said, "No, I don't believe it." Why? Unfortunately, because he was likely taught a form of Scripture teaching where you cast doubt on miraculous events and say they were invented to impress people. This is what Joseph Cardinal Ratzinger, in his famous 1988 Erasmus Lecture in New York, identified as the debilitating effect that Scripture studies had on the catechetical mission of the Church.

The reality in seminary was that the Scriptures were not taught from the point of view of how to preach them and integrate them with doctrine and liturgy. They were taught as an academic subject largely focused upon a German exegetical school which was highly suspicious of the supernatural. Patristics were never really integrated into Scripture studies in my day, and that's most regrettable because the Church's teaching is that the Fathers of the Church left us with a deep understanding of the revelation that is contained in Sacred Scripture. And certainly, many of the Fathers had a deep knowledge of the language and customs of the time so they could communicate that to us.

*How was your seminary formation in terms of the liturgy?*
Liturgy was also not properly taught. Back then, the Old Mass was forbidden. The only ones saying the Old Mass were the followers of Archbishop Lefebvre, so none of us had any access

to it. We certainly liked some of its aspects, but it wasn't a possibility. That came later, after I was ordained.

**Do you remember ever wishing that it would be a possibility?**
There were some aspects of the Old Mass that I liked. I remember as an altar boy, I liked the "Prayers at the Foot of the Altar," and I later came to think that Mass facing East was a good idea. I liked ancillary traditions, which are very vital, like receiving Holy Communion kneeling and on the tongue, and the ringing of bells at the Consecration. Gradually, I began to appreciate the value of the Entrance Antiphon and the Communion Antiphon as being Scripture integrated into worship. This is vital; it's not just an accessory to beautify it. But I had no interest in following Archbishop Lefebvre even though I found some of his arguments to be interesting.

**So, you were aware of Archbishop Lefebvre at the time?**
I was aware of the Archbishop because his positions were commonly discussed. He was suspended *a divinis* but was continuing his activity in the early 1980s. He didn't perform the illicit consecrations until June 1988, so there was a whole period of ferment. When John Paul II was elected, one of the first things he did was to meet with Archbishop Lefebvre, and I had hoped that there would be a reconciliation. As you can guess, I had no interest in guitar Masses and do-it-yourself ad hoc liturgy.

***And your seminary formation in terms of the spiritual life and priestly identity?***
Priestly identity was communicated by the faculty in a good way. The seminarians wore a cassock and surplice at Mass every day. Dunwoodie was known as a traditional seminary in the sense that it maintained traditional ways. The spiritual formation was not adequate, and I thank God that I had a spiritual director from Opus Dei because he gave me a program to follow which was excellent, and I continue to follow it for the most part to this day. It was disappointing that there wasn't communal meditation every day. In other words, it was up to individual seminarians if they went to chapel before morning prayer to meditate in silence.

***Was there Eucharistic Adoration?***
There was Eucharistic adoration once a week, but it wasn't mandatory. The Rosary wasn't mandatory either. I remember complaining that there wasn't enough rigor in the schedule. A good priest said, "We are considered to be rigorous as it is!" I began to realize that the decline that set in after the Second Vatican Council, the questioning of the past and putting it aside to try new things, led to a hesitancy to insist on maintaining things which have value in and of themselves. The fact that they were done in the past is a witness to their presumptive goodness, not to their arbitrary imposition. Unfortunately, as a young seminarian, you'd go to the chapel in the morning and see who's doing a meditation, and not everyone was there. You can't blame them in a certain sense because the seminary didn't train them to value it and to make it a habit.

*If young men at bootcamp weren't expected to wake up early, they generally wouldn't either.*

But the military will train you and insist on it. I remember with a smile what's called the standard Navy lecture: you state what your four points are; you then state point one, point two, point three, and point four; then you would sum it up: the four points we've studied are one, two, three, four. In other words, you constantly reinforce. They didn't do that at Dunwoodie as regards meditation. Things changed after I graduated from there: the communal Rosary was instituted, and they started praying the Angelus aloud. We prayed morning and evening prayer together, and daily Mass was a requirement. But Confession was not available every day, in the sense that there wasn't a priest sitting in a confessional where seminarians could go. I thought there should have been.

Regarding the Divine Office, we were not properly instructed in it, but I've learned more since. The old breviary, the prayer book that contains the Divine Office or Liturgy of the Hours, has advantages over the new; the new has advantages over the old in terms of length, but the value that was found in the Psalms was not really understood by us.

At the time, we also had the bad English translation of the Mass. That was always an annoyance because if you knew Latin, as I did, you realized it was not a good translation; it was grating. But there was good camaraderie in the seminary. We had some excellent candidates from New York and dioceses such as Lincoln, Nebraska. Lincolnites had a good spirit and were well-instructed about meditation and the like. Sad to reflect, but the seminary also took in many men they shouldn't have, who either became sexual molesters or left the priesthood.

***Did you know any of them?***
Yes, of course, because we were in seminary together. In fact, a few of my classmates have been removed from the priesthood and others are under accusation and awaiting possible removal. And I never suspected anything at the time.

***No?***
No, not at all. On reflection, it's clear that at least two of them drank too much. There was a pub in the basement of the seminary where you could go and have a glass of wine or beer in the evening. With others, who left the priesthood, you just wonder why they were in seminary in the first place. Didn't they understand what they were getting into? It's sad. There was a lack of rigor in both training and evaluation.

***Perhaps if it had been more challenging, and the spiritual formation had been more rigorous and intense, those who really weren't going to persevere would have come to the decision that it wasn't for them and left.***
Yes, or the faculty would have judged that they weren't suitable candidates. One thing I learned in the military is what is called the "training environment." There is a reason that the pace at a Marine or Navy training facility is going to be more rigorous than what they are going to encounter in the fleet in peacetime. They want to weed out people who are not capable of the life. When you put people under physical and psychological pressure, you get to see what they're capable of. In seminaries where that pressure is present, men who are not up to the rigors of celibacy, or who are in seminary trying to find themselves, which isn't really the purpose, could be more easily identified.

You could also turn the argument and say, "What about the molesting priests from the forties and fifties, before the collapse of the Church?" To which one could say: "Every system can be gamed, and that's why you have to be rigorous." Men who don't have discipline and an obvious spiritual life and a knowledge of doctrine need to be shown the door for their own good and the good of the Church. We had guys who were not doing well on the academic side, but they let them slip through. This is not in the best interest of the People of God, although there are exceptions like Blessed Solanus Casey, OFM Cap.

If you look at it sociologically, up until the Council, the priesthood was highly esteemed. Parents were proud to have their sons become priests, so there was a lot of social value and esteem to becoming a priest. The job of the seminary is to take men and say, "Look, you're not doing this to look good in the eyes of your parents, or your aunts, or your classmates, and this certainly is not meant to be an easy life. It's to be a life dedicated to a mission rather than serving your own interests. If you're not willing and capable of doing that, the charitable thing is to tell you to leave." That kind of rigor was gone. They panicked in the late 1970s and 1980s, because not so many men sought to enter and a lot of men left the seminary voluntarily, and then they were looking for candidates. In my time in the seminary there were a number of men who were older, many of whom in the old days would have never been accepted because they were too old.

*How old were they?*
They were in their thirties or forties or fifties. In the old days, you didn't just enter the major seminary; you entered minor seminary

at high school or college level. That system basically dried up, so they started other programs. There's nothing wrong with ordaining men with later vocations; many of them are outstanding priests, but some of them were not really suited to the priesthood.

**Did you know seminarians from other seminaries? It sounds like you had a fairly good experience given the circumstances.**
Yes, there were three seminaries in the New York area: St. Joseph's in Dunwoodie, Yonkers; Immaculate Conception on Long Island; and Immaculate Conception, then in Darlington, New Jersey (now in South Orange). Both of the latter were quite liberal. In fact, we had a number of men join Dunwoodie who lived in the neighboring dioceses but didn't want to go to seminary in either of those places, and with reason, because they probably wouldn't have gotten ordained.

**Was it a question of academics and morals?**
It was morality, academics, liturgy, making fun of those who went to Eucharistic Adoration or prayed the Rosary. There was irreverence towards the Blessed Sacrament.

**Do you remember hearing of active homosexuality?**
Not really. You knew in general that that was a reality in the world, but I had such a high notion of the priesthood that I didn't conceive of that happening in the seminary. And in seminary, I had no knowledge of people engaged in that behavior. I was happy because at Dunwoodie they taught the immorality of homosexual activity, and they explained why it is wrong, and it was clear. On reflection, I was twenty-one when I entered the seminary and not cognizant of the problem of clerical vice.

Now, many years later, I see that some people were a problem, a few were later arrested, others credibly accused and removed from the priesthood.

**You were ordained in 1984 in St. Patrick's Cathedral.**
Yes, by Archbishop John O'Connor. He took possession of the Archdiocese in March 1984. He was a good archbishop in many ways because he was the most pro-life bishop that we had in the United States. He started the Sisters of Life, constantly preached about the evil of abortion, and upheld Catholic moral theology. On the other hand, he was a difficult person in some ways personally. I wasn't happy with some of the decisions he made later on. The limelight and focus he got was good for the Church because it drew more attention to the pro-life message. And in the 80s and 90s, the Catholic Church was keeping that issue alive. He was the visible face of it and did a lot of good. Joseph Cardinal Bernardin of Chicago was preaching the "seamless garment" doctrine and claiming that, if you're pro-life, you have to be against the death penalty and other things.

**His spirit is still with us today . . .**
Then you had Bernard Cardinal Law, who turned out to be a disaster. He was also pro-life but lacked courage in some areas, especially in dealing with sexual-molester priests. Cardinal O'Connor was a somewhat distant figure, and things declined financially during his time. He also fired teachers from the seminary in order to please a liberal group of priests in the Archdiocese who weren't pleased with its being conservative. He was listening to the wrong people. It's a temptation of leaders to focus on the institution they're running simply

from the point of view of themselves and their position in it. One of the things in a well-run diocese is that the consultative groups—such as the board of consultors and the priests council—are actually populated by intelligent, informed and courageous men to whom it's made clear that their opinions count and they should freely bring things to the attention of the cardinal or archbishop. Under O'Connor, a self-reinforcing group developed around him. After Geraldine Ferraro made it known that she was pro-abortion, he rightly criticized her, but he later invited her to the annual Al Smith Dinner, a high-profile archdiocesan fundraiser for Catholic healthcare that attracts politicians and big donors.

**What did your mother think about that?**
She wasn't happy about it. None of us were. My interest is to help pro-abortion Catholics realize the path they are pursuing is a danger to their soul and is a cause of social harm and destruction. I'm grateful to Cardinal O'Connor because he ordained me to the priesthood, sent me to Rome to study canon law, and gave me some nice assignments. But I'm disappointed because more could have been done, but it wasn't.

**What are your memories of the day of your ordination?**
It was December 1, 1984. It was a nice cold and sunny day. I remember walking up the main isle of the Cathedral toward the altar during the entrance procession and starting to cry. It was beautiful: I was going to be ordained. At the laying on of hands, I knew that in the mystery of God's providence this simple act, combined with the prayer that is said by the bishop, turns you into a priest. My family and friends were there. In New York the

tradition is that the newly ordained priests go to the seminary for a lunch with the priests and seminarians, and that was wonderful. Then I saw my parents later that evening, but the main celebration for them was the first Mass, the following Sunday, December 2, which was followed by a large dinner with family and friends.

**And what do you remember about your first Mass?**
It was beautiful. I wanted to be as precise and liturgically proper as possible, so I studied the rubrics of the Old Mass to find out details about how you're supposed to do things. The new rubrics didn't answer all the questions.

**Was that suggested to you?**
No, I came to it on my own because I had questions about how the priest was to hold his hands, how he is supposed to stand, etc. Someone afterward said, "You look like you've been celebrating Mass for years." I was happy about that because it meant that I'd prepared well for it. It was very moving and still to this day a great joy.

**And what can you say about your first experience hearing Confession?**
I heard my first Confession right after my ordination in the crypt chapel of St. Patrick's Cathedral. A priest friend of mine told me he wanted to go to Confession, so I heard his Confession still vested in the chasuble and stole. It was a moment of grace for me.

***As a penitent, it's always moving to hear the sacred words, "Ego te absolvo, . . . " but what is it like saying those words for the first time as a priest?***
You realize that you are imparting a gift that is not your own. It is a divine gift. It also brings into relief that aspect of Christianity that Christ encounters us one by one. It's not a mass phenomenon. That's a sign of divine wisdom and mediation. We are born into this world alone but through our mother; we are forgiven alone but through the mediation of a priest; and when we die, we do so alone, but we pray for the angels to take our soul up to God's throne for a merciful judgment.

***What were your greatest challenges and joys as a newly ordained priest?***
I knew Spanish, so I was sent to a Spanish-speaking parish in the South Bronx. I had a wonderful pastor who was a Cuban refugee priest, Msgr. Raul del Valle. He had been the private secretary of Manuel Cardinal Arteaga of Havana at the time of the Castro takeover, and he had to flee Cuba at the time of the Bay of Pigs Invasion in 1961. It's an interesting story. The Americans were in prior contact with Cardinal Arteaga to keep him informed of developments. The cardinal had a custom that he would not spend every night in the episcopal palace. They knew that something was coming, and so he would go visit different diplomats and spend the night at the diplomatic mission. When they knew that the Bay of Pigs was coming, Cardinal Arteaga and Msgr. del Valle went and stayed at an embassy. When it failed the government said, "What are you doing at the embassy?" So, the Holy See negotiated that Msgr. del Valle could leave Cuba.

Msgr. del Valle ended up in Miami, but he said he didn't like Miami because there were too many Cuban spies. He was also not expecting the Castro government to survive, so he thought it would be a brief exile. Monsignor had heard there was need for Spanish-speaking priests in Paterson, New Jersey, but the bishop there put him in a convent rather than a parish. The vicar general told him, "None of the pastors want to have an associate who is a monsignor." So, he told him, "Go to New York. They love monsignors there." So, he did, and he ended up staying in the Archdiocese.

Msgr. del Valle was on the tribunal, as he was a canon lawyer. He also worked in different parishes, including being named pastor of two different parishes in the South Bronx. That's where I met him. I was only with him for seven months, when he was appointed chancellor of the Archdiocese, which is the number three position. Sadly, he had cancer and died just a few years later. He was a wonderful priest and a dedicated, holy man who had been through trials of suffering under Communism and exile. He taught me a lot.

**It sounds like quite an introduction to the priesthood.**
Yes. I said Mass more in Spanish than in English the first year I was ordained. The South Bronx at the time was depicted in the movie *Fort Apache, the Bronx*. It was a time when there were still buildings being burned. I remember standing in front of the church one day seeing in the distance a six-story building on fire. There was a lot of destruction in the South Bronx; it was the poorest Congressional district in America. I was only there, however, for nine months before being transferred to a parish in northern Manhattan, St. Elizabeth's, and was there

for five years. It was also a Hispanic neighborhood that had been an Irish neighborhood, so we had the old timers—Irish, Italians, and a scattering of others—and the Hispanics: Puerto Ricans, Cubans, but mostly Dominicans at that point. The Dominican Republic is a very Catholic country, so at the 11:00 a.m. Spanish Mass on Sunday, you'd have eight hundred people in church. I also worked part-time in the pro-life office of the Archdiocese.

Then, I was administrator of a parish in the Bronx, Nativity of Our Blessed Lady, again for a short period. Then I went to St. Patrick's Cathedral as an assistant for two years, and that was a good learning experience. It was a busy place, with eight daily and Sunday Masses, six priests, and a traditional rectory.

At that point, I had been ordained nine years and had wanted to get a doctorate.

**Was it your decision to study canon law?**
First, I told Cardinal O'Connor that I wanted to study philosophy, then theology. But he said he wanted me to study canon law, so I said, "Okay, I'll do that." It turned out to be a providential decision because it's been a great benefit to have studied canon law, in line with my parents' experience. I spent four beautiful and formative years (1993–1997) in Rome learning canon law at the Pontifical Gregorian University.

**The Jesuit-run pontifical university. Did the Gregorian offer a good program of studies in canon law?**
The canon law faculty was excellent. Some teachers weren't gifted; their material was important, but it wasn't well-presented. Others were very gifted, and it was a thorough all-around

program of canonical studies. Pope John Paul II had promulgated the new *Code of Canon Law* in 1983. I enjoyed studying it.

I also refreshed my Latin by studying with the great Latinist, Fr. Reginald Foster. He was an iconoclast and dressed like a gas station attendant from the 1950s, but he was one of the best teachers I've ever had in my life. I also met all kinds of wonderful priests from all over the United States and elsewhere and got an introduction to the Roman scene and the life of the Church. Back then, it seemed like Pope John Paul II was going to be there for more years to come, which in fact he was, and things were on the upswing in the life of the Church. Things looked good, but there were troubling aspects. There was continued opposition to the pontificate from various quarters.

**Had the storm really hit yet?**
I guess you could say that it had with regard to liturgical abuses. The fight to eliminate them was stronger at the beginning of the pontificate than it was later. As regards doctrine, Pope John Paul's encyclical *Veritatis Splendor*, which is the best document of his pontificate apart from the *Catechism of the Catholic Church*, came out while I was in Rome, and there were other good encyclicals. The expectation was that the teaching was going to be good and helpful and that was always the case. The Pope's Christian witness was also inspiring. I had the opportunity to greet him personally a few times.

**What was the topic of your doctoral dissertation in canon law?**
My doctoral thesis was entitled "Incorporation into and Defection from the Catholic Church according to the Code of Canon Law." It was a study of the canonical norms for how one

joins the Church, which is through faith in Christ and the reception of the Sacrament of Baptism, and what it means to defect from the Church. Defection does not mean that one ceases to be a baptized Catholic, as we are incapable of un-baptizing ourselves. No one can undo God's action in spiritually adopting us in baptism. What defection means is that we lose full communion with the Church by virtue of falling into heresy, schism, or apostasy. Yet the loss of full communion does not mean that we are no longer a member of the Catholic Church. The baptismal character imprinted on our soul is indelible and calls us back to full communion with the Church.

### *Why did you choose this topic?*

I have always been interested in the question of membership in the Church. It is particularly relevant in understanding our relationship with Orthodox and Protestant Christians. They are our separated brothers and sisters in Christ. I also was interested in learning more about the meaning of the canonical penalty of excommunication. People often think that excommunication means that a person has been thrown out of the Church. Similarly, Catholics often think that if they join another religion, they cease to be Catholic. In fact, excommunication does not mean that one is no longer a Catholic but rather that one is deprived of most of the benefits the Church offers to those in full communion, especially the sacraments. If one decides to leave the Church, the Church still regards that person as a Catholic, albeit one who has wandered from the flock. The Church prays for the return of fallen away Catholics to full communion with the Church. As regards our separated Christian brethren, the goal of the ecumenical efforts of the Church is the full communion of all the baptized in the Catholic Church.

***Once you returned from Rome after completing your doctorate, how long did you serve in the tribunal in the Archdiocese of New York?***
When I returned from Rome in 1997 after I had finished my doctorate, I was on the tribunal for half a year.

***That's all?***
Yes. The honest truth is that having studied marriage law and Roman Rotal jurisprudence, I was not going to engage in rubber-stamping annulment petitions because I saw that Rotal jurisprudence was much stricter than what the American tribunals in general were doing, i.e., easily granting annulments for lack of psychological health.

***It's an important issue.***
It's a very important issue. The Rota is the Roman court that receives appeals from American tribunals, so when people appealed an American tribunal's decision to grant a decree of nullity on the basis of psychological incapacity, the Roman Rota very frequently overturned those decisions in those days. This was in the mid-90s. The Rota publishes selected decisions that they make, and I reviewed a year or two of decisions, and approximately 90 percent of the decisions overturned the American tribunals.

***Ninety percent . . .***
Yes. When I got to the tribunal, the work was specifically to judge cases of marriage. It was clear to me that the American standards were too liberal and too expansive. The Church's understanding of human nature is that God created us such

that the average, ordinary person can make a binding commitment of himself or herself in marriage. The Rotal jurisprudence was affirmative of that. The American jurisprudence was essentially, "Anybody who seeks an annulment must have a reason for doing so, so we'll grant it." At the time, there were 800–900 cases per year at the Archdiocesan tribunal.

*That's a large number of cases . . .*
It's now been reduced because people are paying less attention to marriage these days, so they're not seeking to remarry in the Church. I asked the head of our tribunal in New York how many cases of these were annulled. It was 99 percent positive, meaning they were given the rubber stamp—that is, 99 percent of the marriages were found to be null through psychological incapacity to marry. I complained about it, and he said, "Well, not every case that we accept reaches this stage." I responded, "Yes, but is every case that does not reach this stage subject to scrutiny?" They were not. Often people don't pursue the case or don't cooperate, but basically, almost everyone who cooperated and followed up was given a declaration of nullity.

At that point, it was clear that the head of the tribunal wasn't happy. He asked Cardinal O'Connor to remove me. The cardinal agreed to that. I was now free to accept a pastoral assignment. I was pleased to be named the pastor at St. Vincent de Paul Church in 1998, and I stayed there for fourteen years. That was a French national Church, so I celebrated Mass in French.

*Sounds very interesting . . .*
The parish was founded in the 1840s to serve the needs of French-speaking Catholics who were immigrants from France,

Switzerland, and Belgium. But by the 1990s the French people who had settled in New York were not attending the parish in significant numbers. It was largely expatriates, French people who were here in America for job purposes for a few years. So, they made up part of the congregation, along with a handful of long-term French residents. There was also a small congregation of local English-speaking parishioners who attended our English Mass. But the vast majority of people attending Mass on Sunday were African immigrants from French-speaking countries. This gave me great insight into the beauty of the French missionary work for so many decades in West Africa: Ivory Coast, Togo, Benin, Senegal, Cameroon, Burkina Faso, the two Congos, all of these different countries. There is a significant amount of immigration to the United States from African countries and many of them end up in metropolitan areas such as New York City. A typical Sunday congregation would be three-quarters African. Our choir was African.

**Where in New York was the parish located?**
The church was located in the Chelsea neighborhood, which is just north of Greenwich Village on the West Side. Our African parishioners came from the Bronx, Brooklyn, and some from New Jersey. Many of them knew liturgical Latin. We would sing the Gloria and the Creed in Latin. They were serious Catholics and understood religion to be God's gift and not man's plaything. I never had anyone question doctrine among the French-speaking Africans, unlike what you would experience with some Americans or French, for whom the hard teachings are subject to debate.

Traditional societies confirm a lot of traditional wisdom

about honoring parents and grandparents, and children are taught manners and obedience and to work hard. When I read Robert Cardinal Sarah's books, I felt at home because I had seen people with a similar experience: they were grateful for religion, they lived surrounded in many cases by Muslims—some of whom were hostile, others not—so to affirm Jesus Christ is not just to go along and do what everybody does. We did have some converts from Islam to Catholicism. I baptized some of them.

**Did you ever have anyone convert to Catholicism from Islam for whom that was going to mean potential persecution by family members or others?**
I know there was family opposition to some of them, but in West Africa the situation is not as perilous as it is in the Middle East, since you have Christians, Muslims, and pagans living together. And many Muslims go to Catholic schools because they provide a high standard of education. A lot of the French-speaking African Catholics look to France as a cultural reference-point historically. It's understood that France is a Catholic country by heritage, a heritage which the missionaries brought from France to West Africa. The presence of the Church, in addition to bringing so many people to faith in Christ, has yielded a lot of benefits to people in Africa.

**What other aspects of your time in the French-speaking parish stand out?**
Teaching religion in the after-school catechism programs at the Lycée Français de New York and the French-American School of New York in suburban Westchester County. The mothers of the children organized a catechism program similar to those in

France, so I was able to work with those mothers, *les mamans catéchistes*, for fourteen years. I spent a lot of time with the kids, from first grade to high school. There I saw the way the Church works best: when the parents take an interest in the religious formation of their children and work with the parish priest.

**Parents are called to be the primary educators of their children, but so often, at the parish level, parents haven't themselves been formed in order to then educate their children.**
Exactly. We need an educated laity, practicing Catholics who are conscious of the fact that we don't have Catholic schools as much, we don't have as many sisters and priests, so the laity have to make up for this. I met monthly with the catechists, we discussed Church teaching, and I answered questions.

**You also served as a Navy Chaplain?**
Yes, I joined the Naval Reserve Chaplain Corps in 1994. At that point, I was starting my canon law degree in Rome. Cardinal O'Connor, who had been Chief of Naval Chaplains, gave me permission. I had always been attracted to military life. I also thought that, if there were a war, I'd already be trained and ready to serve because, as a young priest, I wanted to be ready to contribute to the spiritual welfare of service members. I was in the reserves for eleven years.

**What did Naval chaplaincy involve?**
It involved going to chaplain school first, which I did the summer after my first year in Rome. I spent seven weeks in Newport, Rhode Island, and learned a lot. You learn military bearing, what it's like to be a Naval officer, the structure of the Navy, Marine

Corps, and Coast Guard. You also learn the history of the chaplain corps and how chaplains have served in the past.

It was my real training in ecumenism because all the chaplains are taught together: Catholic, Protestant, and Jewish. We didn't have Muslim chaplains then, but now they are present. The only really extensive time I've spent with Protestant ministers was at chaplain's school, and we had some really interesting discussions. Then, when I returned to Rome to continue my doctorate, I would go to the US Navy base near Naples, where I also worked with Marines. There was a large Naval presence there—both a Naval base and a North Atlantic Treaty Organization (NATO) base—and I worked with the base Catholic chaplains.

Once I had returned to New York after completing my studies in Rome, I worked with Marines in Long Island, but I had to discontinue that billet in 2000 because I was the only priest at my parish, and the Marine drilling schedule was too demanding to manage both. But it was great experience. The military is an analogous reality to the hierarchical Church. You also learn the virtues of discipline, order, common purpose, and cooperation.

One of the great lessons they taught us in chaplain school was—when you're on a ship— to just go around to the "spaces" and ask the Sailors what they do. It's a happy experience for them to explain to a chaplain the nature of their job. Taking genuine interest in them can be a way to gain the confidence of service members, who then might come to see you in their need. I realized that this can be a sort of Dale Carnegie *How to Win Friends and Influence People* approach, but it has its Christian manifestation in the sense that we don't look at people simply as objects for our pastoral care. We also spend time and talk with them to learn what's important to them and to discover how to bring Christ to their souls and their life.

***Before we go on, you mentioned that you like ice hockey...***
Yes. When I moved from Brooklyn to New Rochelle, New York, in 1968, I discovered the world of ice hockey. In the wintertime, the lakes would freeze, and the kids would skate on the lakes. My grandmother bought me the equipment, so I started playing pond hockey. Then I started playing street hockey, but my high school had no hockey team. At Dartmouth, I played intramural hockey, and that was a lot of fun. Then, when I got to St. Vincent de Paul Church, I joined a men's hockey team and played for ten years in a league at nearby Chelsea Piers.

***As a priest?***
Yes. I ended up performing the marriages of a number of my teammates, helped to prepare them for marriage through Pre-Cana classes, and baptized their children. I had a lot of fun. Our team won the championship twice in ten years, so we had some good players. We had Jewish, Catholic, Protestant, a couple of Mormon players at one point. If someone checked me, the joke was to say, "Do you know you just knocked down a priest?" I love the world of sports because it's part of human nature that we were made to work, and sports are a form of entertaining work, using the body and the mind. Team sports are great because you learn cooperation and the need for others.

***Where were you assigned after St. Vincent de Paul?***
After serving at St. Vincent de Paul for fourteen years, I came to the United Nations Parish, Holy Family Church. It's an

international parish due to the presence of the United Nations and the embassies—they call them "permanent missions"—of the different countries that have permanent representatives at the United Nations. Then there are all the people who work in the various UN offices. Our parish is a business parish, in the sense that we serve the workers at the UN, the diplomats, and the staff members. There are also a lot of business towers in the area, so we serve the businessmen and women in the area. But we are primarily a residential parish for people who live in the neighborhood. It's a busy and interesting parish. Cardinal Dolan sent me here because of my language abilities, so I was grateful for that. I've been here for nine years now and have very much enjoyed it.

***Has the experience given you a lot of insight into how the United Nations works?***
Yes, it has. I remember the French ambassador giving a talk in which he basically said that the UN itself does nothing. The countries do things, he said, and they do them with and through the UN. Americans would tend to overestimate the United Nations as its own organization with its own power. The power really comes from security council members' decisions about what they are willing to support and pay for. The general assembly has ideas about what they want, but the Americans, Chinese, Russians, French, and British have a lot of say in what happens. Now UN agencies do exercise a lot of influence, often against what is morally right. That is a constant source of conflict for the Church.

***What is your view of the Trump administration's presence at the UN? And what is the situation now under the Biden Administration? Is it changing?***

I was very happy that President Trump had restored the pro-life stance of the United States because under the Obama administration the US supported abortion. That is one of the areas I am most familiar with because pro-life volunteers have contact with the parish, and I learn about their lobbying. In addition to representatives from the various nations, you also have non-governmental organizations (NGOs), which send people to meetings to influence the delegates so as to gain their votes. The pro-life strength largely came from the United States. The Muslim world is also basically on the side of pro-life. But the European Union is very hostile to pro-life efforts and is always pushing what they call "reproductive rights," which is a euphemism for abortion. I realized that the Holy See Permanent Observer Mission is one of the most vital organizations that is not a government, because the Holy See is here as a permanent observer, that is, they are not a voting member of the United Nations, but they have a lot of influence in giving the Catholic position. Many countries across the world will pay attention to what the Holy See says because they know it will have a domestic reverberation.

Predictably and sadly the Biden administration has done a 180-degree turn on the abortion question.

***You are a frequent guest on Fox News and are well-known as a member of the "Papal Posse" on EWTN's*** The World Over with Raymond Arroyo. ***How did you get into media?***

I had done a couple of media appearances as a priest in the past, but when I got back to New York after being in Rome, someone recommended me to Fox News. We have to remember that, essentially, cable news was just CNN for so long. Then Fox News was founded. It's headquartered here in New York, and it's more favorable in its coverage to the Catholic Church and more sympathetic to hearing authentic Catholic teachings being presented. So, I started getting calls and went on. When Pope John Paul II died in 2005, I was frequently on Fox News to discuss the pontificate.

**Did you enjoy it?**
I did enjoy it because I was a high school debater and am a canon lawyer, and through these you learn how to present arguments in a concise way. Having studied canon law in Rome, I also had that academic background, which helped me to understand how the Vatican works, the role of bishops in teaching, etc. And, most importantly, they liked me. The producers kept calling me, and I was on many different shows and continue to be until now.

When Pope Benedict XVI resigned in 2013, I got a call from EWTN, and up to that point I hadn't been on EWTN. Someone had recommended me to Raymond Arroyo.

**Did you know Raymond Arroyo at that point?**
I had met him before and had dinner with him but didn't know him well. They asked me if I would join their conclave coverage in Rome back in 2013, and I said, "Yes." I also went on Fox News for the papal election.

***This is when the Papal Posse was founded, wasn't it?***
Yes, the coverage team for EWTN was Raymond Arroyo, Robert Royal, Fr. Roger Landry, and me. Raymond decided to keep inviting Bob Royal and me on to discuss news in the Church. Fr. Landry, in the meantime, was given a new assignment to work at the Holy See Mission to the United Nations in New York, and he became a resident priest at my parish, and I'm very happy that he's here.

The Papal Posse became popular and started to become a once-a-month event. I would go to Washington and meet them in studio or go to a studio in Manhattan with a satellite connection to discuss different events in the life of the Church, which has become quite interesting under Pope Francis. We continue to this day, and for me it's a rewarding experience to be able to explain Catholic teaching to a wide audience.

***After the pontificates of Pope John Paul II and Pope Benedict XVI, have you found it jarring as a Catholic priest to be critical of Pope Francis, and how have you navigated that?***
In the spring of 2016, Pope Francis issued his post-synodal apostolic exhortation *Amoris Laetitia*, which gave permission in a footnote for certain people in invalid, so-called second marriages to receive Holy Communion. So the challenge became, "How do we present the authentic Catholic teaching on the indissolubility of marriage and reconcile it with this new regulation, or law, or policy that Pope Francis has implemented?"

***Do you think it can be reconciled?***
I don't believe you can reconcile it, and I've said that on air and in writing. People who are in so-called second marriages are

not properly disposed to receive Holy Communion until their marriage is canonically regularized. This was a topic, of course, that was debated during the pontificates of John Paul II and Benedict XVI, and there were multiple instructions from Rome indicating that it was not permitted.

When Pope Francis says in *Amoris Laetitia* that, in certain cases, the aid of the sacraments can be given, we have a contradiction with earlier teaching. That's where we have to be forthright and respectful. The way I look at it is: the teaching cannot change because the teaching is God's eternal truth. The way the Catholic hierarchy proposes to uphold that teaching can be deficient and lacking, and, in this case, I think it is. To state that is not disrespectful. It's actually falling back on the foundation of papal authority. The pope doesn't have authority on his own. His authority is delegated to him by Christ. And it would be an imaginary world to believe that popes can never make mistakes, apart from the specific occasions when they issue an infallible teaching, which *Amoris Laetitia* certainly is not. Therefore, to say you cannot criticize a papal decision because it shows a lack of respect to the pope is not correct. The greatest respect you can show to someone is to speak the truth in charity.

I point out frequently on television that Pope Francis himself says he wants Gospel frankness—*parrhesia*. Taking him at his word, I think it's legitimate to say to the Holy Father, "With all due respect, Holy Father, I don't see how you can reconcile *Amoris Laetitia's* provisions with the indissolubility of marriage and the strictures that were placed upon giving Communion to people who are in invalid second marriages by your predecessors." It's the same point that the four cardinals raised in their *dubia* to Pope Francis, meaning the five questions for which they've sought answers based on problematic provisions in *Amoris Laetitia*. Unfortunately, Pope Francis has yet to answer them. The fact that the Pope doesn't want to talk about it, or is convinced that he's right, doesn't mean that all the rest of us have to remain silent. But, of course, the idea of a Catholic priest's contradicting the pope sounds radical. To this, the only thing one can say is that it would only be radical if what the priest was saying were contrary to the teaching of the Church. If the Pope has made a mistake in his interpretation, I think it's necessary to tell him that.

**As a priest of the Archdiocese of New York, you're under Cardinal Dolan. Has he ever told you to tone it down?**
We've never discussed this topic.

**That's interesting.**
Yes, but there are many topics I don't discuss with the cardinal. I see him infrequently and it's usually in order to deal with other matters. He's never asked me to curb anything of my media work or writing—I have a column at *The Catholic Thing* website—and I occasionally write articles for other periodicals. The cardinal has been personally appreciative of my television work, especially at the time of the 2013 conclave.

It's a constant source of consternation for supporters of Pope Francis's new policy that anyone would dare criticize it, as if—in the Catholic Church—whatever the pope says is what we're supposed to believe. It's the other way around. The pope is supposed to say what we all believe, and if he's not doing it, it's a duty in charity to point it out. But the charity doesn't extend simply to the pope; it also extends to all the people who have heard that teaching, to orient them in the proper way because they usually have the impression that whatever the pope says is what the Catholic Church teaches.

***So many people mistakenly think the pope can change the Church's teaching on the ordination of women to the priesthood, on the nature of the sacraments, on various moral issues, etc.***

Sometimes one hears Catholic doctrine and practice being categorized merely as "current papal policy." This expression has its proper application because the Holy See has its own view of world affairs. For example, Pope John Paul II was against the American invasion of Kuwait to liberate the Kuwaitis from the Iraqi invaders. Were all Catholics therefore bound to be against it? Of course not, and nobody would expect it. So, there is a realm where free debate is expected and happens. What's going to be the solution for Jerusalem and Israel and Palestine? The Holy See has its stated policy. Individual Catholics have may have other ideas.

***But in terms of faith and morals . . .***

The indissolubility of marriage has implications for the reception of Communion. People who are in a marriage cannot establish a "second" marriage with someone else and present themselves for Communion because it's a scandal to the community and it's also a false path for themselves, because as St. Paul says, they will be eating to their own condemnation (1 Cor. 11:29). You cannot gain the grace of the sacrament if you're knowingly living in a way gravely opposed to Catholic teaching. And it's clear that most of these people are not acting in ignorance, that is, they know this is against Church teaching. That's the reasonable presumption for anyone who is married in the Church and underwent some Pre-Cana instruction. Everybody, or almost everybody, knows that the Catholic Church doesn't believe a civil divorce ends a marriage.

**You are in a unique position as one of the few priests in the United States who is speaking out publicly.**
I get a lot of support from other priests. I have the microphone and the camera, so it gives me the opportunity to speak, and then I also write. But this is what we were all taught. This point was non-controversial for most of the Catholic world. It *was* controversial for the liberal part of the German Church, and those who followed it since the Second Vatican Council have had a problem with this teaching and think that people who are in invalid second marriages shouldn't be denied the sacraments.

As Archbishop of Buenos Aires, Pope Francis had an orientation towards the German liberal view of things. If Pope Francis had issued *Amoris Laetitia* as Archbishop of Buenos Aires, the Holy See, through the Congregation for the Doctrine of the Faith, would have criticized it—because they did criticize theologians who published those types of ideas. Once you become pope, does this mean you get to change things? The answer is, "No, you don't." And why is that? Because the pope, unlike an elected politician, doesn't represent the will of the electorate, i.e., "The people who got me elected want me to do this and therefore, I'm going to do it." Nor can it be done as an exercise of personal power, i.e., "I'm pope, so I get to make all the decisions and to change what I like."

*This can be a temptation . . .*
That's why pushback is good. And it fulfills what Pope Francis himself has said, that criticism is good because it causes you to reexamine what you are proposing or what you have taught.

*You mentioned that you were on the debate team. What valuable lessons did you learn from that experience?*
I was on the debate team at Regis High School. The Jesuit priest in charge of the debate team sent me and my partner to the Georgetown University summer school for high school debaters in Washington, DC. It was a great experience to live in the dormitory at Georgetown and be trained by teachers who were excellent debaters. That gave me a lot of confidence and knowledge on how to make one's point. Debating sharpens your thinking and teaches you to present your case concisely and convincingly, and to be attentive to the argument posed by the other side.

Probably the most fun was cross-examination, trying to poke holes in your opponent's arguments. That was a good experience. There were different techniques that we learned, but one typical debating technique is to agree with something your opponent says, but to lead him from that agreement to then agree with your interpretation of what it really means. Another technique is to listen to your opponent's argument, then respond saying, "If you and I agree this is true in this case, . . ." and then present an analogous case that contradicts and defeats his broader argument.

Learning to debate is also valuable because contradicting someone or disagreeing with him is today sometimes viewed in the Church as being impolite. Trying to convince someone that he's wrong is also sometimes viewed as disrespectful, but I don't think that's the case at all. Because unlike in a debate experience, where you argue about a topic chosen by whoever is in charge of that particular debate, in the Church it's the doctrine of Christ, communicated to the Apostles and then handed down over the centuries through the teaching office of the Church, that we're defending. It's not a matter of indifference to a defender of the Faith that the Faith is being contradicted, because he correctly sees that as an offense against the truth and also as a self-harm done to the person who denies the truth.

**Sometimes it seems that reasonable and legitimate intellectual argumentation on the one hand and personal attack on the other are conflated.**
It's true, and personal attack is to be avoided because it's an uncharitable and unfair debating technique. It also has the inevitable result of creating anger and even hatred in the person you're debating. On the other hand, startling and jarring observations are useful because oftentimes people can't see the implication of what they are defending unless you present an extreme case showing them the logical conclusions of their thinking.

**Have you ever encountered particular forms of evil as a priest?**
Yes, I remember one time hearing a Confession—and I'm not going to reveal the Confession, of course—but I do remember that it was a face-to-face Confession, which I don't really like, but it is canonically permitted. I was sitting there thinking, "This is bad. There is something demonic here." I can just say that the sense I got, as I was looking at this person making their Confession, was that there was some form of presence of the devil.

This is a mystery, the presence of evil in the world. I certainly see it, as we all do, with horrible criminals who commit grievous crimes—but occasionally you do get that sense. I'm a big believer in appealing to the Sacred Heart—I love the short prayer, "Cease, the Heart of Jesus is with me!"—and asking God to be with us and the Holy Spirit to guide and protect us. I remember the priest at Dartmouth used to say that the Real Presence of the Lord in the tabernacle throughout the world is a great hindrance to the devil's activity. Paganism is much more likely to be associated with diabolical activity because it's a false religion and can be easily manipulated. In Catholicism, on the other hand, we have a definite awareness that the devil is trying to attack the Church at all times and undermine the people's faith, but the solution is at hand. God comes to our assistance when we turn to him.

**May we talk about your life of prayer as a priest? You said you were influenced by Opus Dei in seminary and during the early years of your priesthood.**
Yes, having had an Opus Dei priest as a spiritual director as a seminarian, I learned the spiritual practices that Opus Dei recommends to its members and anyone who participates in their activities. It involves a half an hour of meditation in the morning before Mass. As a priest I celebrate the Mass every day, pray the Rosary every day, do fifteen minutes of spiritual reading every day, make an examination of conscience at noon time and pray the Angelus, and also make a short visit to the Blessed Sacrament to spend time with the Lord apart from Mass. I think it's essential that we constantly remind ourselves of the Real Presence of Jesus in the Blessed Sacrament so that

we are aware that God is present in his house, the Church. We go and visit him as we would visit anyone in their house. As a priest, I also say the breviary, which is the Liturgy of the Hours or Divine Office, and try to say it with devotion and attention.

**Do you say the new or the old breviary?**
I say the new breviary, but at some points I have said the old. It's more of a time commitment, and as a busy pastor in Manhattan, I appreciate the abbreviated form of the new breviary. I go back and forth in my mind on this question. When I retire from parochial management and have less busyness in my life, it would be good to go back to the old breviary.

Opus Dei also encourages one to develop your intellectual appreciation of the Faith, so I do try to read things to deepen my knowledge of theology and philosophy.

**What are you reading now?**
I'm reading Edward Feser's *Scholastic Metaphysics*, which is an excellent book. I'm reading a book called *The Architecture of Law: Rebuilding Law in the Classical Tradition* by Professor Brian McCall. I'm reading *The Everlasting Man* by G. K. Chesterton. I do tend to read a number of books at the same time.

In the internet age, I also follow the Catholic news in the media. It's important to be ready if I'm asked to comment on news.

**Do you celebrate the Traditional Latin Mass?**
I celebrate the Traditional Latin Mass occasionally. At Holy Family, we only have Mass according to the Missal of St. Paul VI, but my neighboring parish, St. Agnes, has the Tridentine

Mass every Sunday, so people in the neighborhood can go there. When I was in Rome studying canon law, I almost always celebrated the Old Mass *sine populo*, "without the people," because I do love offering the Old Mass.

**When did you learn it?**
When the Fraternity of St. Peter priests first came to the United States, I got to know some of them. In the summer of 1988, Pope John Paul II gave a wider permission to offer the Old Mass through his apostolic letter *Ecclesia Dei*, and then I started studying it and attending some Old Masses, and then learned it on my own. One of my priest buddies is ten years older than I, so he knew the Old Mass and helped me to learn it. Local bishops could give permission, so I got permission from the Archdiocese of New York. I would say the Old Mass occasionally at another parish in those days.

**Did it affect your priesthood?**
As a priest, you certainly learn more about the nature of the Mass by offering the Old Mass. The Mass is not primarily a dialogue between people and a priest. It is a prayer offered to God the Father, with people and priest together praying. We celebrate the New Mass *ad orientem*, facing East, here at Holy Family parish. The New Mass said *ad orientem* communicates the same message as the Old Mass because the focus is not on us (*non nobis Domine, non nobis*),[2] and as Pope Benedict XVI observed, the closed circle, with everyone looking at each other,

---

[2] Taken from Psalm 115:1: "Not to us, O Lord, not to us; but to your name be the glory."

is a bad idea. The priest becomes the celebrity-host. It's not what the nature of worship is.

The Old Mass also taught me the riches of Scripture and the Old Testament roots of so much of what's in the Mass. Part of the problem that I experienced, as a priest, was not simply that the New Mass was ritually diminished in that it was a cut-down version of the Old Mass. There was also its vulnerability to sloppiness and particularly liturgical abuse. Sloppiness could also be present with the Old Mass, but with the New Mass—since it's in English—the priest can very easily ad lib and rework the ritual as he wants. Learning the Old Mass was a real eye-opener in terms of the order and regulation of movements, and the focus on the Real Presence of Christ in the Blessed Sacrament once the Consecration occurs. I always liked the reception of Holy Communion kneeling and on the tongue. The aspects of reverence do not have to be invented by the celebrant; they are present if you conform to the rubrics and the spirit of what you're celebrating.

**May we talk about your sister's death?**
Yes. My sister Margot, who was the second child, was a year and a half younger than myself. In 1991 she had to have surgery for a condition called an arteriovenous malformation. She had had her first child that spring, a baby girl. At one point in the summer of 1991 she fainted, and we weren't quite sure what it was. The doctors discovered that there were arteries in part of the brain that failed for some reason to develop properly, and if blood goes into them, because they aren't properly formed, they can bleed, and it can cause serious injury or death. She

decided to have surgery to remove it, and the surgery was unsuccessful. She was in a coma for eighteen months.

*So her death wasn't sudden?*
No, and we hoped that she could recover.

*Did this test your faith?*
No, thank God my faith was strong. It was a sorrow and very difficult for my brother-in-law, for my mom and dad, and for my other sister and me. I remember that morning a few days after the surgery when Margot's condition became grave and she went into a coma. I rushed to the hospital to go visit her, and then later that day I said Mass back at St. Patrick's Cathedral, where I was assigned. It was very dramatic saying Mass thinking that your sister might die that day. It was a deep human sorrow but a reminder that we have no lasting city here.

*Did you give your sister last rites?*
I did. I also anointed my dad, years later, when he was dying. As a priest, you're a priest for everybody, including your family members. It was a blessing.

*Did your sister's death, and your father's death some years later, make the reality of the afterlife more real for you?*
As a priest, we deal with so many people dying. We visit people in their homes as they're about to expire or just after they die. We visit people in emergency rooms and intensive care units. I remember once anointing someone in the intensive care unit and, immediately after I had anointed him, the screen flatlined. I thought, "Thank God I got here in time."

The priest prepares people for the eternal journey. We do so many funeral Masses and wakes at funeral homes, so it's a reality we're more conversant with.

When it comes to your family members, it's more shocking, but the consolation of Catholicism is that this earthly life is not the whole story. If it were, it would be a horrible story: you work your whole life, and you end up dead. What's the point of working hard and building up a business or a family or an academic career or anything, and then, in the end, it's meaningless? If there's no afterlife, there's no accountability to a Creator. The idea that God would create us at the same level as the animals that go out of existence when they die . . . the Faith teaches us the exact opposite, and that's an unfailing consolation. "Life is changed, not ended," it says in the preface for the funeral Mass, and for me that's a great cause of joy.

**Have you ever had anyone resist as they were being anointed?**
Yes, I had the case of a man who was conscious. He believed but was not someone who had much time for prayer. At that point in his life, I think he was happy to receive the anointing, but once that was done, he said, "Okay, that's enough prayers." The great thing about Catholicism is that we have a great tolerance for different levels of participation!

**Do any other stories come to mind?**
I remember once going to an apartment in upper Manhattan to anoint a woman who had just died. She had died within the hour of when I got there, and the Church teaches that you can still do the anointing because death is a process, and it's not evident how long it takes for the soul to leave the body. I remember her

husband saying, "Fr. Murray, I hope there's a priest like you to come and anoint me when I'm about to die." That sort of thing reminds you that we are all instruments in the hands of God.

When as a priest you go to these deaths in apartments, sometimes the fire department is there, or the police are there, and that's one thing we don't always think about: fire fighters and police officers see a lot of death. It's good for them to see a priest and strengthen their faith that there's more to this life than the unhappiness of someone's being shot and killed, or dying of a disease or in a car accident. The Faith brings many consolations, and this is one of them: knowing that, no matter how life ends, if you cross the tape believing in Christ and are sorry for your sins, you've got nothing but happiness ahead of you. You might have a little stop in Purgatory, but that's not forever.

*Chapter 2*

# AGE OF CONFUSION

"And behold, there arose a great storm on the sea." (Matt 8:24)

**In The City of God, St. Augustine calls Babylon, the City of the World—the eternal enemy of the Church—the "city of confusion." Today confusion seems to reign in the world and the Church, too. Fr. Murray, why is this an age of confusion?**
The essential problem we face in the Western world is the loss of reality. We have entered into a nihilistic view of the world in which nothing is what it is, where there is no such thing as "what something is." According to this view, something only becomes what it is when we determine it. It is called the "plasticity of reality." Everything is subject to man's reshaping or designating of value.

We have adopted a philosophical outlook that rejects metaphysical realism, which is the foundation of Western civilization. Metaphysical realism is an essentially Aristotelian view of the world, which, when combined with the Roman legal mind, produced Western civilization in the pre-Christian period. Christianity then added the supernatural understanding that correctly guides sense perception. Understanding accurately the nature of things is complemented by the supernatural understanding of the divine purpose of creation.

*Can you say more about metaphysical realism?*
God created the world and gave man natural intelligence and the ability to understand the world. The world is intelligible, and it exists apart from man's mind. When we attempt to understand, we can go only so far with natural reason, but that is sufficient to create a social order that is essentially just. But there's more to reality and justice than what man can figure out on his own, and that's why natural religion cedes to supernatural religion. The correct and fuller understanding of creation and the natural order is ultimately found in Christ's revelation. Natural understanding can be shortchanged and lead to cruelty.

I am only a student of philosophy, but the ancient Greek philosopher Aristotle taught that the material world that we see can be understood through observation and analysis, and that categories of being are inherently present in creation. So, in discovering what things are, we can find out what their purpose is, i.e., why they exist. Aristotle taught that we can understand reality based on the study of how things function. The world is not a shadow dreamworld, as Platonism understands it, where reality is hidden from our eyes—although Plato had many good things to say otherwise.

Reality is intelligible, and categories exist, and therefore creation has a commonality. The stone I see in China is the same thing I see in North America, and they can be acted upon in similar ways and produce similar results. In other words, creation is mysterious, but it isn't unintelligible. That leads to some definite conclusions. For example, when we examine the human body and the way the human mind works, we see that we're meant to act in certain ways and not in others and that, if we act in accordance with our nature, it will produce well-being. This can happen also on the social level, where people cooperate to produce common well-being. All of this leads to definite conclusions about what should and should not be tolerated in society.

**Why ought a concept like "metaphysical realism" matter to the average person?**
Because reality is the key to anything in life: happiness, flourishing, achievement, wisdom, and love. All of this depends on a proper encounter with reality, on understanding the nature of what is given, and then conforming to that according to our capabilities. Reality is predictable because it has a nature. If you eat and sleep right, you're going to be a healthy person. Disease may arise, but if you cooperate with the way God made us, you're going to flourish.

The same thing goes for study: if you put the energy and effort into it, you're going to learn things, and based on that knowledge, you're going to be capable of doing other things which will benefit you and others.

The Aristotelian point of view was essentially adopted by St. Thomas Aquinas, but it is also in conformity with the Roman legal way of life. In other words, the Roman Empire functioned on the social level, on the basis of a similar metaphysical realism, on a commonly shared appreciation of a given reality. Christianity brought all of this to completion through the revelation of God the Creator and his law for his creation.

**When did this perspective shift?**
The Enlightenment largely rejected the God-centered understanding of creation and redemption and replaced it with a man-centered perspective in which human genius would no longer seek to know the truth of creation but would rather redefine reality. This arrogant usurpation of the Creator's sole prerogative predictably has led to skepticism and relativism. It led to the basic proposition that modern thinking in so many ways reflects, i.e., that the world is whatever I want it to be, and I can and will use force to make it so, because the only reason it isn't the way I want it to be is because some evil opponents are stopping me and my friends from accomplishing it. And that's basically what we have today in the "woke" cancel-culture revolution.

**Didn't the problems begin before that, with the Reformation and even as early as the Renaissance?**
According to Protestantism, Christianity had to be remade according to various theories of how the "primitive Church" was lost amidst Catholic accretions but would now re-emerge through the action of the Holy Spirit in guiding the reformers. The central Protestant principle of private judgment, meaning that God would lead each believer to correctly understand the Holy Scriptures apart from any ecclesiastical authority, has had the devastating consequence of making Christianity an essentially individual endeavor unbound by any external authority.

The Renaissance had good aspects but also had an element of self-worship that was devastating. Self-worship is a modern variant on the pagan practice of creating gods who embody human virtues and vices. Human achievements are now worshipped at the altar of self-aggrandizement.

**And how have the social theories of Communism, socialism, fascism, and anarchism—things we are now familiar with in a way we never expected to be—contributed to the present age of confusion?**

These coercive, violent ideologies have produced untold misery in the pursuit of remaking man as the "new man" who would "perfect" the world. This utopian effort failed, and at such a horrible price in persecution, death, and destruction, yet there are those today who would go down the same route in pursuit of the power to "re-create" the world.

**It does seem that many problems we face today boil down to man claiming for himself the right to decide the nature of things.**

Exactly, and the perfect example is gender ideology. The idea is that I'm going to treat something in a certain way because that's the way I think it should be. I'm going to determine that something is this way, and if you disagree with me, then you are a hateful person who has to be coerced or somehow constrained or even "cancelled." This is the gender-ideology fascism that we're going through today, where if you travel to a certain region and you're instructed that Miss Jones is now Mr. Jones, if you ever call her "she," you're going to be fired, fined, or perhaps arrested. That's a coercive use of power in order to enforce an imaginary worldview which is, of course, false. It's really a pathological view that's now being elevated to a legal status in our country.

Gender ideology is just one example of the flight from reality. The same can been seen in the case of abortion. It's not a baby because *I don't want it to be*. The same is true for so-called same-sex "marriage." It's a marriage because *I want it to be a marriage*. No, it isn't. The same is true for "gender non-conformity," the idea that there can be a "transgender" person, someone who says he's a male but really is biologically female, or the idea that there's something beyond male and female ("non-binary"). It's all a denial of reality and a failure to make proper use of the intellect to conform one's thinking to what is true.

**You have identified the Enlightenment and, before it, the Reformation and Renaissance, as key historical moments which have led to the present-day loss of reality. What do you see as the pivotal points in recent decades that have ushered in this age of confusion?**

The sexual revolution in the 1960s is one of the starting points for the current decline. The broader perspective in the twentieth century goes back to the two world wars during which Europe largely self-destructed, meaning that one part of Europe tried to destroy another and the other fought back. In the process, however, the one did such damage to the other. European man and people in the European sphere lost confidence in European culture. The Catholic Church remained faithful to her teaching but came under pressure from the idea that we have to create a new world and a new Europe.

The Second Vatican Council was an attempt to incorporate the idea of finding a new way to exist in the post-war world. Beyond this, however, the idea was to try to come up with a new way of conceiving of the order of Christian society in Europe.

But it largely failed on this score because it wasn't done in a vacuum: the Communist world and Socialist ideology wanted to get rid of the Christian worldview that had become subject to doubt after two world wars. Confrontation with atheistic ideologies on the level of ideas gave way to finding a form of co-existence, which has had disastrous results.

This came across the ocean and arrived on American shores. Couple this with the libertine philosophy that led the way in the breakdown of a common understanding of sexual relations, marriage, and family. In the United States, this was combined with a rejection of authority, and a necessary reckoning with racial injustice that led some to reject the whole American social order as unjust. "Tear it all down" was the revolutionary cry.

**You mention a rejection of authority. How do you think most people understand authority today, and what is its classic meaning?**
For most people, "authority" is the institution that has legitimate coercive power over the community. In other words, it is the institution that controls the police and the military and the jails. But this is an inadequate view of authority. Authority is the representation of a just order in society and the guarantor of that justice, when it acts in accord with the nature of man and the nature of the material creation, that is, in accord with God's purpose in creating man and the rest of the world.

***So, authority has a definite place and purpose in reality, in the metaphysical realism you just described . . .***
Yes, authority is the manifestation in society of the real nature of things as established by its Divine Author, for the purpose of organizing society at its different levels for cooperative activity. Authority is a good thing and is meant to ensure that justice is fostered and vindicated when violated. It's a necessary thing because man is a social being.

The original society was Adam and Eve and their children, and there was a hierarchy present in their family. That hierarchical nature then extends to social groupings, tribes, clans, etc. When meta-groupings such as cities and states arise, an authority must be found to guide the people according to reality, but it must have legitimate coercive power to govern the populace it oversees. In other words, a government must have the power to compel those who violate just laws to change their behavior or be isolated from society.

So, authority is necessary, but it can be misused if injustice is being proposed and enforced.

To return to what I was saying before, the Civil Rights Movement opposed an unjust segregationist system. The unjust social and legal order had to be reformed. Authority had misused its power to oppress black people. At the same time, the sexual revolution had started in Europe and migrated to America, and it was essentially a rejection of Christian moral authority, which stigmatized immorality and promoted morality. Christian moral authority got cast aside through birth control, pornography, mass divorce, and other aspects that have now devolved into "transgenderism," same-sex "marriage," and the like. Christian moral teaching was treated as another unjust imposition on society by authority. This false idea has caused untold havoc in our world.

**How is authority generally undermined?**
Authority can discredit itself by not being true to its mission, or people can reject the notion of authority because they believe it's going to infringe on their ability to be happy in life. Both of those are regrettable. That is why authority is always called upon to conform its use of power to what is true, right, and just.

In baseball, everyone is horrified when the umpire misses a call at first base. That is why they want to use electronic means to determine things—any way to get to the absolute truth because it lets things play out fairly. The umpire is not an evil actor. Unless he's being paid under the table, he just made a mistake, but people are outraged if the call isn't right.

If you transfer that to the realm of ultimate questions: How should I treat my neighbor? What do I owe to the poor? How should I raise my children? What are my duties to society? What am I supposed to do when I or my loved one get sick? How do I get to Heaven?—in all those areas, we need authorities who are going to actually tell us the truth and guide us well, and we have to have confidence that authority is acting truthfully and justly.

**To what extent do you believe the breakdown in paternity, i.e., fatherhood, in the West, has affected the way we view authority?**
There is no question that there is a crisis in fatherhood in the West. Male leadership, which should take its inspiration from the way a good father protects, guides, and provides for his

family, is deprecated as "toxic masculinity." Gender ideology necessarily attacks both motherhood and fatherhood. God the Father is the ultimate target of those who rebel against the created order.

*In his September 2006 Regensburg address in Germany, Pope Benedict XVI said that reason plays a part in the foundation of Western culture and that the Church was a driving force in understanding God as Wisdom.[1] In his memorable lecture, Benedict connects the loss of reason with the dissolution of society. Do you think it's not so much a crisis of faith we're living through as it is a crisis of reason?*

As regards the origin of the crisis in theology, one of my professors in the seminary, Msgr. William B. Smith, said that, at root, all theological problems are philosophical problems. By that I think he meant that speaking correctly about God presupposes that you have a correct understanding of God's creation and man's part in it. So, if you fail to understand the nature of reality and man's ability to understand, interpret, or explain reality, then you really can't speak intelligently about the meaning of revelation or natural law. So, it is very much a philosophical crisis.

When Pope Benedict spoke in the Regensburg address about the Western world, I think he understood that the wisdom of the Greeks, particularly Aristotle, was to make clear that the world is intelligible and ordered and has purposes and

---

[1] Pope Benedict XVI, "Faith, Reason and the University: Memories and Reflections," University of Regensburg (September 12, 2006), https://www.vatican.va/content/benedict-xvi/en/speeches/2006/september/documents/hf_ben-xvi_spe_20060912_university-regensburg.html.

meanings inherent in it. Therefore, it is not subject to manipulation by man. It's susceptible to understanding, and then man cooperates with creation. This goes against the magical thinking that is typical of non-rational and idealistic thinking processes, which, quite frankly, the West was triumphantly able to overcome in large measure because it had the philosophical basis of realism combined with the true knowledge of revelation that allowed for a complete explanation of what the earth is, why we're here, and what we're supposed to do.

**Pope John Paul II opened his 1998 encyclical on the relationship between faith and reason, Fides et Ratio, with these memorable lines: "Faith and reason are like two wings on which the human spirit rises to the contemplation of truth; and God has placed in the human heart a desire to know the truth—in a word, to know himself—so that, by knowing and loving God, men and women may also come to the fullness of truth about themselves (cf. Exod 33:18; Ps 27:8–9; 63:2–3; John 14:8; 1 John 3:2)."[2]**

The crisis of reason has to do with the Church's continual struggle to overcome philosophical errors and, primarily in our own time, errors of the Enlightenment. As regards the crisis of faith, that has to do with the Western world's rejection of Christian culture and belief as the basis of daily life, and that comes under many forms: militant atheism, and as John Paul II always used to talk about, the consumeristic atheism of people who get by

---

[2] Pope John Paul II, Encyclical Letter on the Relationship between Faith and Reason *Fides et Ratio* (September 14, 1998), https://www.vatican.va/content/john-paul-ii/en/encyclicals/documents/hf_jp-ii_enc_14091998_fides-et-ratio.html.

in life and don't need God's help. The deeper a Catholic culture is rooted in the customs and usages of a society, the harder it is for that militant atheistic philosophy to overcome it, as was the case in Poland. But consumeristic atheism soon leads to a soft tyranny, which we basically have in many places in Western Europe, where the biggest defenders of secularism seem to be Catholics or ex-Catholics.

**And the United States . . .**
The United States is becoming that way, although the resistance to the abortion license, for instance, is much more notable in the US than in Europe, and that's a sign of the relatively greater vitality of Catholicism and Christianity in general, but it's an ongoing struggle.

**The consequences of sin are the darkening of the intellect and the weakening of the will. At times, it seems there's almost a satanic veil that has fallen over the Western world and is impeding man's power to reason.**
The mystery of iniquity is manifest precisely in the devil's trying to trick men into thinking in ways that will lead them to deny God and his revelation and certainly to deny the Church in its role as a mediator between God and man. And that is an age-old problem that starts with the beginning of world history. Certainly, the Apostles faced this reality, and we do too.

Where is it going in our own society? We have the paradox of the highest level of technical knowledge ever achieved by mankind in the history of the world, witnessed by cellphones and spacecraft on Mars, but we have among the most ignorant populace as regards basic categories of right and wrong, reason and unreason. A sign of that is the ever-present and growing fascination with pagan ideas, superstitions, a relentless fascination with moral deviancy, the titillation of seeing people violate the moral law that is treated as somehow indicative of a brave new world when it's simply a regression into pagan lifestyles and ways of thinking.

*It sounds eerily similar to a cross between Hilaire Belloc's essay, "The New Paganism," and George Orwell's 1984. In the former work, Belloc writes that the two most prominent marks of the new paganism, i.e., of Western society's abandonment of the heights of Christian civilization, are "the postulate that man is sufficient to himself, that is, the omission of the idea of Grace; the second, despair."[3] Belloc continues:*

> *The New Paganism is the resultant of two forces which have converged to produce it: appetite and the sense of doom. Of the forces which impelled it into being, the appeal of the senses to be released from restriction through the denial of the Faith is so obvious that none will contest it, the only controversy being upon whether this removal of restriction upon sensual enjoyment, declining every form of reticence and exercising the fullest license for what*

---

[3] Hilaire Belloc, "The New Paganism," in *Essays of a Catholic* (London: Sheed and Ward, 1931), https://www.catholic.com/magazine/print-edition/the-new-paganism.

***is called 'self-expression,' is of good or of evil effect upon the individual and upon society.*** [4]

Yes, it's interesting because, at the same time, we have a tremendous self-confidence about the ability of scientists to make life better and more convenient—and in many ways they have—and a complete explosion of drug use, and other forms of addiction and "stupefaction." In other words, we have forgotten—or are trying to forget—ordinary life as a way of enjoying oneself. And this is revealing the hole in men's hearts when they don't have God. Because what do they have then? Only themselves. And what is self-worship but completely frustrating, because we know that we're not worthy of worship even if we pretend that we are.

**Contrast that with many of the peoples in Africa, who may be very poor but who often radiate joy and seem to understand what is truly important in life.**
And joy comes from a certain knowledge about the way creation exists, where I fit in, what's going to happen to me when I die, what I have to do now in order to die well, and those things are immediately evident to people who hear the Gospel and believe it is true.

People in the Western world have become adept at trying to exempt themselves from the demands of the Gospel and give themselves free passes to do whatever they want, and then they find people who justify it, even in the Church, and the result is sadness, neurosis, and self-destructive behavior.

---

[4] Belloc, "The New Paganism."

*One realm in which this manifests itself today is in married life and sexuality. When there is the proper ordering of the relationship between a married couple, it brings real joy to the couple and to the family. But when that order is lost, it leads to sadness in the family and in the wider society.*

Absolutely right. Christian solidarity means we try to strengthen one another in our belief and in our practice. Married couples who are generous in receiving children and then raising them in a Catholic manner give strength to everyone who knows them because everybody knows it's sacrificial to have a large family.

*When we talked about your life, you mentioned that Catholicism was so different in your parents' time. How did things go wrong specifically in the United States over the past decades?*

Before the 1960s, by and large Protestant culture was hostile to Catholicism for reasons of religious belief. The classical Protestant belief was that the pope of Rome was a usurper, and that the Catholic Church made things up and led believers away from Christ and the Gospel. That conviction was held by many, but in general, we could say that the culture of Protestantism in the United States was not hostile to the moral claims or basic religious purposes of all of Christianity, including Catholicism, which is to worship God and to serve our neighbor, in view of salvation.

That all fell apart when mainline Protestantism endorsed the sexual revolution, and then the Catholic Church defended its position against that, but oftentimes without winning the battle among Catholics. So many Catholics defected to a very hedonistic lifestyle, and this is at the root of a lot of religious alienation. Part of it is also that religious practice among mainline

Protestants declined and is now miniscule. I come from the Northeast, which is basically defined by Episcopalianism historically. That now is a shell of what it was a hundred years ago.

Catholicism was vibrant with a great number of people going to Sunday Mass. There were many Catholic schools and religious orders. When the Catholic Church did not successfully win the cultural war around the sexual revolution but in many ways surrendered to it—at least in practice, not in teaching—the results were disastrous. Catholics today use birth control at rates equivalent to secular society. Abortion rates are very high among Catholics, and Mass attendance is pathetic compared to what it was in 1960. This is all due to caving into the trends of secular society.

Nowadays, if you embrace Catholicism as a package-deal, meaning, "I believe it all and practice it enthusiastically," you're considered to be a conservative, right-wing extremist because you're not willing to make compromises. And that's false. To live out our Faith as it is written down and taught is to live it in its essence, and that's one of the great things that is evident in the efforts of those derisively called "Catholic Cultural Warriors." It should just be called "Catholic Normalcy," but the normal becomes the extreme in the view of those who want to tear it down.

**Today there is dramatic disunity, not only in the world but in the Church, too, seemingly riven by factions. And the hostility of the world to the Church is much more overt and unapologetic than it was sixty or seventy years ago. What is the cause of this disunity and this hostility?**

In the Western world, the Christian foundation was altered tremendously by the Protestant Reformation, but it still remained the foundation of both religious and public life. That foundation has been eroded over time. One of the notes of the twentieth century, in the European world, is the rejection of its Christian foundation. This is manifest in the European Union's 2004 Constitution, which intentionally avoids any reference to the Christian roots and history of Europe, as if it were a matter of shame.

It's a matter of historical record that Catholicism is the religious, philosophical, and cultural foundation of European society. The rejection of the Christian foundation led to a split on moral questions, primarily between what civil governments and the Church were proposing. It's most clearly manifested in the left-wing Communist rejection of morality, but it's likewise manifested in secularist views of the world, which can even be based on conservative economic principles or ideas that are hostile to leftism but are nonetheless very secularistic. Here we would talk about an a-religious conservatism, which is essentially libertarianism. These erroneous ideas, predominant in many areas of the world, are fighting against the remnants of the Christian worldview. Again, this is most manifest in morality, so we see laws attacking family and sexual morality, and now human identity.

Pope John Paul II always insisted on the inherent dignity of the human person, i.e., that everyone created by God has value, apart from any judgment by anyone else.

That split leads to different ways of looking at how society should be ordered, and the result is a power grab, primarily by the Left, and it is not always opposed by those who consider themselves friends of tradition. America is not as advanced as Europe in this regard but is catching up quickly. We've had presidents since 1968 who have been more or less favorable to a Christian worldview, but our laws and customs are sliding away.

***Can you give an example?***
Abortion is the prime example, and it's to the credit of the pro-life movement, which is almost entirely inspired by religious motivations, that this is still a lively political issue in America and is discussed at every election. In Europe, it is basically a dead letter, apart from small public gatherings of pro-life people. But there is no general political movement or intellectual ferment in favor of the pro-life movement in Europe, and this is where the United States could head if we keep imitating the secularist worldview.

***St. John Henry Newman wrote: "In proportion as you put off the yoke of Christ, so does the world by a sort of instinct recognize you and think well of you accordingly. Its highest compliment is to tell you that you disbelieve."[5] Why then should we desire "unity" with the world?***

[5] St. John Henry Newman, "Discourse 8: Nature and Grace," in *Discourses to Mixed Congregations* (1849), no. 166, https://www.newmanreader.org/works/discourses/discourse8.html. In a similar vein, Newman also wrote:

> Is not the world in itself evil? Is it an accident, is it an occasion, is it but an excess, or a crisis, or a complication of circumstances, which constitutes its sinfulness? Or, rather, is it not one of our three great spiritual enemies, at all times, and under all circumstances and all changes, ungodly, unbelieving, seducing, and anti-Christian? Surely we must grant it to be so. Why else in Baptism do we vow to wage war against it? Why else does Scripture speak of it in the terms which we know so well, if we will but attend to them?

The Church is meant to transform the world, precisely because, by worldly standards, the only *good* Catholic is a *bad* Catholic. The quest for unity apart from Christ is in vain, and Catholic instinct teaches that. We can have pacific relations between Christians and non-Christians, and we can have the application of laws to guarantee rights and duties, but in the end, true social harmony among men is going to be based on a common recognition of God and his providential design for creation, meaning the Church. Where that is present—which was the goal of Christendom, the Social Kingship of Christ—you will have a society in which sin is not praised or legalized and virtue is supported, lauded, and held forth as an example.

Conversely, in a Communist society, which denies Christ's Kingship and even God himself, the powerful lie and steal and those without power are victimized by it. This would

> St. James says, that "the friendship of the world is enmity with God" (Jas 4:4), so that "whosoever will be a friend of the world is the enemy of God." And St. Paul speaks of "walking according to the course of this world, according to the prince of the power of the air, the spirit that now worketh in the children of disobedience" (Eph 2:2); and exhorts us not to be "conformed to this world," but to be "transformed by the renewing of our mind" (Rom 12:2); and he says that Christ "gave himself for our sins, that he might deliver us from this present evil world" (Gal 1:4). In like manner St. John says, "Love not the world, neither the things that are in the world. If any man love the world, the love of the Father is not in him" (1 John 2:15). Let us be quite sure, then, that that confederacy of evil which Scripture calls the world, that conspiracy against Almighty God of which Satan is the secret instigator, is something wider, and more subtle, and more ordinary, than mere cruelty, or craft, or profligacy; it is that very world in which we are; it is not a certain body or party of men, but it is human society itself. This it is which is our greatest enemy. (Newman, "Sermon 7: Faith and the World," in *Sermons on Subjects of the Day* [Longmans, Green & Co.: London, 1902], 79–80, https://www.newmanreader.org/works/subjects/sermon7.html.)

be viewed as a successful accomplishment by a Communist government. In a truly Christian society, if you had leaders stealing and lying, they would be rebuked and called to repent, and if they failed to, they would be removed.

**It would be a betrayal of the authority entrusted to them . . .**
Yes, because they have not conformed to God's will, and they've done so in violation of the laws which, over the centuries, Christianity had promulgated to uphold that will in the everyday life of society. In a way, that's the undergirding of the Christian worldview: we may be sinners, but we don't praise sin. Whereas, in the materialist world, there is no sin. There are simply contrary claims, which can only be enforced if you have power. Therefore, your goal is to gain power so as to have your claims enforced. We see this now in the university world, where radical left-wing professors dominate the scene. They are no longer interested in debating the people they used to debate with when they were in the minority. Now, they stigmatize their opponents and demand that they be fired because debating was only a necessary pause on the road to gaining power. It wasn't a common effort to arrive at truth.

That is why it's dangerous when Communists and people like them take power in a nation—because there's no appeal to conscience or to legal standards. It's simply: submit, flee, or be killed. The only way they can be overthrown, then, is by outside and eventually inside pressures that undermine their ability to maintain their control. For example, the fall of the Soviet Union happened when they lost the police and the military supporting Gorbachev's Glasnost policy, which was a failed self-preservation mode that led to the Communist Party collapsing. Cuba is an example of where outside pressure has not been able to overcome the Communist dictatorship. Island nations can be more resistant to outside influences.

**What do you think is the core of disunity between different factions in the Catholic Church?**
I think the primary cause of disunity in the Church is the importation of the Protestant notion of private judgment as the interpretive mechanism for understanding God's revelation.

Therefore, the authoritative determination of the Church is not treated as definitive and final but is considered "another approach." This attitude is manifested in every heretical movement from the beginning of Christianity, in which some people willfully assert contradictory teachings based on private judgment and their understanding of the Scriptures and the Tradition of the Church.

That became the principle of the Reformation, and it is the operating principle of Protestantism that there is no ultimate authority and that each person forms his own opinions on the meaning of the Scriptures and what it means to be a Christian. There are generally agreed upon things, that people should agree to, but even those are not strictly held to because there is no authority to uphold them. Whereas in the Catholic Church, when you start claiming that the Bible justifies A, B, and C, and the teaching authority in fact teaches that the Church does not authorize A, B, and C, then you have a conflict if the claimants do not submit their judgment to that of the Church.

Each believer has to make an act of faith in the Creed and in the teachings of the Church, so we are believers who enter into the embrace of the Church and therefore believe together with all other Catholics. Our belief is determined by the doctrine proposed by the teaching Church, so the teaching Church tells us what we need to believe in and how to understand it as best we can.

When people arrogate to themselves the right to disagree with the teaching Church, the source of disunity is not the teaching itself but their refusal to recognize that the Church is endowed by God with the ability and right to require us to conform our belief to a certain way of thinking, which is to profess the Creed according to what it really means.

**Can you give an example of this?**
The perfect example is the Holy Eucharist. The Church teaches that when the priest says, "This is My Body," transubstantiation occurs, and the bread becomes the Body of Christ. Any thought that contradicts that has to be removed from the mind of the believer because it prevents him from embracing the truth that the Church teaches.

Christians in the Protestant world interpret this differently, and in fact they don't have a valid priesthood and most merely see the Eucharist as a symbol. Unfortunately, there are also many ignorant Catholics who go along with the Protestant view of the Eucharist. The people who would justify that erroneous teaching can never do so in a Catholic way because the authority has already spoken. So, it's not an open question. It's not subject to revision. But sad to say, on this and many other issues, this is where certain teachers in the Church have misled people since the Second Vatican Council and even before it. The results, seen in surveys, show that actual belief in the Real Presence, in transubstantiation, is often a minority position among Catholics. Many people also reject in practice the belief that Catholics must marry in the Church. The need to baptize your offspring is rejected in practice, as are other teachings.

In the end, it comes down to a question of authority, because the authority is God. So, the question is: How has God determined that we should accomplish his will? And he's determined it by sending his Son into the world, and the Son taught authoritatively, then told the Apostles, "He who hears you hears me" (Luke 10:16). He gave the Apostles under and with St. Peter this responsibility and that is why, in the Catholic Church, you can say there is one point of reference that cannot be overridden: papal authority. Papal authority is the final word, and the pope's duty is to teach precisely what has been taught by the Church from the time of the Apostles, to explain it, and to meet new challenges.

In the Protestant world, you can come up with your own understanding of what it means to be a Christian. People may criticize you for it, but there's no compelling reason why you should listen to or even agree with their criticism because they have no more authority over you than you have over them. Whereas in the Catholic world, the pope has authority over me, and I have no authority over him.

**What do you see as the origin of the current storm through which the Church is passing?**
It goes back again to the Reformation and the Enlightenment. It's a combination of interior and exterior rejection of visible authority for the Christian world, and the rejection of the common inheritance of the realist metaphysical view of the world, which leads to definite conclusions, laws, and customs

that result in societal arrangements in which the natural order is upheld and supported. The Enlightenment is the source of modern skepticism and rationalism, relativism, these theories which deny objective truth or any common natural law to guide behavior. And when those things are denied, it essentially comes down to who's in charge here, who has the power. Here authority is not based on what is good and natural according to the order of creation. It comes down to, "You do what I want, or I'll arrest or kill you." And that's the paradox: when there's no external standard that is accepted as the reference point, then it's simply a game of king of the hill.

**Domination instead of debate . . .**
Exactly.

**Is it also the presence of the "world" in the Church that has caused division between different factions?**
I think it's the adoption of ways of thinking among Catholics that were reprobated in the past, and this goes back to Enlightenment thinking and the notion of the perfectibility of man and his ability to comprehensively understand creation and then modify it according to the best of human thinking.

That's sort of the impetus behind socialism, i.e., we've got to "rationalize" the market, meaning we've got to control the market. Well, anywhere socialism is tried, it produces misery and often violence, and it doesn't work—and when possible, people flee it and go elsewhere.

In the religious sphere, the idea that if we become less hostile to Protestantism and more ecumenical, then Protestants will desire full unity with the Catholic Church has certainly not been realized. I think that was a naïve presumption because hostility to Protestantism didn't mean hostility to Protestants. What it meant was a rejection of Reformation errors and a reaffirmation of the necessity and vitality of dogmatic beliefs in the life of the Church. In other words, we believe things that other people deny. In order to attract them to believe it, we shouldn't downplay the value of those dogmas, saying "Well, don't let that be an obstacle to being fully united to the Catholic Church because dogma is not the most important thing." If you do that, you're on a suicide path because if we don't know what we believe, then why would anyone want to be a Catholic? It's a lot easier, humanly speaking, to be in a religion where they make no demands on you or in a religion where they tell you salvation is assured and there's no such thing as going to Hell.

*In his 1907 encyclical on the doctrines of the Modernists, Pascendi Dominici Gregis (Feeding the Lord's Flock), Pope St. Pius X called Modernism "the synthesis of all heresies" and added that "their system means the destruction not of the Catholic religion alone but of all religion."[6] Modernism, he explained, sets aside intelligible truths in favor of a religious sentiment that can be expressed in different concepts from one age to the next. Is Modernism still alive today, and how do we see it manifest in the current doctrinal confusion and disunity in the Church?*

Pope St. Pius X issued in 1910 "The Oath against Modernism,"

---

[6] Pope Pius X, Encyclical on the Doctrines of the Modernists *Pascendi Dominici Gregis* (September 8, 1907), § 39, https://www.vatican.va/content/pius-x/en/encyclicals/documents/hf_p-x_enc_19070908_pascendi-dominici-gregis.html.

which was formerly sworn to by all priests. It includes this: "I sincerely hold that the doctrine of faith was handed down to us from the Apostles through the orthodox Fathers in exactly the same meaning and always in the same purport. Therefore, I entirely reject the heretical misrepresentation that dogmas evolve and change from one meaning to another different from the one which the Church held previously."

The theory that dogmas can "change and evolve" plagues the Catholic world today and gives rise to such absurdities as the blessing of unions or so-called marriages of same-sex couples. When the Holy See reaffirmed in March 2021 the impossibility of blessing such unions, numerous Churchmen in Europe publicly rejected this and called for a change in the Church's teaching and practice. That is Modernism in action.

**In the early Church there were factions. Is there something different about the factions now?**
Well, there will always be different interest groups and different apostolates and different emphases, and that's all good if we're all united in our common pursuit of salvation and our common belief in the doctrine of the Faith. Today, the factionalism in the Church is essentially made up of people who want to change Catholicism versus those who want to defend Catholicism. The most scandalous thing is when the people who are entrusted with defending the Church actually try to dismantle it, which is what's happening in Germany right now and is happening in other places.

Cardinal Newman spoke about how, in the Arian crisis, the faith of the ordinary believer was the perduring witness of the catholicity of the Church, at a time when so many of the bishops had defected into Arian belief. And how often today the most vocal and eloquent defenders of Catholic teaching are not bishops or priests but lay people. That's a sign, I think, of divine providence, that God is once again raising up brilliant and dedicated and faithful defenders of the Church in ways that were not necessary in the more recent past because the hierarchy was vigilant. Nowadays, some bishops aren't vigilant, and some bishops are undermining the Church.

***Do you think some factions have more influence in the Church right now? And do you see the Church trending towards one direction?***

Many of the people who control institutional aspects of Catholic life—the hierarchy, the professoriate in Catholic universities, religious orders and their vast network of operations—are hostile to the Faith and practice that was commonplace in the 1950s in the Church. They would consider Pope Pius XII to be someone to be forgotten, not looked to as an inspiration. And that is a shame because Catholicism doesn't change with the calendar year. Their idea seems to be that some things become obsolete and out-of-date and are to be discarded. That is not the supernatural Faith that is proposed by Christ.

The Church has many areas of strength, mostly among those who joyously and happily want to defend the integrity of the Faith and the seriousness of Catholic piety and worship. Attendance at the Latin Mass—meaning those both young and old who have been drawn to the Tridentine Mass since Pope Benedict XVI encouraged its widespread celebration in *Summorum Pontificum*[7]—is growing by leaps and bounds,

---

[7] Pope Benedict XVI issued this motu propio in 2007.

attracting many young people and young families, and producing many vocations to the priesthood.

**We have been talking about secularization and disunity within the Church. What did Christ mean when he said we should be "in the world but not of the world"? What is the way for the Church to balance those two commands?**
To be in the world means that we are living in God's creation and in the human society in which we are born, with a desire to be a good influence on and to guide our fellow man in the way of salvation. In other words, it means trying to convert non-believers and to help create laws and customs that reflect the mind of Christ.

The worldly spirit is the spirit of disbelief and is man-centered, meaning that humanity figures it all out and is only answerable to itself. Since the unredeemed world is subject to the devil, it largely reflects diabolical preoccupations, which prominently include unbridled sex, power, the acquisition of money, and the use of violence to promote oneself and to dominate others. That's basically what we see today. Christianity has not always lived up to its vocation because Christians have also lived this sort of lifestyle, but they have not justified it as being God's will. Whereas the worldly spirit is the spirit of wantonness, recognizing no authority but itself.

**Some today might say, "Why not just let the storm come and be visible, since the division in the Church is real, and to suggest otherwise is unreal?" Pretenses of unity are just that, proponents of this argument would claim. "Enough with the attitude of not wanting to face the storm, of continually**

*giving the benefit of the doubt in order to maintain what is only a superficial calm." The storm has to come, they say, or it will never pass.*

The analogy of a storm is imperfect because no one controls the weather. Will Rogers said, "Everyone complains about the weather, but nobody does anything about it."

The storms in the Church are the result of the decisions people make in what they are going to teach and how they are going to live. Those are influenceable; you can influence people through words and, if necessary, through legal penalties. It's never good to be passive in the face of heresy being taught or immorality being practiced. The authority of the Church needs to remind people that the salvation of their souls is at stake, and that the bad influence they're having on others is a grave sin and a grave cause of harm to others. But that takes courageous shepherds who are convinced of the value of confronting evil in the life of the Church and not simply standing by or saying, "I'll pray that things get better, but I'll do nothing," because that's not enough.

*In* **Heretics,** *G. K. Chesterton said that every heresy is focused on one truth to the exclusion of others. How does confusion arise when people focus on one truth and not others?*

Confusion arises when people look at the body of Catholic doctrine and cast a doubt on its integrity. In other words, they say, "I find so much attractive in this religion, but some things I just can't accept, but I think that's all right because the rest of it is good, and I go along with that. But there are other things that I don't really want to accept, and I'm not going to make an effort to understand why the Church teaches that. I'll simply say I don't agree with that, but Catholicism means a lot to me and I'll stick with that."

This is a common approach, and the task of the shepherds is to make clear that believing in eight out of twelve articles of the Creed is not good enough. In other words, you can't just say, "I believe in most of it." Because it is a "package deal." I use this kind of secular expression, but when the Lord said to the Apostles, "Go therefore and make disciples of all the nations, . . . teaching them to observe all that I have commanded you" (Matt 28:19–20), he said "all"; he didn't say "the parts they find most compelling." Because Our Lord Jesus is not a negotiator or someone who proposes a set of ideals, and if you only want half of them, he'll be satisfied with that.

**It's not "the art of the deal" with Jesus.**
Exactly, it's not the art of the deal, and human reason is limited, so even though we're smart and we can think of objections, that doesn't mean that they are determinative of the truth we are considering. A Catholic instinct is to say, "If the Church teaches something, and I find it difficult to believe, the benefit of the doubt goes to the Church who knows what she's teaching. I just have to understand it better. And the Church, because she's a loving Mother, will answer my difficulties if I really want to have them resolved." That's what apologetics is: it seeks to explain to people the teachings of Catholicism that may not immediately be embraced or self-evident.

**It would seem that there's a parallel, then, between the scientific world—i.e., between man believing that creation is intelligible but mysterious and takes time to discover, and**

*that it's not for man to determine or manipulate the nature of things—and the world of Catholic doctrine. Faith ought to seek understanding, but we shouldn't expect to immediately understand everything, and Catholics ought to be disposed to trust in the Church and in the goodness of the integrity of her Faith.*

That's an excellent point. By analogy, you don't have to know how your iPhone works in order to make a call. It's similar in the world of Catholic doctrine: if you don't understand what it means, that doesn't mean you can't believe it. And in divine providence, God has raised up brilliant saints like Thomas Aquinas, Augustine, and others who explained things in a profound way. If one takes the trouble, one can read them, but your faith doesn't require you to have their same level of knowledge to believe.

*Even among the doctors of the Church themselves, we have a St. Thomas Aquinas and St. Thérèse of Lisieux. One has all the academic learning and the other, in addition to knowing her catechism well, had infused wisdom. Yet both are given to us so that we might come to better understand the Faith.*

Exactly, and in our own day I look at Robert Cardinal Sarah's writings as a perfect example of how, in a crisis, God raises up voices and writers to explain things and to make them clear. But remember, religion is not purely reason. It's the act of faith, and the act of faith demands that we recognize the reasonableness of what we're taught but we don't demand a complete explanation of things that are mysteries.

For instance, when the priest says, "This is My Body" over a piece of bread, it becomes the Body of Christ. How does that happen? Well, on the simplest level it happens because

Jesus gave the power to the priest to make it happen. How it happens otherwise the Church has explained through "transubstantiation" and other doctrinal explanations on the power of the priesthood and the nature of the Mass. But you don't have to have a complete understanding of transubstantiation in order to believe in the Eucharist and to love receiving Communion. We shouldn't think people are wrong to want to know what it means, and, on the other hand, we shouldn't say to people, "Until you come to that profound knowledge, your faith is lacking." No, each person believes with the power of God's grace in a way that can always improve but is not necessarily deficient in and of itself.

**Catholics aren't required to have a complete understanding of transubstantiation in order to receive the Eucharist, but they are required to believe in all of the dogmas of the Faith to receive Communion, aren't they?**

If we believe that Jesus Christ is the eternal Son of God, who is "the way, and the truth, and the life" (John 14:6), then everything he taught is true. And if he gave the power to teach to the Apostles, then we also believe that everything the Church defines and proposes as dogmas of the Faith must be believed in in order to be saved. So people who have rejected any part of that faith, if they are men and women of integrity, should refrain from receiving the Eucharist because they should be conscious that the Church teaches that God is not pleased with those who say, "I believe 80 percent of what you said, Lord, but 20 percent I disbelieve."

Why would the Lord teach something and ever give you permission to disbelieve it? Therefore, what you're doing is not in accordance with God's will. It's an act of disobedience, and disobedient people have put themselves at odds with the person they refuse to obey. To ask God, "Bless me with your Holy Body while I consciously disobey your law" is inconsistent. If you want to be a man or woman of integrity, you will refrain from receiving Communion if you do not really believe that Jesus is the infallible Teacher of Truth. If you do not believe this, then maybe he was wrong when he said, "This is My Body." How can you be sure he wasn't?

**Chesterton also writes (in Heretics) that "the word 'heresy' not only means no longer being wrong; it practically means being clear-headed and courageous. The word 'orthodoxy' not only no longer means being right; it practically means being wrong."**
This has been fulfilled in how society organizes itself and social life. We have the expression "cutting edge" to mean the thing towards which everyone should strive. Yet, when you continually cut away at a garment, you eventually destroy it. What really counts in life is to be united to what is true and possesses integrity and strength, and when something is strong and has confidence in its own mission, which the Church by nature has, fads and the like get judged by the Church and not the other way around.

Look at the idea of women's ordination: what's the reason we should ordain women now, when that's not happened in two thousand years in the Church? The standard answer is, "Times have changed, and women deserve it as much as men." One can say, "But how does that relate to how the Church herself exists? The Church wasn't founded by the Apostles themselves by saying, "Let's create something in the memory of Jesus, and then we'll figure out the rules later."

We have a very secularistic and worldly view, that whatever man can possibly control, he should. The Christian view, which sees nature as coming from God, means that our use of nature and all created things has to be subject to God's rules, and those rules are the natural law and revelation. For the Church, these two things are the foundation of proper living.

**Let's turn to Vatican II. In 1988, Cardinal Ratzinger remarked, "The Second Vatican Council has not been treated as a part of the entire living Tradition of the Church, but as an end of Tradition, a new start from zero. The truth is that this particular council defined no dogma at all, and deliberately chose to remain on a modest level, as a merely pastoral council; and yet so many treat it as though it made itself into a sort of super-dogma which takes away the importance of all the rest."[8] How did this unfortunate representation of Vatican II take hold and what have been the consequences?**

The question of the Second Vatican Council and its aftermath is a principal focus of interest right now in the life of the Church because we are trying to figure out why the Catholic Church has declined in so many areas and so rapidly. Was it due to the Council? Was it not? Is it something that can be blamed on the Council Fathers and what they wrote?

The Council did not teach anything heretical. I think it did not teach everything as well as it could have, and I think

---

[8] Cardinal Joseph Ratzinger, "Address to the Bishops of Chile" (July 13, 1988). As reprinted in *The Wanderer*, June 22, 2000, https://www.catholicculture.org/culture/library/view.cfm?recnum=3032.

that sections which could be subject to further explication would not involve contradicting the Council but explaining better its teaching. The issue of religious liberty is one example of where this could be done.

**Archbishop Carlo Maria Viganò seems to be of the mind that the Council should be forgotten. By contrast, Bishop Athanasius Schneider has stated that while he believes there were positive elements about the Council and we must respect it as an event of the Church, we cannot close our eyes to what is evidently ambiguous or even potentially erroneous in some of the texts. Where do you stand?**

The Council's Declaration on Religious Liberty, *Dignitatis Humanae,* is subject to serious critique, I agree, and that critique has been carried out in the Church. One thinks of Fr. Brian Harrison, or of the French Benedictine monk from the monastery of Le Barroux, Dom Basile, who wrote his doctoral thesis on this topic. *Dignitatis Humanae* was a compromise document because of what it states about individual rights. It left intact the duties of the State to the true religion. It's a complicated issue, but essentially it boils down to the teaching that there is one true Church, and we are all obligated to join it, but that you can't be compelled to join it. On the other hand, can you restrain the public expression of some religions if that is judged necessary to protect the Faith of others? But that becomes a difficult question in the modern world because we don't have a monarchical form of government in which Catholic kings have subjects whom they seek to protect.

More broadly, as Cardinal Ratzinger alludes to in the passage you referenced, the Second Vatican Council set in motion an expectation that "change for the good" was necessary because past practices needed to be updated. It would be arrogant to say that everything was perfect in the life of the Church in the late 1950s and that therefore nothing should have been changed. On the other hand, the dynamic of change took over and eliminated many good things in the life of the Church that were not the intention of the Council Fathers to overturn. The dynamic of change that was embraced by Pope Paul VI allowed, for instance, for liturgical changes which I consider to be a bad execution of the Council's intent.

**Such as . . .**
Such as the complete rejection of the Latin language, which was never intended by the Council Fathers (see *Sacrosanctum Concilium*, no. 36). The extensive rewriting of the Mass is another example. I don't think that's what the Council Fathers intended. We can say that the New Mass was the fruit of the committee that wrote it[9] but not of the Council itself. The Council gave indications on liturgical reform, and then the committee came up with their own work.

**You mention the rewriting of the Mass. The Catechism of the Catholic Church no. 78, says:**

> **This living transmission, accomplished in the Holy Spirit, is called Tradition, since it is distinct from Sacred Scripture, though closely connected to it.**

---

[9] "The Council for the Implementation of the Constitution on the Liturgy," usually referred to as the "*Consilium*."

*Through Tradition, "the Church, in her doctrine, life and worship, perpetuates and transmits to every generation all that she herself is, all that she believes." "The sayings of the holy Fathers are a witness to the life-giving presence of this Tradition, showing how its riches are poured out in the practice and life of the Church, in her belief and her prayer."*

*Only 20 percent of the 1970 Missal appeared in the Missal of 1962. How is this "living transmission"?* [10]

Each ecumenical council can overrule a previous ecumenical council as regards disciplinary matters. Additionally, the composition or approval of prayers is the prerogative of the supreme authority, the pope, so that's legitimate. Was it wise to eliminate huge swaths of the old prayers? I don't think so. The prayers themselves are good.

*But is the Church's liturgy merely a disciplinary matter? The Second Vatican Council's dogmatic constitution on Divine Revelation,* Dei Verbum *(n. 23) presents the Church's liturgies as if they were akin to the writings of the Fathers.*[11] *And*

---

[10] "If anyone says that the received and approved rites of the Catholic Church, accustomed to be used in the administration of the sacraments, may be despised or omitted by the ministers without sin and at their pleasure, or may be changed by any pastor of the churches to other new ones, let him be anathema." The Council of Trent, Decree Concerning the Sacraments & Decree Concerning Reform, canon 13, https://www.ewtn.com/catholicism/library/decree-concerning-the-sacraments--decree-concerning-reform-1497.

[11] "The bride of the incarnate Word, the Church taught by the Holy Spirit, is concerned to move ahead toward a deeper understanding of the Sacred Scriptures so that she may increasingly feed her sons with the divine words. Therefore, she also encourages the study of the holy Fathers of both East and West and of sacred liturgies."

**Pope St. Pius V expressly eschewed all novelty in the Missal of 1570 (i.e., the Tridentine Mass), saying that he had rather "restored the Missal itself to the original form and rite of the holy Fathers."[12]**

My opinion on the New Mass is that there's nothing heretical about it but that it is inadequate, in comparison to the Old Mass, in communicating with depth and richness the patrimony of the Church's public worship. In issuing *Summorum Pontificum* in 2007, Pope Benedict XVI hoped the liberalization of the celebration of the Tridentine Mass would redound to the benefit of the New Mass. Perhaps that indicates that someday there will be a combining, such that some praiseworthy elements of the New Mass are incorporated into the Old Mass, with the result that we will again have only one expression of the Roman Rite. That may not happen in our lifetime, but it's manifest to me that, through the experience of the reformed liturgy employing the bad translation that we formerly had in English, people lost touch with the profoundly mystical and supernatural worship found in the Tridentine Missal, and that wasn't a good thing.

**Going back to the Second Vatican Council more generally, it's been said that the attempt of the Council was to win over the world, but the world won over the Church. Do you believe this is true?**

---

Second Vatican Council, Dogmatic Constitution on Divine Revelation *Dei Verbum* (November 18, 1965), § 23, https://www.vatican.va/archive/hist_councils/ii_vatican_council/documents/vat-ii_const_19651118_dei-verbum_en.html.

[12] Pope Pius V, Apostolic Constitution on Promulgating the Tridentine Liturgy *Quo Primum* (1570), https://www.papalencyclicals.net/pius05/p5quopri.htm.

It reminds me of what an Australian priest wrote years ago in *Catholic World Report*, that in the past the question was, "What can the Church teach the world?" But after the Council it became, "What can the world teach the Church?"

There's a lot of truth in this, in the sense that we now attempt to answer modern concerns by trying to incorporate those concerns into our own approach in teaching and shepherding. That becomes a dangerous proposition when the presuppositions of secular points of view are not identified and clearly understood. For instance, take the proposition that the Church should embrace feminism, or what was called "women's liberation" when I was a kid. Certainly, I'm all in favor of equality in the workplace and in educational opportunity. I think it's wrong to say young girls should not get an education or be allowed to have a career. But the anti-motherhood aspect of feminism, the embrace of abortion and birth control, the stigmatizing of fatherhood as "patriarchy" that's oppressive, all this must be rejected. The Church should never in any way be associated with those ideas. But how many religious sisters and ordinary lay people now embrace these ideas?

**What's the way out of this?**
The way out is through the exit! The way out of the crisis of the Church is to teach the fullness of the Faith and to do so with confidence and conviction and to express the life of Catholic prayer and charitable living in a way that is consistent with our Faith.

We're not in a position to say that we don't know how to live Christianity well because it's been lived well at many points in Christian history. It's not being lived well now by so many. We should ask why and then change those things that we think are at the origin of the problem. Certainly, irreverent liturgy is one of them. Doctrinal deviation is another problem. The absence of an active spiritual life which is replaced by gimmicks and the imitation of pagan spiritualities is another.

The loss of reverence is another. Bishop Athanasius Schneider has been so insistent that reverence for the Eucharist is the key to the renewal of the Church.[13] I agree with that. It would restore faith and devotion. How do you do that? In the United States, in the Catholic school system there were religious women who devoted themselves to teaching the Christian religion to their students every day. That's by and large gone in most places. In the early 1960s, the Mass attendance percentage was somewhere in the vicinity of 75 percent of Catholics. It's by going to Church on Sunday and bringing your children and being reverent that you communicate the Faith.

**Critical discussion and debate on Vatican II and its aftermath seem to have become much more mainstream in recent years.** For me that debate has been going on since the beginning. Dietrich von Hildebrand wrote a book called *Trojan Horse in the City of God*. It was published in 1967. Archbishop Marcel Lefebvre (1905–1991) talked about it right from the start. It's undeniable that Vatican II and its aftermath produced notable effects in the life of the Church. The statistics show that Mass attendance is down, sacramental participation is down, an unbelievable number of priests and religious left Holy Orders or the religious life. In some places, the figures for seminaries

---

[13] See also Bishop Athanasius Schneider in conversation with Diane Montagna, *Christus Vincit: Christ's Triumph over the Darkness of the Age* (Brooklyn, NY: Angelico Press, 2019).

are pathetic. Religious orders were decimated. The number of Catholic schools in the United States has been cut by one half to one third. In other words, in the aftermath of the Council, the results were not favorable to the continuance of the Catholic life that flourished in so many ways before the Council.

Why is that, and how do we reverse it? Debate is good. I don't think we should forget the Council because it's in the living memory of many people, and certainly we have to say that since the documents of the Council are good, we need to make use of them as best we can. But in the end, what really counts is living the Faith well and communicating it well. By and large, the Council documents don't have great relevance for even well-educated Catholics who have scanty knowledge of their teaching. And that teaching is often not evidently significant or memorable. *Lumen Gentium* is certainly one exception. It is the most important document of the Council because it talks about the nature of the Church.

The challenges facing the Church today are not primarily a matter of how we are going to implement Vatican II. The challenge facing the Church is how are we going to revive Christianity within the Catholic Church among a people who are losing interest. That's where the Catholic laity are often leading the way and the many Catholic apostolates are doing a tremendous amount of good. Certainly, the most influential figure in the Catholic Church media-wise since the Council is Mother Angelica. And that is a testimony to divine providence: that a contemplative nun from Cleveland, Ohio, who moved to Alabama to found a new monastery, would end up being an international TV superstar promoting Catholicism in its fullness is a great grace from God.

**Little Rita[14] . . .**
God is good. I repeat that constantly. Therefore, in the process of trying to accomplish his will when we have disagreements, if we conduct them properly, we're serving God's goodness because our goal is not personal aggrandizement but rather the promotion of the mission of Christ's Church.

**You say that our challenge is not to implement the Council but to revive Christianity. Yet even under the current pontificate we continue to hear about the need to implement Vatican II, with little reference to pre-conciliar documents or Tradition, as if the Council really was "a new start." Do you think it's time to rediscover pre-conciliar teaching?**
I think there's always a need to go back and read Christian history and teaching documents down through the centuries. The implementation of the Vatican II documents, for most people, meant changes in the liturgy. For nuns, it meant reform of the religious life. For priests and bishops, it meant some new ways of acting that didn't involve any significant changes.

In the intellectual life of the Church, there is a notion of a more biblically-grounded teaching, which is fine. But the Bible alone is not sufficient to communicate the Church's teaching, because we have Sacred Tradition, and the magisterium is entrusted with interpreting and proposing both Scripture and Tradition in response to modern concerns, so we need to know them. We need to know what the magisterium teaches. We should never take the view that Christian history began at the close of the Second Vatican Council, and that it was the

---

[14] Rita Rizzo is Mother Angelica's birth name.

break-off point with the past. Too often, that has been the experience of the Church. Older people will say, "The Catholicism I grew up with in the 1940s and 1950s is now unrecognizable." We have to say there were certainly some deformations and problems in the past, but Catholicism doesn't change, and its teaching doesn't change.

When debates arise and people propose changes in doctrine, then we should do what any good shepherd does. We say, "No, here's the truth. Let me show you what it means. If you think I'm wrong, try to convince me. But matters of doctrine are not subject to debate, in the sense that they are not subject to being reformed and overthrown."

Practices in the life of the Church can be taken up or cast aside, but then we have to consider the wisdom of doing so. Was it wise or not? In the old days, you couldn't eat or drink anything from midnight until receiving Communion on Sunday. The rigor of early Christianity was not something that was embraced in the post-Vatican II Church, even though we're supposed to be "returning to the sources" of Christian life. But should there be a one-hour fast, which essentially is no fast? Or should we go back to three hours as under Pope Pius XII? That's a good subject to debate. I'd say we could easily go back to three hours. Make people conscious that receiving Communion involves physical preparation of the body as a reminder of detachment from things of the world, and particularly detachment from sin.

Before the Council, the practice of Confession was also much more widespread. Since then, it's not. Is that a good thing? No, and we need to fix that.

*Why do you think that is?*
Well, there were theories taught that basically minimized mortal sin or its consequences. There was a certain psychologizing of sin, which claimed that things that you think are wrong are not necessarily offensive in the way you once thought. Instead, sin is depicted as "self-defeating behavior." Or people were told they "weren't living up to their potential," but at least they were trying.

*Where did these ideas come from?*
One of the underlying dynamics at the time of the Council was the preoccupation of European theologians with answering existential philosophers and secularists who rejected Christianity or rejected the moral order or rejected metaphysical realism. There was an attempt to engage in a constructive dialogue with atheistic forms of thinking, in an attempt to clarify the reasonableness of Christianity. I would say this can be worthwhile if it's carried out with a serious and rigorous attempt to defend Christian theology and its philosophical support in Thomistic realist thinking. But there's often a capitulation to categories of thought and modern ways of thinking, and an attempt to make Christian practice and belief somehow congruent with that. That's a naïve and destructive way of acting.

The idea that we have to "open the windows" and let some light and air into the Church is a popular theme often used to identify what Vatican II was trying to do. But I think some theologians took that as a starting point and wanted to basically get rid of Thomistic-based theology and enter into new ways of looking at things—the so-called "turning to the subject" which, in place of a Christian theology which focuses on the objective truth taught by God, focuses on the subjective reaction of mankind to nature and revelation and goes from there to try to figure out the meaning of Church teaching. I think that was a terrible mistake. It's a horizontalism in the world. You have these crazy notions of process theology.

**How would the average person identify process theology? What does it look like?**
Process theology can be summed up in this way: One day Monsignor is wearing his cassock and saying the breviary, and the next day he's in a Hawaiian shirt and has a guitar and is singing a strange hymn. In other words, the certainties of Faith that the Church teaches us are set aside, and then everything gets subject to questioning. The humorous analogy is meant to demonstrate that in a process theology mindset, former ways of dressing, acting, designing buildings, and artistic creation are all cast aside in search of a new, ever-evolving way of looking at things. The primitivism movement in the 1960s—which imitated art that was representational but not developed—is an analogy of how some wanted to look at doctrine. The idea was that "we're in the process of developing doctrine, we have to look at things in a new way, in a new fashion," but that's playing games with the most serious thing in life, which is the question, "What do I need to know in order to be saved?"

A very crazy notion emerges where people think any church that asserts it has the truth can't for that very reason have it because it's proud and imperious, and everybody is seeking the truth, but nobody can say that they alone have it in its fullness and completeness. The Catholic Church would respond, "Absolutely not." Jesus said, "I am the way, and the truth and the life" (John 14:6); "He who hears you hears me" (Luke 10:16); "Go therefore and make disciples of all nations" (Matt 28:19). In other words, we have a definite mission and definite content to communicate, and we do so *not* because of a superiority complex based on our success ratio, but because we know that this is what God wants. So, why would I question it?

**We talked about how confusion arises by focusing on one truth to the exclusion of others. Do you think that this happened at Vatican II and in its aftermath?**
Well certainly after Vatican II, some people started proposing things that had never been taught by the Church, but in fact were taught by Protestant communities or were even ancient heresies. So, a lot of the crisis in the Church focused on moral teaching obviously. But if you don't believe that the Church is the teacher of truth on morality, how can you be so sure she is the teacher of truth on dogmatic teachings? So, the whole body of Catholic teaching gets called into question. We're at this stage now where many people look at the Church not as the divinely protected teacher of truth but rather as a collection of people who believe in Jesus—but each decides what they're going to believe in.

The "German Synodal Way"[15] document that recently

---

[15] The German Synodal Way is a series of conferences which began in December 2019 and brings together German bishops and laity of the Central Committee of German Catholics to discuss four major topics: how power is exercised in the Church ("Power and Separation of Power in the Church—Joint Participation and Involvement in the Mission"); sexual morality ("Life in Succeeding Relationships—Living Love in Sexuality and Partnership"); the priesthood ("Priestly Existence Today"); and the role of women ("Women in Ministries and Offices in the Church").

came out showed that they proposed that there could be, in the Church, conflicting sets of beliefs, but that this posed no problem because that's the way the Church is meant to be. That, in itself, is a heresy because it's claiming that there is no teaching mission of the Church but simply a secretarial role which is, "Find out what everybody believes, write it down on paper, and then say, 'Okay, you have your choice. This is what your fellow believers think. Maybe you find proposition number fifteen true, whereas someone else believes in the contradictory proposition number seventeen. Each one decides what to believe.'"

**So, it undermines the whole divine constitution of the Church.**
Yes. Everything is undermined when you begin rejecting teachings based on the claim that the Church has no right to teach one thing and reject its contradiction, that everybody has the right to believe whatever they think is right. But that's the way we are going, certainly in Germany, and it's very dangerous.

**It's an interesting question that you raise about how the Church is seen now as compared to how she was viewed in the past.**
The Church was seen by Catholics before Vatican II as the divinely-appointed guardian and promoter of the religion founded by Jesus Christ, which over the course of almost two thousand years had many opponents, break-away groups and others, and the Church remained firm in explaining her teaching and defining what Catholics believed in, and what they could and could not do.

***How do you think that people outside the Church used to see her? There was certainly some hostility, as we've discussed, but wasn't she a beacon of light and a moral compass for the world, even for non-Catholics who didn't want to embrace the Catholic Faith?***

I think you're right. I think the knowledge most non-Catholics had about the Catholic Church came via observing their Catholic neighbors. When they saw them living the teachings of the Church, going to Church, sending their children to Catholic school, praying, giving money to the poor, sending their sons and daughters to seminaries and convents, having large families, and Catholics making considerable social welfare efforts before government social welfare programs were prevalent, that all had an impact. So, not just the saints, but everyday ordinary Catholics who lived a consistent Catholic life had a great influence. I think that seeing them impressed people because the message that was conveyed was that these Catholics take seriously what their Church proposes, they live according to it, and they seem to be as happy, or even happier than most everybody else—and that was a compelling social witness. It didn't mean that those people were going to leave their religion or embrace Catholicism, but some did, and the Catholic Church could not be dismissed as simply an interest group that was interested in political power, which is how many secularists conceive their own mission, i.e., to seize power and use it in a coercive way to get their point across and make laws.

The Catholic Church always pointed to the proposition that we have no lasting city here, so we'll do the best we can, but we really want to prepare people to meet their Maker, and that involves the whole realm of spirituality, practice, and belief.

***And was the Church more unapologetic about being the one true Faith then as compared to our own day?***
Yes, we often hear people reducing Catholicism to just one more version of Christianity but which makes no claim to be the one true Church of Christ. The goal of reincorporating separated Christian ecclesial communities into the Catholic Church is now rejected by many. Reinhard Cardinal Marx recently said in an interview, "An ecumenism of return is completely impossible and was neither a goal of the ecumenical movement nor of the popes. What is clear is that we want to walk a common path. What a differentiated consensus means remains open. We do not have a clear model of unity to strive for."[16] He is completely wrong. Vatican II's document on ecumenism states plainly: "When the obstacles to perfect ecclesiastical communion have been gradually overcome, all Christians will at last, in a common celebration of the Eucharist, be gathered into the one and only Church in that unity which Christ bestowed on his Church from the beginning. We believe that this unity subsists in the Catholic Church as something she can never lose, and we hope that it will continue to increase until the end of time."

This is why the German idea of giving Communion to non-Catholic Christians is so wrong— because to receive Holy Communion is to receive the sacrament of unity, precisely because it means that believers accept the teaching about the nature of the Eucharist and the place of the Eucharist in the

---

[16] Jeanne Smits, "German Cardinal: Ecumenism of Return to Catholicism 'Is Completely Impossible,'" LifeSiteNews, May 10, 2021, https://www.lifesitenews.com/news/german-cardinal-ecumenism-of-return-to-catholicism-is-completely-impossible.

overall structure of salvation. The Eucharist comes from the Church, and the Church comes from Christ. Without the Church there is no Eucharist, and the Eucharist is not what I believe it to be based on my own determination. It's what the Church tells me it is, and I believe that because that's what God wants me to do. And I have ample evidence that that's what God wants me to do because I believe Jesus rose from the dead, and therefore his instruction to his Apostles is not just "another approach." It is in fact God's truth, and no one can demonstrate that any other church can lay rational claim to being the unique intended fruit of what happened when Christ made St. Peter and the other Apostles the first priests and then sent them out. All Christians are called to be one with Christ with Peter and under Peter.

**If Vatican II is as unproblematic as some Catholics claim, why does the debate rage on?**
It's a great question, and the answer has different aspects. One aspect, of course, is that you had the Council *and* the aftermath. In other words, who was put in charge of implementing the reforms that were proposed and voted on in the Council?

The control of those reforms under Pope Paul VI was generally put into the hands of people who were hostile to the traditional liturgical formulations. The Roman Curia was then updated and reformed to include departments to deal with ecumenism and interreligious dialogue. Those in general have no real impact on the day-to-day life of your average Mass-going Catholic, but they are important for the theological discussions that go on, the doctrinal agreements that have been reached, and the constant battle that went on under the pontificates of

John Paul II and Benedict XVI to assure that Protestantizing efforts in the Church would not succeed. That's where the German hierarchy has been a constant source of irritation and continues to be so with their demands for things that have nothing to do with Roman Catholicism but are in fact experienced widely in Protestant churches, such as women clergy, married clergy, lay power in the church, things of this sort.

Again, the problem as I see it is that the Council set in motion an expectation for constant change, the presupposition of which is that things *needed* to be changed. But as with everything, we have to ask: What determines "need" and what makes change "necessary"? Usually in the Church, you change things if they either don't reflect properly the doctrinal patrimony or the spiritual identity of the Church, or you alter things that are contingencies that aren't useful anymore, ways of acting that become antiquated in the sense that they are no longer part of the general experience of the life of the Church.

**Such as . . . because this argument is often made regarding the traditional liturgy.**
The early Church had an organizational structure that included archdeaconries, for instance, and deacons in Rome oversaw charitable works in designated sectors. That experience was never brought into the United States, for instance. Cathedral chapters common in Europe were unknown in the US. I'm talking about these and other canonical structures that existed in the past and continue in some places. The Council of Trent mandated, for instance, that every diocese had to have its own seminary and all the minor orders should be put into effect in every diocese so that you should in every parish have men in

the minor orders such as lectors, acolytes, etc., things which reflected what was done in the early Church but did not really take hold.

The expectation of change always has to be controlled, because man loves novelty. The love of novelty is something that is an aspect of human existence—everyone likes reading the newspaper—but it needs to be guided and shepherded. Love of novelty, when applied to "itching ears" seeking new doctrines "to suit their own likings," as St. Paul says (2 Tim 4:3), leads to disaster because the doctrine of the Faith is not a human creation arrived at through wise deliberation over time by a group of intelligent people, who say to themselves, "There was a man named Jesus, and what do we think he was trying to do?" No. Jesus gave the message, entrusted it to the Apostles, and said, "Go therefore and make disciples of all nations . . . teaching them to observe all that I have commanded you" (Matt 28:19).

Our divine Savior communicated divine revelation, and then entrusted to the Apostles and their successors the promulgation of his teaching, and also the further explication of its meaning over time, because the richness of revelation was not fully understood at the beginning. Since the Church is the living voice of Tradition, as Cardinal Newman said,[17] the Tradition has to be applied in circumstances that present themselves over time, and challenges need to be met.

There's a great aphorism on this question—I don't remember who said it—but it was taught to me by my history professor in college. The statement was: "The Holy Fathers do not defend what is not attacked." The point is that not every doctrine

---

[17] See St. John Henry Newman, *An Essay on the Development of Christian Doctrine.*

has been fully explicated from the start because what wasn't attacked was docilely received and accepted. Therefore, defenses and deeper explanations of its meaning, and the reason for the teaching and its obligatory nature, weren't necessary. But when people challenged the divinity of Christ, the Church rose to the occasion. When challenges arose regarding the Petrine authority, or the Real Presence in the Eucharist, or the Marian dogmas, or the Protestant objections to the sacrificial nature of the Mass, or to the seven sacraments, all these things had to be defended over time. The job of the hierarchy is to respond to these challenges, not to invent or theorize about what Christ meant.

**And yet perhaps more than any other council, the Second Vatican Council has led to a pluralism of interpretations of its documents, with members of the hierarchy interpreting them in various ways. The Church has traditionally been seen as a rock, but it seems that Vatican II and its aftermath put the Church into a state of fluidity, and it would seem that we're living in a perpetual fear of what might happen next. People feel more like they are living in a bunker experience waiting for the next bomb to hit rather than in a springtime. What went wrong in the hierarchy to allow this to happen?**
It goes back to the liberalizing tendencies that were present, a Catholic version of liberal Protestantism. In other words, some Catholics were influenced by the development of a non-dogmatic religion that occurred in the Protestant world over the course of the nineteenth and twentieth centuries and fell into that mode of thinking. It is the fruit of bad philosophy.

One of the main attacks in the modern era is the attack on the notion of truth itself. What Christ taught is unassailable.

You cannot change that and claim it's the will of Christ. The intellectual ferment after the Second World War still had the remnants of the modernist spirit, and Pius XII spent a good portion of his magisterial teaching trying to defend traditional doctrine and identify the roots of errors springing from Modernism.[18] Not every liberal theologian is a modernist, but many of them express sympathies with ideas that had previously been treated as errors. The doctrinal confusion combined with the sexual revolution and the anti-authoritarian spirit of the 1960s in the United States and in Europe led to a free-for-all. The Catholic Theological Society of America published a book (*Human Sexuality: New Directions in American Catholic Thought: A Study*) that justified bestiality, for instance.

**Do you think it was reasonable at Vatican II to open the Church to the world and not expect secularization?**
As an overall exercise, the Second Vatican Council manifested a confidence that, following the Second World War, Europe could reorganize itself in such a way as to advance human progress and create peaceful, harmonious conditions that would be appealing to everyone and would be self-evident and therefore everyone would willingly participate in it. One of my keys to the interpretation of Vatican II was that it was done in the same spirit as the foundation of the United Nations, even though the Church has had councils from the beginning.

The horror of the Second World War was the result of a

---

[18] Pope Pius XII, Encyclical Concerning Some False Opinions Threatening to Undermine the Foundations of Catholic Doctrine *Humane Generis* (August 12, 1950), https://www.vatican.va/content/pius-xii/en/encyclicals/documents/hf_p-xii_enc_12081950_humani-generis.html.

murderous pagan superstition becoming the ideological foundation of the regime in Germany, which led to millions of people being killed and destruction on an unprecedented scale. When the Allies won the war, the proper providential perspective was to see this as God not permitting the triumph of genocidal paganism in the world, and that called for renewed faith. But that renewed faith should not be in the ability to create a perfect world but rather a world more directed to God.

I think the Fathers of the Council did want to direct the world to God and overcome divisions in Christianity. But there was a naivete in thinking that, if we somehow "open the windows" and let the winds of new thinking to come in, that this would somehow help the Church to figure out how to carry out her mission. That's manifestly not happened.

Optimism is not bad per se, but when an optimistic spirit proposes we can realize results that have not historically been seen according to the way the Church operates, it's a problem. For instance, we think we can take a new approach to Protestantism by adopting Protestant ways in our liturgy and claim that this is going to cause the unification of the Church. But we end up imitating Protestant ways of acting and thinking and antagonize Catholics who are repelled by that, particularly converts who say, "I left a non-dogmatic religion to embrace a religion with dogmatic certainty, and now you're telling me that the Protestant way of doing things is the way we need to act."

**Are there Protestant elements in the New Mass (sometimes referred to as the "Novus Ordo"), and how would you explain to the average Catholic in the pew how and why this happened?**

Yes, there are Protestant elements. The vernacular liturgy is one of them. A completely vernacular liturgy was not intended by the Council Fathers (see *Sacrosanctum Concilium*, no. 36), but the people who reformed the liturgy after the Council got rid of Latin completely in part because it was a distinctive difference between Protestant worship and Catholic liturgy. The Mass facing the people (*versus populum*) is another aspect of that. The casualness that crept into and was experienced with liturgical changes regarding the handling of the Holy Eucharist, such as Communion in the hand, Extraordinary Eucharistic Ministers, and a married diaconate. All things that were not part of the Catholic experience ever but were certainly present in the Protestant world.

**How is the married diaconate a Protestant element?**

The married diaconate was not the historical experience of the Latin Rite Catholic Church. The innovation after the Council was a laudatory attempt in some ways to resurrect the second grade of major orders in the old system (subdiaconate, diaconate, priesthood). According to the mind of the Council, the married diaconate was designed for mission territories, where there was a lack of priests. In the past, they would have designated catechists, i.e., trained laymen. Later we ran into problems because married deacons have to embrace celibacy in the event that their wife dies, but what happens when a man says, "I've always been married, I have young kids, and I need a wife and a mother for my family"? Should they be dispensed from that commitment and be able to marry? For a while the Vatican was giving dispensations, but the tradition of the Church, East and West, is that men in major orders cannot contract marriage. It's an area of difficulty. The Vatican has stopped granting those dispensations as far as I know.

**Would you include female altar servers, i.e., "altar girls" in the Protestant elements that were introduced into the New Mass in the aftermath of the Council?**
Sure. I don't think this innovation is inherently wrong because the Church can decide on a disciplinary matter, such as if girls can serve as altar servers. But I don't think it's a good idea.

Altar boys in Italian are called "little clerics" (*chierichetti*) because they are substituting for acolytes, men who were ordained to minor orders; acolytes were to serve at the altar.[19] Since there were no acolytes, you put young boys in their place, dressed in cassock and surplice, so they were honorary clerics. It was a substitutionary role and was not designed as a means of recruiting vocations. It had that effect, however, because it exposed young boys to the work of a priest. I was an altar boy. It was a good thing. But they got rid of the minor orders. It used to be you became a cleric by receiving tonsure and then were ordained to the minor and then the major orders. The minor orders were all done away with. I think it was a mistake. Even in the revised liturgical rites, when they got rid of the minor orders, they created two ministries: acolyte and lector, both of those

---

[19] These minor orders still exist in the Extraordinary Form of the Mass and in the Eastern Rites.

until very recently were restricted in Church law to men.[20] One could say, "Oh, Father, we have women lectors." Well, right from the start even though the ministries of acolyte and lector were restricted by law to males, women were permitted to *act as* lectors.

**How did that happen?**

There was a request made to Rome asking why, if we can have lay people reading at Mass, it has to be reserved to males only. The response said that women can do it even though they don't receive the ministry of lector. In fact, those two ministries were not simply to be restricted to men studying for the priesthood. They were supposed to be given to males who would serve at the altar and read, but that fell out of fashion immediately, in part because it was restricted to men in the case of lectors, and there was no need for acolytes when you have sufficient altar boys.

**Females serving at the altar seems to have been excluded by previous popes on doctrinal rather than merely disciplinary grounds (e.g., St. Gelasius I, Innocent IV, Benedict XIV).[21] Does their authority not trump the later concessions?**

---

[20] Pope Paul VI, Motu Proprio on First Tonsure, Minor Orders, and the Subdiaconate *Ministeria Quaedam* (August 15, 1972), https://www.ewtn.com/catholicism/library/ministeria-quaedam-9006.

[21] In his encyclical *Allatae Sunt,* Pope Benedict XIV writes: "Pope Gelasius in his ninth letter (ch. 26) to the bishops of Lucania condemned the evil practice which had been introduced of women serving the priest at the celebration of Mass. Since this abuse had spread to the Greeks, Innocent IV strictly forbade it in his letter to the bishop of Tusculum: 'Women should not dare to serve at the altar; they should be altogether refused this ministry.' We too have forbidden this practice

In matters of discipline, the popes have the power to change the decisions of previous popes. This power should be exercised carefully and sparingly, and only for very good reasons when it is a matter of changing practices that go back to the earliest days of the Church, such as the restriction of service at the altar to clerics who are all males. There were doctrinal reasons for this restriction to be sure. Those reasons do not cease to have persuasive force when they are no longer determinative of Church practices. Innovations often lack the similarly persuasive reasons and thus are subject to ongoing criticism, which is not unreasonable.

**As a woman, when I see girls or women in the sanctuary it's rather jarring. The liturgical action in the sanctuary is the action of Christ the High Priest and Bridegroom of the Church vis-à-vis his Church, so having women in the sanctuary seems to confuse this relationship and these roles, and the deeper mystery of the liturgy.**

In the traditional understanding of the Church, only clerics were in the sanctuary carrying out the liturgical worship. Christ the High Priest acted through the ordained priest at the altar, and everyone around him was, as it were, an extension of the priest, i.e., doing things to assist the priest in carrying out his task. Since Christ is a male, the priest is a male, clerics are male, everyone serving around the altar should be a male because they are serving in a role that has a ministerial aspect to it.

Regarding the experience of lectors, there was no previous history of lay people doing readings at Mass. In the Old

in the same words in Our oft-repeated constitution *Etsi Pastoralis*, sect. 6, no. 21." (Encyclical On the Observance of Oriental Rites *Allatae Sunt* [July 26, 1555], § 29, https://www.papalencyclicals.net/Ben14/b14allat.htm).

Mass, the subdeacon proclaims the Epistle at a Solemn Mass, but this was commonly carried out by a priest, not a layman, in the absence of a subdeacon.

Therefore, seeing a woman or a man go up and serve as lector at Mass after the Council was seeing something completely new. Yet female lectors didn't have the same visual impact as seeing a girl wearing a cassock and surplice, which are clerical garments, but it was jarring.

In the sociological experience of the Church, I think the proponents of altar girls are not so interested in girls serving at the altar because generally feminists don't like women serving as a category, particularly serving males. They think it's submissiveness. But the goal there is to shock people into seeing that women can do the same things that men do, and so that's why there's a push for the female diaconate as a stepping-stone to the female priesthood.

**Why did the bishops allow this to happen, and why don't more of them push back?**
Some bishops are in agreement with these changes and think they are good. They think that the traditional way of doing things was too restrictive and needed to be changed.

This may be controversial to say, but I think most lay people would be happy if the priest did all the readings at Mass because on a purely practical level, in most cases, there's a likelihood they'll be read well by someone who is used to reading in public. Some lectors are really not up to the job. Many, if not most, are good, but it's not always the case.

The lector issue is rather minor, but it is symbolic of the fact that, after the Council, there was an expectation of change but then no indication of where that change would end. I think that is why, fifty-plus years later, women religious are still asking Pope Francis, "Can we please have a female diaconate?" When they didn't get it, Pope Francis said he'd form another committee to study it. Enough already.

### And Extraordinary Ministers of Holy Communion?

We need to remember that Extraordinary Ministers of Holy Communion were not part of the liturgical reform at Vatican II. It was not envisioned, and it's certainly not integral to having a reformed Mass. It is an add-on. Again, it goes back to the minor orders because acolytes did have the role of bringing Holy Communion to those unable to attend Mass in the early Church. But they were clerics. They were set apart by tonsure and were recognized as being separated for the service of the altar and of the Church.

There is nothing inherently wrong in Eucharistic ministers, so I'm not saying the Church is doing something inherently wrong in having them. But I think it's pastorally unwise. Experientially in the Church, it's also become an opportunity for liberalizing elements in the Church to say, "This is how lay participation in the Church is supposed to be experienced," which is taking on the roles of the priests. Lay participation in the life of the Church after the Council is not meant to be taking on the roles of the priest. John Paul II said that, Benedict XVI said that, and Francis has said that. And the Council never said that the laity was to fulfill its role in the Church by taking over priestly activity, in its direct or derivative aspects.

Bringing Communion to people is a role of the priest and in many ways imitates Christ's visits to the sick. The indiscriminate use of Extraordinary Ministers of Holy Communion to make the distribution of Communion go quicker is an abuse. Christ feeds his people, his people don't feed each other, and that's what it comes down to. Even though they are designated as Eucharistic ministers, they are still lay persons and are not sacramentally conformed to Christ the High Priest.

It's not per se wrong to do it, because the Church allows it, and there is an analogous experience in the early Church of non-priest acolytes, who were still clerics, who did this, and in wartime and other emergencies the Holy Eucharist can be entrusted to people to be transported in times of persecution. But, again, the dynamic of the Extraordinary Eucharistic Minister of Holy Communion was meant to habituate people to a new way of conceiving how the Church conducts worship. It's not a good thing to have lay people dressed in liturgical albs, imitating priests standing around the altar and then distributing Communion.

The same thing goes for Communion services conducted by lay people, which are allowed by the Holy See but, again, are unwise because they create the impression that we have a lay version of the Mass. That is, everything except the Consecration, versus the priestly version of the Mass, i.e., everything, including the Consecration. It's not helpful.

**It seems that there's a pattern of behavior here: A request is made to Rome and the Holy See in turn grants permission, at least as an exception. Most Catholics will therefore think, "Well the Holy See gave permission, so it must be fine."**
The responsibility falls on the Holy See which decides on these matters. These are for the most part largely decisions of

governance rather than doctrinal pronouncements, but they are decisions about how the everyday life of the Church should be carried out. It introduces new ways of acting that have theological justification—or not—and that's what we debate.

But apart from the intention of the Church leadership when they approve or disapprove of something, we have to ask what is the dynamic that led forward to a demand in some quarters for this change. For instance, the act of giving Communion in the hand was never practiced in the Church after the Council of Trent and for many centuries before that. The Eastern Church doesn't have it. But they had it in the Protestant churches.

It was also suggested that we are now a more "adult" Church, and more "mature," and mature people are not treated like infants who have to have food placed in their mouths.

**What do you suppose St. Peter might say to that? He told the early Church, "Like newborn babes, long for the pure spiritual milk, that by it you may grow up to salvation; for you have tasted the kindness of the Lord" (1 Pet 2:2).**
We are all children of God, and Christ feeds us, and Christ acts through his priest.

Then there is the aspect of reverence. Particles from the Holy Eucharist can fall to the ground because the Host is placed in the hand. People can walk away with the Host without consuming it, as has happened. People drop the Host. These are problems that never existed in the life of the Church but have been introduced through a change in discipline, and there's no justification sufficient to say that while those problems exist, they are outweighed by the plain benefits of giving Communion in the hand.

The first three vital steps to the renewal of the Church

are: Communion on the tongue, Communion received kneeling, and the priest saying Mass facing East. If you do those three things, you will increase Eucharistic faith and piety just by osmosis. An important additional step would be to restore the three-hour Communion fast.

**You've described the present storm as one of doctrinal confusion, moral confusion, liturgical abuse and ignorance, and disciplinary laxity.**
Yes, and I would also add in spiritual tepidity. The demands of the Christian life in terms of prayer and sacrifice have been lessened, and as regards the spiritual life as guided by the Church, a certain laxity that has entered in among Catholics. Many people don't go to Church, many don't go to Confession, people don't pray as much as they did in public, e.g., in public processions. The practice of daily Mass was much more prevalent in the past than it is now, and fasting is more or less gone from the Latin Church through a decision to make it easier.

**And among the Catholic clergy and hierarchy?**
The formation of seminarians was not as spiritually rigorous after the Council as before, and there is not a focus on serious spiritual practices, as there used to be.

The spiritual life has suffered, and this is caused by a "horizontalist" vision of the life of the Church, i.e., that we should spend our energies on charitable works and trying to arrange social structures so as to favor a Christlike spirit, which is all to the good but it's not the main mission of the Church. Her main mission is the salvation of souls and that has to do with preparing people for a heavenly life. That starts with being in living union and in conversation with Christ, striving to seek constantly to grow in the grace of God.

**To what extent is the chaos and division within the Church today due to a loss of the supernatural and a neglect of the primacy of the supernatural in the life of the Church?**
The loss of a supernatural sense lies at the root of so many problems in life of the Church. We need to be reminded constantly of our eternal destiny, and the need to live in God's grace in order to prepare ourselves to die well. The sacramental system given by Christ to the Church is the wellspring of grace for believers. When we neglect prayer and sacraments we can easily slip into a worldly view of Christianity as being primarily, if not exclusively, a promoter of human solidarity and an agent for the relief of the various miseries of life on planet earth. Preaching salvation and the forgiveness of sins is so often cast aside in favor of purely worldly concerns.

A supernatural outlook will certainly include promoting the works of charity and justice as acts pleasing to God and showing effective love to our neighbor. But that is not the primary reason why Christ founded the Church and sent forth the Apostles.

**How much of the present crisis do you think may be attributed to a loss of the sense of sin? And what is the best way to recover it? Some suggest that more emphasis needs to be placed on seeing sin according to the Old Testament understanding, i.e., as adultery against God to whom every baptized soul is wedded in the sacrament of Baptism.**

Sin is an ever-present reality in the life of every man, woman, and child on the face of the earth. We can deal with our sins either by seeking forgiveness or by pretending that they are not really sins at all. Man needs to face reality, not flee from it, if he would be happy. God stands ready to forgive us, but he leaves it up to us to freely ask for forgiveness. Living in sin is truly to embrace unfaithfulness to the good God who made us and redeemed us. The recognition of that is the first step in returning to the One who is never far from us, no matter how far we wander away from him.

*In his 1931 essay, "The New Paganism," Hilaire Belloc wrote,*

> *Our civilization developed as a Catholic civilization. It developed and matured as a Catholic thing. With the loss of the Faith it will slip back not only into Paganism, but into barbarism with the accompaniments of Paganism. . . . It will find gods to worship, but they will be evil gods as were those of the older savage Paganism before it began to advance towards Catholicism. The road downhill is the same as the road up the hill. It is the same road, but to go down back into the marshes again is a very different thing from coming up from the marshes into pure air. All things return to their origin. A living organic being, whether a human body or a whole state of society, turns at last into its original elements if life be not maintained in it. But in that process of return there is a phase of corruption which is very*

*unpleasant. That phase the modern world outside the Catholic Church has arrived at.*

**When Belloc was writing, he took for granted that this was a decadence characteristic of those outside the Church. Since then, it seems it has entered her walls. In 2017, Pope Emeritus Benedict XVI even likened the Church to a boat that "has taken on so much water as to be on the verge of capsizing."[22]** A holy Franciscan priest I highly respected was wont to say of the Church that "the world is too much with us." The chaos observed in so many parts of the Church shows how destructive ideas have entered the minds of many Churchmen, ideas which have nothing to do with the Gospel. The pagan spirit Belloc rightly saw as afflicting the world is now an affliction within the household of God. It must be resisted for the good of souls.

---

[22] Pope Emeritus Benedict XVI, Message Delivered by His Personal Secretary, Archbishop Georg Gänswein, at the Funeral of Cardinal Joachim Meisner at the Cologne Cathedral, (July 15, 2017), https://www.ccwatershed.org/2017/07/15/benedict-xvi-funeral-joachim-cardinal-meisner/.

*Chapter 3*

# CROOKS AND HIRELINGS

"The boat was being swamped by the waves."
(Matt 8:24)

**Fr. Murray, many people today are scandalized by the presence in the Church of bishops and priests who teach false doctrines by word or example and lead people into sin and error. But in St. John's Gospel (10:7–9), Our Lord expressly talks about the presence of thieves, inside the sheepfold as well as within his flock, who have come to steal and kill and destroy. Would it be fair to say, then, that outside the sheepfold there are also sheep who have not yet been brought in but are not opposed to the Church (men of goodwill), while inside the fold there are only the Lord's flock and his enemies?**
The Lord also said a few verses on, "And I have other sheep, that are not of this fold; I must bring them also, and they will heed my voice. So there shall be one flock, one shepherd" (John 10:16). The message of Christ as preached by the Church is inherently attractive and intriguing for all men of goodwill. The

warning by Our Lord, the Good Shepherd, of the presence of thieves and hirelings who prey upon the flock or who flee when wolves appear should not unduly sadden or cause us to lose our peace. Rather, we take courage knowing that the Good Lord is always with us. We must beg him to send us good shepherds after his own heart who will fearlessly stand in defense of the Faith, protecting the flock from those who would seek to lead them astray from Catholic doctrine by preaching alien beliefs and practices. The voice of the Lord is heard when the Church's teaching is proclaimed by faithful bishops and priests.

**The storm hit the Catholic Church in the United States with particular force in early 2002. The Boston Globe published an explosive article on serial child abuser, Fr. John Geoghan, which became the catalyst for the criminal prosecutions of other priests in the Archdiocese of Boston and thrust the sexual abuse of minors by clergy into the national spotlight.[1] As a priest and canon lawyer, how do you explain how things went so horribly wrong?**

Priests were sexually abusing people for many generations, but it was not commonly known because it was covered up and hushed up. Beginning in the 1980s, stories began to come out about different priests being prosecuted for criminal sexual behavior. Generally, this reporting came through the secular media. As you mention, the crisis that broke in 2002 with *The Boston Globe* requesting the unsealing of court records related to Fr. Geoghan's crimes.

---

[1] Global Spotlight Team, "Church Allowed Abuse by Priest for Years," *The Boston Globe*, January 6, 2002, https://www.bostonglobe.com/news/special-reports/2002/01/06/church-allowed-abuse-priest-for-years/cSHfGkTIrAT25qKGvBuDNM/story.html.

We then found out about hundreds of priests who were accused. The bishops' response was typically to minimize and explain away what they did because there's been a history of protecting criminal priests by moving them around, having them accept early retirement or granting retirement for reasons of health when, really, they were being put aside rather than prosecuted for their crimes.

Almost all of the cases involve homosexual activity with post-pubescent boys. According to the 2004 John Jay Report,[2] 87 percent of all cases involved males over the age of thirteen. For twenty years, there has been a hesitancy among many, because of a pro-homosexual attitude, to make any connection between homosexuality and what they call "child abuse." But this is not abuse of pre-pubescent children. This is abuse of teenagers. They invented a category called "ephebophilia" to psychologize what was, in fact, male homosexuals seeking attractive young victims who are sexually mature or maturing—not pre-pubescent children, in whom sexual potency has not been realized.

I remember going to a "Virtus" training session at which we were told it would be wrong to connect homosexuality with sexual abuse of minors. I thought, "This is propaganda we're being told." Indeed, the John Jay study revealed that—in almost nine out of ten cases—homosexual male priests sought and abused teenage male victims.

The whole sexual abuse crisis, and not just the sexual abuse of minors, is a horrible story of deceit, lying, and fraud

---

[2] This report was done by the John Jay College of Criminal Justice, and it was commissioned by the U.S. Conference of Catholic Bishops (USCCB).

that involved using diocesan money to pay victims and then making them sign non-disclosure agreements so they couldn't talk about it. And we know from the case of former cardinal Theodore McCarrick, as well as others, that important people in the Church were accused and then protected.

**Why is some of the hierarchy reticent to admit a connection between homosexuality and the sex-abuse crisis?**
Some members of the hierarchy have the attitude that there are homosexual priests, and we don't want to rock the boat.

**How big of a problem do you think homosexuality is among the clergy?**
It's a problem. We know from experience that some young men who have homosexual tendencies seek the priesthood either to get over their temptation, thinking if they grow closer to God that will help, or it's a place to hide from the perpetual question of why you aren't getting married. Others know there is a homosexual subculture in the priesthood, and they want to join it. This is not merely my suspicion. It's common knowledge, and everyone knows—because of the revelations of the last twenty-plus years—that there have been, and must still be, active homosexuals in the priesthood.

If someone has a homosexual problem and lives a chaste life and doesn't cultivate a homosexual identity, that's a person to be praised. I've worked with the Courage apostolate,[3] for instance, which helps people to deal with temptation and affectivity problems. But those who confuse this issue, such as

---

[3] To learn more about Courage, visit their website at https://couragerc.org/.

Fr. James Martin, S.J., who is teaching that "homosexual identity" is what people *are* as opposed to a problem that they *have*, do great damage to the Church's ability to have a common voice and witness to proclaim the truth about homosexuality. And it encourages priests to think that perhaps homosexual activity isn't that bad because "that's the way God made me."

**Are there homosexual bishops?**
Obviously. McCarrick was certainly one of them, and there are others. There's a list of bishops who have been convicted, or admitted, or have been credibly accused of engaging in homosexual behavior, who are no longer in their dioceses.

**But do you think there are others, who still hold their office and who are compromised?**
Statistically, there must be. The former bishop of the Diocese of Orán in Argentina, Bishop Gustavo Zanchetta,[4] was not indicted in Argentina for sexual misconduct with females. He is under indictment for alleged sexual misconduct with male seminarians who are not minors but who were under his authority. The Zanchetta case is emblematic of a certain paralysis in the Vatican right now.

---

[4] Bishop Gustavo Zanchetta was appointed Bishop of Orán by Pope Francis in 2013. In July 2016, Bishop Zanchetta abruptly left his diocese, justifying his departure on grounds of health reasons. After Bishop Zanchetta resigned from his diocese in 2017, Pope Francis appointed him "councilor" to the Administration of the Patrimony of the Apostolic See (APSA), the curial department dealing with Vatican investments and real-estate holdings. See Edward Pentin, "More Questions Surface regarding Argentinian Bishop Appointed to Vatican Post," *National Catholic Register*, January 22, 2019, https://www.ncregister.com/blog/more-questions-surface-regarding-argentinian-bishop-appointed-to-vatican-post.

*Nearly two decades after the Boston Globe's first report, the Church is still dealing with the crisis. In January 2018, Pope Francis defended Chilean bishop Juan Barros against accusations of cover-up, which subsequently turned out to be true.[5] The following June, revelations began to emerge regarding disgraced former cardinal, Theodore McCarrick. In August of the same year, the former apostolic nuncio to the United States, Archbishop Carlo Maria Viganò, issued his first testimony alleging an extensive cover-up of the McCarrick case which included Pope Francis and Donald Cardinal Wuerl.[6] This cascade of disturbing revelations compelled the convening of a "Meeting on the Protection of Minors in the Church" at the Vatican in February 2019. At the event, journalists pressed organizers on the findings of the John Jay Report, but they denied any causal connection between homosexuality and the abuse of post-pubescent boys, and said decades of widespread homosexuality in US seminaries had "nothing to do with the sexual abuse of minors."[7] How can trust in the*

---

[5] In January 2018, during Pope Francis's visit to Chile, he defended Chilean bishop Juan Barros—whom he had appointed Bishop of Osorno in 2015—against accusations of a cover-up in the case of Fr. Fernando Karadima, saying there was "not one piece of evidence against him" and that "everything is slander." A massive public outcry from the laity led the Pope to open a Vatican investigation into the case, which found Barros guilty. Pope Francis apologized to the victims and summoned the Chilean bishops to Rome.

[6] Diane Montagna, "Pope Francis Covered Up McCarrick Abuse, Former U.S. Nuncio Testifies," LifeSiteNews, August 25, 2018, https://www.lifesitenews.com/news/former-us-nuncio-pope-francis-knew-of-mccarricks-misdeeds-repealed-sanction.

[7] Diane Montagna, "Cardinal Cupich: Vatican Majority of Clergy Abuse Is Homosexual, but Homosexuality 'Not a Cause,'" LifeSiteNews, February 18, 2019, https://www.lifesitenews.com/news/cardinal-cupich-concedes-majority-of-abuse-is-homosexual-but-denies-causal. See also

*hierarchy be regained when, to many, it doesn't appear that there's a real commitment to get to the heart of the problem?*
The faithful will trust in the hierarchy when the bishops demonstrate by word and action that homosexual activity among the clergy will not be tolerated, excused, or covered up. That means that unchaste clergymen who use their authority to sexually victimize people entrusted to their pastoral care will be removed from the priesthood without any chance of ever returning. Wolves in shepherd's clothing should be expelled and never let back into the role of shepherd in the sheepfold. The faithful who are horrified by what has gone on will only trust their bishops when they see that they, the bishops, truly share that same reaction of horror to sexually predatory clerics.

*Two months after the Vatican sex-abuse summit, in April 2019, Pope Emeritus Benedict XVI published a lengthy essay in which he explained "what he sees as the roots of the crisis, the effects it's had on the priesthood, and how the Church should best respond."[8] What is the significance of Benedict's letter in helping us understand the crisis?*
Pope Emeritus Benedict's letter essentially identified the sexual abuse crisis as being at root the invasion of a 1960's secularistic mentality into the Church. Bad ideas led to bad actions.

---

Diane Montagna, "Vatican Summit Organizer: Gay Subculture in Seminaries Has 'Nothing to Do with Sex Abuse of Minors,'" LifeSiteNews, February 22, 2019, https://www.lifesitenews.com/news/vatican-summit-organizer-gay-subculture-in-seminaries-has-nothing-to-do-wit.

[8] Edward Pentin, "Benedict XVI Breaks His Silence on the Catholic Church's Sex-Abuse Crisis," *National Catholic Register*, April 10, 2019, https://www.ncregister.com/news/benedict-xvi-breaks-his-silence-on-the-catholic-church-s-sex-abuse-crisis.

Churchmen entranced by new ways of thinking that were directly opposed to Christ's teaching felt emboldened by the sweeping changes in society to demand that the Church go along with those ideas so as to be relevant. It was a total disaster.

**One of the problems with the 2002 Dallas Charter, drawn up by the US bishops, including then-Archbishop of Washington, DC, Cardinal McCarrick, was that it made priests accountable but left bishops to monitor themselves. Are the measures that followed the Vatican's February 2019 meeting, such as those laid out in Pope Francis's motu propio Vos Estis Lux Mundi,[9] sufficient in holding bishops and senior clergy accountable for how they've handled sex-abuse cases?**

The provisions of *Vos Estis* are good and make possible a simplified reporting mechanism for sexual abuse, including for the abuse of episcopal authority to protect the abusers. There is now a publicly known accountability system. The question that remains is whether the Holy See will follow the provisions of this law and deal with the accusations against bishops in canonical trials or administrative processes that yield a publicly known decision with resultant penalties. A number of cases that have been presented to the Holy See have, in fact, been concluded without canonical trials or administrative processes reaching a published verdict or decision. Rather, accused bishops were asked to submit their resignations, thus avoiding any canonical sanction. That is legally and morally unsatisfactory. Crime

---

[9] Pope Francis, Motu Propio *Vos Estis Lux Mundi* (May 7, 2019), http://www.vatican.va/content/francesco/en/motu_proprio/documents/papa-francesco-motu-proprio-20190507_vos-estis-lux-mundi.html. The document came into force on June 1, 2019, for a three-year experimental basis.

needs to be treated as a public offense against the victims and also against the good order of society. Early retirement is not a punishment and allows the accused bishop to pretend that he retired so as to spare the diocese further upset, which may even be characterized as a "generous" act on his part.

*Do you think enough has been done for the victims of the sex-abuse crisis?*
No, clearly not, because the victims are not just those who have been abused but the entire Catholic community who were taken advantage of by bishops, who used the money and goodwill they got from those faithful laity to hide and protect homosexual (and some heterosexual) predators in the priesthood rather than come to a full accounting. The situation has not been resolved by any means. More needs to be done, and I would say that canonical trials and public accountability for criminal behavior that constitutes canonical crimes should be clearer and swifter and more publicly engaged in.

The McCarrick case, for instance, was handled by Rome as an administrative process rather than a canonical trial. The results were summed up in a two or three paragraph statement. That's not a sufficient way, in my opinion, to inform people of what happened and why he was punished. The good of the Church would have been better served if McCarrick had been canonically tried so that his crimes would have been exposed and his victims given the satisfaction of knowing that they had their day in court and were able to confront the evildoer who had done so much damage to themselves and to the Church as a whole. Those victims should also have been free to reveal their testimony in public, and the record of the proceedings should have been made available after the verdict had been given. If the administration of justice is to be exemplary and instill confidence in the community, then the public needs to know how and why a decision was reached, in this case convicting a former cardinal of horrendous crimes.

**Should the State be handling these crimes, or does the Church have enough in her own legal system to handle them?** Criminal behavior that violates the laws of the State must be prosecuted by the State, and the Church should cooperate with that if the local government is a just government and operates according to standards of justice.

Canonically, the punishments involve depriving clerical criminals of their office in the Church, subjecting them to a penal life of prayer and penance, or removal from the priesthood. The Church could also command restitution to be paid to victims. But the Church's law depends on the cooperation of the parties involved. If the priest flees his diocese and will not acknowledge any communication from the Holy See or the diocese, then there's not much they can do in terms of getting him into a canonical courtroom. He should then be declared absent, the trial concluded, and the canonical verdict should be published and put into effect.

**What does the Church do at that point?**
Generally, if his guilt is established, they would act based on the evidence they have and give him a canonical penalty. Or if there is a civil crime, they should turn that over to the State. The state has a legitimately coercive legal authority to arrest people, detain them, and then try them, whereas the Church doesn't

have that kind of coercive power to physically seize someone and put him in, say, a diocesan jail and bring him to trial. This happened in the past. That is not possible now. Vatican City State has a jail cell, but it is for crimes against the civil criminal law. Or, for instance, if a nuncio commits a crime in a foreign country he can be prosecuted in Vatican City.

**What more do you think needs to be done?**
Given what we have seen worldwide for the past twenty-plus years, there needs to be a new codification of canonical laws related to sexual immorality and abuses of authority to cover up those crimes. Procedures used should meet current standards of justice in democratic societies. The law needs to be comprehensive and simple to understand. Mechanisms to prosecute these crimes need to be clearly identified. The current arrangements are incomplete, often obscure, and not transparent. Justice is served when justice is seen at every stage of an established process that is conducted impartially and transparently. The Church should also clean her own house by pro-actively revealing past crimes that have been hidden.

The revelation of historical crimes in each diocese is largely the fruit of pressure from the civil government, even in the form of allowing plaintiffs to sue beyond the statute of limitations.

**Are you in favor of that?**
Yes, I am in favor of that, given the history of "turning a blind eye," when even the civil authority would not prosecute priests but delivered them back to the bishop, saying, "He'll take care of the problem to avoid scandal." Often, people who worked

in government were Catholic or didn't want to be seen in the position of persecuting the Church even though that was a mistaken interpretation in my opinion.

The Holy See should send visitators to every diocese and do a historical investigation. The Holy See should then issue a report about how dioceses have handled these crimes in the past, who was involved, and what they knew, because what happened in the past, in so many cases, was a grave offense against justice.

**The former cardinal and now laicized Theodore McCarrick was at the center of abuse and corruption for decades, both in the US and at the Vatican. How much of this is a symptom of the crisis or part of its cause? Why is the McCarrick cabal (i.e., all of McCarrick's motley crew who abetted him and kept him going) so significant? And what, to you, are the most disturbing aspects of this network of which he was the head?**

I am not sure that there was a cabal acting in sync with McCarrick. McCarrick was in many ways a loner who bought influence and protection with the money he raised. He was the ultimate manipulator. He used people his whole life. I am sure he never had a real friend among his fellow bishops. That was how he wanted it. The McCarrick scandal reveals the deeply entrenched problem of clerical homosexual abuse of minors and adults who were under the authority of a bishop and cardinal such as McCarrick. The report on the McCarrick scandal published by the Holy See reveals that he was protected and even promoted over the years despite very credible claims against him. When Pope Benedict decided to discipline him, he did so in a private way that allowed McCarrick to carry on his official duties without anyone knowing that he was a sexual abuser. It was a terrible mistake not to put him on trial. He should have faced justice long before his criminal acts were revealed due to a former altar boy victim coming forward to lodge a complaint to the sexual-abuse compensation board set up by the Archdiocese of New York.

**Stepping away from those unspeakable evils which inflict psychological and moral harm on those in the care of the Church, let us turn to false teaching. As the Lord says, "Whoever then relaxes one of the least of these commandments and teaches men so, shall be called least in the kingdom of heaven; but he who does them and teaches them shall be called great in the kingdom of heaven" (Matt 5:19). Some people have accused Pope Francis of having taught people to break the commandments, most recently by his alleged endorsement of same-sex civil unions. In October 2020, the secular media erupted when Pope Francis said in a documentary that premiered in Rome, "What we have to create is a civil union law. That way [same-sex couples] are legally covered. I stood up for that."[10] Are we witnessing the repeated use of a tactic**

---

[10] In a letter to papal representatives, the Vatican Secretariat of State asked bishops to provide context regarding Pope Francis's comments on civil unions. In doing so, it confirmed that he supports legal provisions for such unions, even though he opposes same-sex "marriage." See CNA Staff, "Vatican Secretariat of State Provides Context of Pope Francis's Civil Union Remark," November 1, 2020, https://www.catholicnewsagency.com/news/46431/vatican-secretariat-of-state-provides-context-of-pope-francis-civil-union-remark. See also English translation of "Guide to Understanding Some of the Pope's Expressions in the Documentary Francesco," in Kathleen N. Hattrup, "Vatican Secretariat of State Clarifies Pope's Civil Unions Comments," Aleteia, November 2, 2020, https://aleteia.org/2020/11/02/vatican-secretariate-of-state-clarifies-popes-civil-unions-comment/.

*whereby the Pope advances an agenda without irrevocably committing himself to it in such a way as might provoke a reaction?*

The pope is, by definition, the chief teacher in the Church. Therefore, he has to exercise this role with great precision and care so that he upholds Catholic doctrine and does nothing to lead people astray by saying things that contradict or are not supported by the Church's perennial teaching. That means that Catholics, who by nature reverence and respect the office of Peter and the person who occupies that office, are now at times required by the Faith to critique and even contradict certain statements by Pope Francis because what the Pope is teaching conflicts with what the previous popes have always taught.

On the matter of civil unions for so-called "same-sex couples," Pope John Paul II taught very clearly, through the Congregation for the Doctrine of the Faith, that Catholics cannot support these civil unions in any way because they are a pseudo-marriage.[11] Furthermore, supporting this legal institution would scandalize people by falsely indicating that the Catholic Church approved of immoral behavior and was encouraging homosexual couples to enter into sinful relationships which would enjoy legal approval.

So, when Pope Francis expressed support for these civil unions—and he clearly said it because it was recorded and broadcast—I wrote a column criticizing him for doing this.[12]

---

[11] Congregation for the Doctrine of the Faith, Considerations Regarding Proposals to Give Legal Recognition to Unions Between Homosexual Persons (June 2, 2003), https://www.vatican.va/roman_curia/congregations/cfaith/documents/rc_con_cfaith_doc_20030731_homosexual-unions_en.html.

[12] Fr. Gerald Murray, "Pope Francis Oversteps the Papal Office," *The Catholic Thing*,

I don't believe this was a failure on my part in respect or charity to the Pope, because the highest charity we owe to someone is to remind him of what is true. The Pope himself has said that he welcomes criticism and has said it on a number of occasions. One memorable occasion was at the 2014 Extraordinary Synod on the Family. In his greetings to the Synod Fathers, Pope Francis said, "One general and basic condition is this: speaking honestly. Let no one say, 'I cannot say this, they will think this or this of me.' . . . It is necessary to say with *parrhesia* [i.e., to speak candidly] all that one feels." The Pope continued: "After the last consistory (February 2014), in which the family was discussed, a cardinal wrote to me, saying: what a shame that several cardinals did not have the courage to say certain things out of respect for the Pope, perhaps believing that the Pope might think something else. This is not good, this is not *synodality*, because it is necessary to say all that, in the Lord, one feels the need to say: without polite deference, without hesitation."[13] Taking the Pope at his word is, I think, an important sign of respect, and he himself has said that he welcomes criticism. On one occasion, he said it helps him to evaluate what he's said.[14]

Similar respect is owed to bishops and priests, but we now live in an age when some bishops and priests say things which

---

October 24, 2020, https://www.thecatholicthing.org/2020/10/24/pope-francis-oversteps-the-papal-office/.

[13] Pope Francis, Greeting to the Synod Fathers during the First General Congregation of the Third Extraordinary General Assembly of the Synod of Bishops (October 6, 2014), http://www.vatican.va/content/francesco/en/speeches/2014/october/documents/papa-francesco_20141006_padri-sinodali.html.

[14] Pope Francis's In-Flight Press Conference: Full Text," Vatican News, September 10, 2019, https://www.vaticannews.va/en/pope/news/2019-09/pope-francis-in-flight-press-conference-full-text.html.

are manifestly either heretical, or erroneous, or contradictory to the Faith and that would, if put into effect, damage the mission of the Church.

**Fr. Murray, as a member of The World Over's "Papal Posse" on EWTN for the last several years, you've weighed in on some of the most important and controversial events in the Church. What effect do you think the current pontificate has had on the Church today?**

Pope Francis came into office saying that he wanted to "make a mess" in the sense that he's encouraged people to stir things up, and I think he's consciously done that himself. A mess or a stir, however you want to describe it, that's what we have. The Church is very unsettled now. People are wondering if we're going to be changing more things; they are wondering about the political focus of so much of what the Pope says on environmentalism and the economy. They are wondering about internal Church governance. So, there are all kinds of questions about how things are going in Rome that puzzle people, and I believe this isn't a result of papal inattention. I think he does want to stir things up as his *modus operandi*, which can be traced in some ways to his Jesuit formation because Jesuits do like to challenge people to think and defend their positions. But part of it also, I think, is that his vision of the Church does involve a heavy interest in economic and environmental issues that were only lightly focused on in the last two pontificates.

*To what extent do you believe the Church should be weighing in on economics, climate, and other issues that pertain more to the temporal order?*

The Church's role is to present the treasure of her doctrinal heritage as it bears on economic life and man's relation to his environment, and there's a full body of teaching, dating back to the Church Fathers and then the medieval theologians. There are ways of applying the doctrine of the Faith as regards the economy and the environment based on the morality of human acts. The essential issue here is: What should people do to have a good impact economically and environmentally? That is, in part, based on virtuous action, but a large part of it is based on accurate information regarding how you obtain outcomes that are good and what your presuppositions are. For instance, on economics, is your presupposition that the existence of economic inequality in the world is itself a sin and a sign of disorder, or is the phenomenon of economic inequality a natural result of how human society exists, that there are some who will earn more than others in virtue of their work or their talents or abilities or opportunities? What is the influence of factors such as geography, social arrangements in a society and its laws? All of those are factors worth studying and understanding, but they are largely matters that inform people making moral decisions. They are not matters that have one definitive answer to be given by a religious authority, i.e., "You must do this in order to obtain an economy that is sound, just, and beneficial."

The same is true for environmentalism. What will result in man's making good use of the natural gifts that God has given to the world? What are your presuppositions? What is a good outcome: more trees, more people, more food, less disease, things of that sort? There's no such thing as an "environmental teaching of the Church" that requires all people to agree that we must do the following ten steps. No. You have a teaching about how man must make just and good use of the creation God has given him, but there are a variety of ways in which that will depend on who is involved and what his particular needs are.

**Some people might ask, "Isn't it good to shake things up and make people question the Church's approach to issues?"** Our Lord shook things up, and so should we, but not every innovation and challenge to the way things are is good or necessary. The faithful transmission of the Church's teaching is our primary obligation. The encouragement of personal holiness and the need for charitable living are essential. The hope of Heaven must always be before our eyes. Actions or words which undermine the tranquility of the faith of believers should be avoided.

**Far more dramatic have been the novelties ascribed to Pope Francis in the interviews he has conducted with Italian journalist and avowed atheist Eugenio Scalfari.[15] But in these cases, there is a higher level of deniability, given that the ninety-seven-year-old doesn't record the interviews or take notes. One might have thought that, were the interviews inaccurate, the Holy Father might have issued a firm denial and reiterated**

---

[15] James Roberts, "Scalfari Claims Pope Does Not Believe Jesus 'the Man' Was Divine," The Tablet, October 10, 2019, https://www.thetablet.co.uk/news/12111/scalfari-claims-pope-does-not-believe-jesus-the-man-was-divine. See also Edward Pentin, "Pope Allegedly Says Hell Doesn't Exist in Latest Scalfari 'Interview,'" National Catholic Register, March 29, 2018, https://www.ncregister.com/blog/pope-allegedly-says-hell-doesn-t-exist-in-latest-scalfari-interview.

*Catholic doctrine or stopped granting such interviews. How should a Catholic respond to these interviews?*

Pope Francis plainly likes being interviewed by Eugenio Scalfari even when Scalfari attributes to Pope Francis shocking statements, including the claim that Pope Francis told him that Hell does not exist and that the souls of those who die in serious sin go out of existence. This is a double contradiction of Catholic dogma. Did Pope Francis really say that? I hope not. The Holy See issued a very weak statement saying that we should not trust everything that Scalfari writes. If that is the case, it is extremely imprudent in my opinion to grant any more interviews. Pope Francis obviously disagrees, as he has continued to talk with Scalfari.

**Many of Pope Francis's statements, especially his interviews and in-flight press conferences, are said not to be magisterial statements. But what are the consequences of these statements, and how much are they undermining the authority of the papacy?**

They are not solemn teachings, nor are they given in the manner of a formal papal teaching, but, on the other hand, they *are* being taught by the Pope. These statements therefore indicate the mind of the Pope, and he obviously makes them with the confidence that what he's saying does not contradict Catholic teaching. He's saying he thinks this is what Catholics *should* believe, for instance, on the topic of same-sex civil unions, or on the question of Communion for the divorced and remarried. And he has made clear that he doesn't believe that the death penalty is moral. What he's indicating in these occasional statements, i.e., which are given on an occasion rather than in a solemn teaching document, is what he believes the faithful *should* believe and do, and that has consequences. Most people assume that if the pope says something, then Catholics have to believe in what he says. But that is not what the Church teaches. The pope is a servant of the Word of God, not its master (CCC 86). He can have personal opinions on matters that are subject to debate and discussion. But his teaching role as pope does not include compelling us to agree with him on such matters. That is why popes have traditionally avoided unscripted or off-the-cuff pronouncements on matters of doctrine.

**Famed Italian journalist and author, Vittorio Messori, who came to prominence in 1985 with his published interview with Joseph Cardinal Ratzinger (The Ratzinger Report), more recently in 2017 publicly criticized Pope Francis for mirroring modern society by turning the Church into a place where "everything is unstable and changeable."[16] But Messori noted that "in a 'liquid world' where everything becomes uncertain, precarious, provisional, it is precisely the stability and firmness of the Catholic Church that all humanity needs, and not only believers." To what extent do you believe Pope Francis is simply implementing the "dynamic of change" that took over in the aftermath of the Second Vatican Council?**

Messori is onto something profound here. Pope Francis contributed to the sense in the Church that everything is subject to revision by his endorsement in *Amoris Laetitia* of giving Holy Communion to some divorced-and-remarried Catholics. If

---

[16] Edward Pentin, "Messori: Pope Francis is Creating a 'Liquid Society' Church," *National Catholic Register*, November 8, 2017, https://www.ncregister.com/blog/messori-pope-francis-is-creating-a-liquid-society-church.

the Church can change that, people say, then what else can be changed. I am firmly convinced that the Pope does not have the power to authorize the administration of Holy Communion to those living in adulterous so-called second marriages. But other people think he does, and others do not know what to think. That is a perfect example of the instability introduced into the life of the Church by Pope Francis. It stands in sad contrast to the way of acting of his immediate predecessors, who guided the Church through the "liquid world" of disintegrating modernity with great care to defend her doctrine and practice.

**There has been a lot of talk about the need to formally correct Pope Francis. What form should such a correction take? Should it involve cardinals? Should it have already happened? Or do you see it as potentially happening in the future?**
Raymond Cardinal Burke discussed issuing a formal correction of Pope Francis's teachings in *Amoris Laetitia*, but nothing ever came of it. The *dubia* that he and three other cardinals submitted included an analysis of why each *dubium* was posed. Those analyses in themselves serve as a corrective to the mistaken teaching concerning the permissibility of administering Holy Communion to some of those living in invalid second marriages. The justifications given in *Amoris Laetitia* for this radical departure from the constant practice and teaching of the Church are refuted ably by the *dubia* analyses and by many other critiques that have been written by knowledgeable theologians and canonists. It was very disappointing that only four cardinals presented the *dubia*. This is now a matter for the next pope to address as Pope Francis has indicated his unwillingness to answer the *dubia*.

*In the late twentieth century, a kind of hypothetical universalism has become popular, which proposes that we can reasonably hope and pray for the salvation of the total number of all men. Whereas in the past it has been taken for granted that the concrete reality of damnation was a revealed fact—and even the concrete reality of damnation for most men.[17] It is clear that this shift has coincided with a falling off in missionary activity in the Church. Do you think that has contributed to this decline? Do you think that annihilationism (the belief that the souls of the damned cease to exist rather than suffering eternal torment) is a heresy? How should the faithful respond when prelates openly espouse universalism or annihilationism?[18]*

The salvation of souls is the mission of the Church. This can only mean saving souls from perdition. Perdition means eternal damnation in Hell. God is the just judge who renders perfect justice with perfect mercy. The mystery of his love for mankind includes the existence of both Heaven and Hell. Our Lord spoke of Hell frequently and came to offer the way to avoid Hell and gain eternal life in Heaven. Any denial of the existence of Hell is heretical. The notion that no one goes to Hell stands in plain contradiction to the way the Church has always understood Our Lord's warnings, i.e., he was not engaging in

---

[17] "For although [the faithful] are few compared to the unfruitful multitude of the damned, according to Matthew, '*narrow is the way that leads to life, and few find it* (Matt 7:14).'" St. Thomas Aquinas, *Commentary on St. Paul's Letter to the Romans,* vol. 37, 12:2 (Lander, WY: Aquinas Institute for the Study of Sacred Doctrine, 2012), 333.

[18] Eugenio Scalfari, "Il Papa: 'È un Onore Essere Chiamato Revoluzionario,'" La Repubblica, March 28, 2018, https://rep.repubblica.it/pwa/esclusiva/2018/03/28/news/il_papa_e_un_onore_essere_chiamato_rivoluzionario_-192479298/?ref=RHPPRB-BH-I0-C4-P1-S1.4-F4.

hyperbole or stating a mere hypothetical possibility of eternal damnation but rather a real possibility for each and every one of us fallen creatures (Our Lady excepted). He refers to Judas as the "son of perdition" (John 17:12). As for annihilationism, the Church has never taught that God returns to nothingness what he has created out of nothing. "God saw everything that he had made, and behold, it was very good" (Gen 1:31). Why would God totally destroy what he created? In addition, the Church affirms that Hell is an everlasting reality (CCC 1033).

**In the Church's liturgy for Holy Thursday for more than a millennium, the damnation of Judas is presumed: "O God, from whom Judas received the punishment of his guilt, and the thief the reward of his confession: grant unto us the full fruit of thy clemency; that even as in his Passion Our Lord Jesus Christ gave to each retribution according to his merits, so having cleared away our former guilt, he may bestow on us the grace of his resurrection: who with thee liveth and reigneth."[19] And it seems to be the consensus of the Fathers that the meaning of the Lord's words in John 17:12 was that Judas was lost. What are we to make, therefore, of modern clerics who preach the salvation of Judas?**

The common opinion in scriptural commentaries in the history of the Church has either taken the view that Judas is in Hell or is likely in Hell. That is based on the Lord's own words: "It would've better for that man if he had not been born"

---

[19] Peter Kwasniewski, "Damned Lies: On the Destiny of Judas Iscariot," Rorate Caeli, March 30, 2015, https://rorate-caeli.blogspot.com/2015/03/damned-lies-on-destiny-of-judas-iscariot.html.

(Matt 26:24). The only possible thing better than existence in Hell is non-existence. If he's going to suffer eternally in Hell, the only better alternative would have been if he never existed. On the other hand, we have a true understanding that the fate of souls is judged by God alone and that he alone knows the motions of the will and intellect at the moment of death and whether Judas expressed repentance to God for his sin, so the Church has never definitively taught that Judas is in Hell.

**Even the Vatican's own semi-official newspaper, L'Osservatore Romano, ran a cover on Holy Thursday 2021 promoting this view of Judas Iscariot.[20] What do today's attempts to rehabilitate Judas say about the modern view of sin, mercy, and truth?[21]**

The sentimental fable that somehow Judas was not responsible for his sins is a fruit of modern-day theories in which someone who inflicts evil upon someone else is, in reality, just as much a victim as the real victim. It is the denial of personal responsibility for choices in life and reduces man to a robotic actor who bears no responsibility but likewise gets no credit for anything he does. This obvious falsehood is dehumanizing and irreconcilable with Biblical religion.

---

[20] Andrea Monda, "Judas and the Scandal of Mercy," *L'Osservatore Romano*, April 1, 2021, https://www.osservatoreromano.va/it/news/2021-04/quo-074/giuda-e-lo-scandalo-br-della-misericordia.html.

[21] Msgr. Charles Pope, "Mercy and the Scandal of Judas," *National Catholic Register*, April 25, 2021, https://www.ncregister.com/blog/mercy-and-the-scandal-of-judas.

*In 2018, the English musician Sting composed a "Dies Irae"[22] for a multimedia show at the Vatican on Michelangelo's* The Last Judgement. *Discussing it in an interview, he said he admired Pope Francis's emphasis on a God of mercy and so "took liberties" to amend the original text, putting* Deus Misericordia *(God is mercy) at the end. "With the Last Judgment, if God is mercy, then there's no judgment at all, just forgiveness," Sting said. "I was surprised that the authorities seemed to like it and let it go."[23] This is perhaps just one example of how, these days, mercy tends to eclipse justice. Have we forgotten about God's justice or adapted it to our own image to make it more palatable?*

If there is no judgment by God that someone has done wrong, then there is no need for forgiveness either because there is nothing to forgive and everything is morally meaningless. If that is the case, there is no need to be good in this life as God will not hold anyone accountable for the evil they have done. Being good requires sacrifice and self-restraint. Why bother if none of that is important? A world without God's judgment is not the world that the good God created and redeemed by sending his Son. If everyone gets into Heaven no matter what they have done, then life is essentially meaningless, and we become simply beasts who prey upon each other to stay alive.

---

[22] Literally, "Day of Wrath." A hymn regarding the Judgment Day.
[23] Edward Pentin, "Sting: 'The Church's Music and Liturgy Fed This Artistic Soul,'" *National Catholic Register*, August 8, 2018, https://www.ncregister.com/blog/sting-the-church-s-music-and-liturgy-fed-this-artistic-soul.

*Orthodox Catholics feel a bit battered around the head by the various things Pope Francis has said about them since he was elected, e.g., that they're too "rigid"; they're "doctors of the law"; that traditional Catholics are "sick" and need to be healed; that they "breed like rabbits"; that he doesn't look at conservative blogs because they "do my head in"; that young priests in traditional clerical garb harbor "moral problems" and "imbalances"; ridiculing those who wear the saturno as "all stiff" and wearing "the planet Saturn on their heads."[24] What are Catholics to make of this? And what do you say to those who don't feel they have a spiritual father in Pope Francis?*

The popular, and reasonable, expectation is that the pope is going to choose his words carefully and is going to say things designed to promote spiritual growth or reform. Offhand comments which may be jokes or joking ways to criticize others, and certainly insults and uncharitable inferences, are not expected from the pope and, I would say, are really not useful and should be avoided. We must always pray for our pope, and when his words are either cruel, or at the least thoughtless, we must not hold a grudge against him but rather forgive and forget. Emotional resentments are not compatible with a peaceful Christian spirit.

*Without wishing to draw too much negativity around this pontificate, there have been occasions when Pope Francis has drawn the world's attention in positive ways. One thinks of the early images of the Pope embracing the Italian man*

---

[24] Dorothy Cummings McLean, "Pope Criticizes Young Traditional Priests' Clothes: Cassock Suggests 'Moral Problems,'" LifeSiteNews, September 27, 2019, https://www.lifesitenews.com/news/pope-criticizes-young-traditional-priests-clothes-cassock-means-moral-problems.

*with a deformity, his Friday acts of mercy, or inviting the homeless to Santa Marta for his birthday.*

Pope Francis deserves our thanks for showing Christlike charity to those who suffer greatly in this life for various reasons. We must not take our blessings for granted and forget the needs of our fellow man. Pope Francis always concludes his speeches and talks with the request that we pray for him. This reminder that we depend upon God's grace is very timely in an age in which God is too often forgotten or ignored.

*Jeffrey Sachs is an American economist and longtime advisor to the Vatican who exercises considerable influence. In October 2021, Pope Francis appointed him a member of the Pontifical Academy of Social Sciences (PAS). At a PAS meeting, he announced that potential funding partners for Pope Francis's Global Education Pact include Bill Gates and the International Monetary Fund.[25] The Pontifical Council for Culture, headed by Gianfranco Cardinal Ravasi, has in recent years hosted global health conferences at the Vatican featuring pop stars such as Katy Perry, who talked about the benefits of transcendental meditation for children,[26] and the CEOs of COVID-19 vaccine manufacturers Pfizer and Moderna, but with no effort to communicate the Church's*

---

[25] Diane Montagna, "Vatican Urged to Partner with Top Population Controllers on Pope's Global Education Pact," LifeSiteNews, February 14, 2020, https://www.lifesitenews.com/news/vatican-urged-to-partner-with-top-population-controllers-on-popes-global-education-pact.

[26] Diane Montagna, "Vatican Invites Katy Perry to Talk about Transcendental Meditation," LifeSiteNews; May 2, 2018, https://www.lifesitenews.com/news/vatican-invites-katy-perry-to-speak-on-meditation.

call for non-abortion-tainted vaccines. When pressed on the latter decision, Msgr. Tomasz Trafny, the Vatican's chief organizer of these conferences, said, "So if we blame others and condemn others, what can we really achieve? No one cares today about our condemnations."[27] How much should the Church be engaging with these groups and individuals? Where should the line be drawn? And has the Church lost her force as a moral compass for the world, precisely because her shepherds don't push back hard enough against worldly values?

The allegation that some people do not care when the Church boldly proclaims the demands of God's law is not a reason to stop proclaiming the truth. It is unseemly and potentially dangerous to seek funding for Vatican events and meetings from individuals and institutions that are hostile to the Church's teaching. Bill Gates, for instance, is a prominent supporter of spreading contraceptives in poor countries. The Catholic Church should not conduct herself as one more international lobby looking to gain influence and funding from globalist centers of power that are, in fact, using the Church to burnish their reputations.

*On May 8, 2021, Pope Francis sent a message in support of "Vax Live: The Concert to Reunite the World."[28] The concert included LGBT propaganda and, in at least two acts, the sort*

---

[27] Edward Pentin, "Catholic Perspectives in Short Supply at Vatican Health Conference," *National Catholic Register*, May 12, 2021, https://www.ncregister.com/news/catholic-perspectives-in-short-supply-at-vatican-health-conference.

[28] Pope Francis, "Video Message to the Participants in 'Vax-Live: The Concert to Reunite the World,'" May 8, 2021, https://www.vatican.va/content/francesco/en/messages/pont-messages/2021/documents/papa-francesco_20210508_videomessaggio-vaxlive.html.

*of sexually explicit dancing which plagues pop culture today and is corrupting the minds and hearts of young people. One can only assume that the Pope had no idea about this before sending a video-message to the concert. How should we make sense of this, and should anything be done given that many are scandalized by it?*

Great care must be taken by the Holy See in endorsing events that could include scandalous and immoral performances. Due diligence before endorsing will usually identify possible red flags. It is scandalous and demoralizing for a family trying to raise their children in a Christian way to learn that the pope is listed as a supporter of a concert that they would never let their children attend out of legitimate concern for the kind of entertainment likely to be included in the program.

*This would never have been accepted before the Second Vatican Council, or even during more recent pontificates. Why is it accepted now with little or no opposition?*

Engagement with the world has slipped into submission to the worldly standards of our contemporary society. When a Vatican official, as cited above, appears to be more upset with Catholics who criticize the immorality that is rampant in our world than with those who promote such immorality, we have arrived at a sad moment in the history of the Church. Our Savior did not go "hat in hand" to the people of his time and seek to cut deals or find common ground. He proclaimed God's truth and called men to repentance. That should be our program in any age of the Church. When other things become priorities the faithful must protest for the good of souls.

*In February 2021, Italian journalist Aldo Maria Valli penned an article provocatively titled "Rome Is without a Pope."[29] Valli argued that although the Pope has been ubiquitously featured in Catholic and secular media, he is representing himself, i.e., Jorge Bergoglio, and not Peter. Valli further argues that the God whom Pope Francis presents is a "caricature of the God of the Bible." Scripture, Valli writes, teaches us that God "is indeed patient, but not lax. He is indeed loving, but not permissive; he is indeed caring, but not accommodating. In a word, he is Father in the fullest and most authentic sense of the term." Do you think this is a fair criticism?*

I thought it was a good article. The provocative title is indicative of the point Valli is making: that Peter and his successors have always understood their role to be that of representing the teaching of Christ in consistency with the magisterium of the Church, and that this Pope has, on occasion, said things that cannot be justified according to the magisterium. When the Pope is criticized for it, he refuses to defend his position beyond, for example, on *Amoris Laetitia*, asserting: "It's very Thomistic." He publicly infers that people who are what he would call "traditionalists" or "rigorists" have emotional problems and are hiding behind dogma. It's not serious engagement with your critics to say, in effect, "You've got a problem; just leave me alone."

---

[29] Aldo Maria Valli, "Rome Is without a Pope," Duc in Altum, February 21, 2021, https://www.aldomariavalli.it/2021/02/21/rome-is-without-a-pope-roma-senza-papa-anche-in-inglese/. See Aldo Maria Valli, "Roma senza Bergoglio. C'è Bergoglio. No C'è Pietro," Duc in Altum, February 20, 2021, https://www.aldomariavalli.it/2021/02/20/roma-senza-papa-ce-bergoglio-non-ce-pietro/.

*What is the duty of the cardinals as the pope's counselors in this regard? You mentioned that Pope Francis has invited constructive criticism and we should take him at his word. But the reality is that he hasn't convened the cardinals in several years now. What is the responsibility of the cardinals, and how do you think they can best exercise their duty under the present circumstances?*

The cardinals as a body are called, in canon law, the senate of the Church, and a senate in the Roman understanding was a body of wise and experienced men who had the best interests of the State at heart. They would meet to discuss matters of importance to the State. Similarly, in the Church, the cardinals have a role of advising the pope. It depends on the pope to convoke them as a body to meet. Pope Francis has shown a reluctance to do that and, in fact, hasn't done it in at least five years.

*Just after the four cardinals sent the "dubia" to Pope Francis, asking for clarity on* Amoris Laetitia.[30]

Yes, even though the last time he met with the cardinals he told them they would assist him in the proposed reform of the Roman Curia. But since then, they've never met as a group to discuss the proposal that is right now in the hands of the Pope regarding the Roman Curia. Cardinals, however, are not merely passive. They have a duty to defend Catholic teaching as does every Catholic bishop, and it's laudatory when cardinals take up the pen or speak in front of a microphone or camera in order

---

[30] Edward Pentin, "Four Cardinals Formally Ask Pope for Clarity on 'Amoris Laetitia,'" *National Catholic Register*, November 14, 2016, https://www.ncregister.com/news/four-cardinals-formally-ask-pope-for-clarity-on-amoris-laetitia.

to defend the integrity of the Faith and to give advice to the pope as individuals. That was certainly what Cardinal Sarah did regarding the question of optional celibacy at the Synod on the Amazon. Cardinals have a right and a duty to use their office to promote the Faith in the unique way they can as men with important responsibilities in the life of the Church who will elect the next pope.

*Moving on to other prelates, the most notorious examples today are, of course, the German bishops. In his papal bull* Exsurge Domine, *which condemned the errors of Martin Luther, Pope Leo X said how unfortunate it was that this heresy had broken out in Germany when its people are so naturally "germane to the Catholic faith."[31] Some might observe that a lot of water has flowed under the bridge since then. St. Paul famously warned the bishops of Ephesus that "after my departure fierce wolves will come in among you, not sparing the flock; and from among your own selves will arise*

---

[31] Pope Leo X, Papal Bull Condemning the Errors of Martin Luther *Exsurge Domine* (June 15, 1520), https://www.papalencyclicals.net/leo10/l10exdom.htm:

> These errors have, at the suggestion of the human race, been revived and recently propagated among the more frivolous and the illustrious German nation. We grieve the more that this happened there because we and our predecessors have always held this nation in the bosom of our affection. For after the empire had been transferred by the Roman Church from the Greeks to these same Germans, our predecessors and we always took the Church's advocates and defenders from among them. Indeed, it is certain that these Germans, truly germane to the Catholic Faith, have always been the bitterest opponents of heresies, as witnessed by those commendable constitutions of the German emperors on behalf of the Church's independence, freedom, and the expulsion and extermination of all heretics from Germany.

*men speaking perverse things to draw away the disciples after them" (Acts 20:29–30). In view of the current situation regarding the German bishops and their "Synodal Way," is this a case of Reformation redux?*

As I wrote in a column at *The Catholic Thing* website, "An attempt at what can only be called the self-destruction of the Catholic Church in Germany—and beyond—is being carried out by the country's bishops, in tandem with the officially recognized national organization of Catholic laity, the Central Committee of German Catholics." This refers to the German Synodal Way, which is an ongoing series of meetings producing policy documents meant to lead the Church in Germany in new paths. Those new paths, however, are far from new and simply rehash the teachings of liberal Protestantism. The fact that the majority of German bishops have so far not rejected this act of self-destruction is indicative of the gravity of the situation. Similarly distressing was the failure by many German bishops to condemn the nationwide ceremonies "blessing" homosexual couples, a direct repudiation of the recent prohibition of such sacrilegious provocations by the Congregation for the Doctrine of the Faith, which was approved by Pope Francis.[32] Episcopal support for, or tolerance of, heretical teaching is a sure sign that the German hierarchy is plainly failing to carry out its duty to teach, govern, and sanctify the flock of Christ. This must be dealt with firmly by the pope or things will only get worse.

---

[32] See "Responsum of the Congregation for the Doctrine of the Faith (CDF) to a Dubium Regarding the Blessing of the Unions of Persons of the Same Sex," March 15, 2021, https://press.vatican.va/content/salastampa/it/bollettino/pubblico/2021/03/15/0157/00330.html#ing.

*As you mention, the Vatican gave a definitive "no" to same-sex union blessings in March 2021, and yet many of the bishops in Germany, including the president of the episcopal conference, appear willing to defy such a clear ruling. How can we make sense of this? Can we make sense of it?*

The blessing of same-sex "unions" proposed by some German bishops is completely wrong. What are they blessing? They are blessing a relationship based on the promise to sodomize each other, which is horrible. There is no same-sex marriage; it's a myth. It may be a legal institution in civil society, but it has no grounding in reality.

*What do you think about efforts to decriminalize or de-penalize homosexuality worldwide, which has also been supported by senior Vatican officials in recent years?[33]*

We don't believe in the death penalty for sodomy. The intent of laws that criminalize homosexual acts is to teach people that this behavior is bad and socially damaging and personally damaging. The law is designed to uphold the common good, and the individual good is part of the common good.

The whole Christian heritage in the West included criminalization of certain deviant sexual activity, and we should not get rid of that. We criminalize the deviant sexual behavior of non-consensual sex (rape) and sex with minors. We also

---

[33] Edward Pentin, "President of Pontifical Academy for Life Backs Italian Anti-Homophobia Bill," *National Catholic Register*, July 1, 2021, https://www.ncregister.com/blog/president-of-pontifical-academy-for-life-backs-italian-anti-homophobia-bill.

criminalize incest. We criminalize bigamy. So, there are sexual sins that are subject to criminal law and for a reason, because those behaviors are bad and harmful. If a society doesn't want to promote homosexual activity, we have to look at it this way: no one is naturally homosexual, and no one has a right to homosexual activity, so you're not violating anyone's "right" to freely commit acts of sodomy by making this behavior illegal. The harshness of some laws we would not endorse. The Muslim world freely administers the death penalty in many cases in a way the West does not. We reject that. But the law is a teacher; that's one of its functions.

Those laws are also helpful to people who get trapped in the world of prostitution, child trafficking, and things of that sort, because you can use them to prosecute people. And we have to face the fact that formerly colonial Third-World countries that inherited Western legal systems and have not updated them in the way the West has are subjected to great pressure to do so for one main reason: to legitimize homosexual activity and the homosexual lifestyle. The way they are resisting that is by saying, "We're not going to change our laws."

See also Francis DeBernardo, "Vatican's Cardinal Turkson: 'Homosexuals Should Not Be Criminalized,'" New Ways Ministry, October 24, 2015, https://www.newwaysministry.org/2015/10/24/vaticans-cardinal-turkson-homosexuals-should-not-be-criminalized/.

> As the Church in Germany continues to defy Rome, whether it be by allowing same-sex union blessings,[34] shared Communion with Protestants,[35] or vying for women's ordination,[36] what should the Pope and the Vatican be doing? Should the Pope threaten the bishops in question with excommunication? Gerhard Cardinal Müller, former prefect of the Congregation for the Doctrine of the Faith, has said that by allowing shared Communion, they're "no longer Catholic." Have they in effect excommunicated themselves latae sententia, i.e., automatically?

Bishops are subject to the pope, and Pope Francis should ask these men to recant their immoral propositions regarding the legitimization and blessing of homosexual activity. This should be done immediately because the scandal only grows when it appears that the Vatican isn't concerned about bishops encouraging people to live an immoral lifestyle. Similarly, the Church's discipline forbidding the reception of Holy Communion by Protestants—except in very specific and usually rare conditions—must be upheld by the Holy See, or the Church in Germany will make such defiance the norm, to the harm of souls. The matters at hand are not merely

---

[34] Francis X. Rocca, "Catholic Priests in Germany Bless Gay Couples, Defying Pope," *The Wall Street Journal*, May 10, 2021; https://www.wsj.com/articles/catholic-priests-in-germany-bless-gay-couples-defying-pope-11620662111.

[35] Edward Pentin, "Catholics and Protestants Share Communion at German Ecumenical Convention," *National Catholic Register*, May 17, 2021, https://www.ncregister.com/news/catholics-and-protestants-share-communion-at-german-ecumenical-convention.

[36] Fr. Gerald E. Murray, "Germany's Schismatic Synodal Way," *The Catholic Thing*, February 22, 2021, https://www.thecatholicthing.org/2021/02/22/germanys-schismatic-synodal-way/.

disciplinary but are based on Catholic dogmas, which must be defended by the Church's supreme authority, the pope. The question of automatic (*latae sententiae*) excommunication needs to be examined if the German bishops refuse to desist from all disobedience and endorsement of heretical ideas.

**Was that traditionally done by the Holy Office?**
Yes, by the Holy Office, now known as the Congregation for the Doctrine of the Faith, operating as the Pope's agent. But the Pope could also call these men in directly and tell them, "When you leave here, you recant what you've done, or you resign, or you will be deposed." If they really believed that God wants homosexual activity to be blessed, they already know the Catholic Church doesn't accept that, so they should resign from a leadership role in a Church they no longer consider to be the divinely appointed teacher of God's truth in the matter of homosexuality. They should not be allowed to make use of their positions as Catholic bishops to undermine and subvert Catholic doctrine and practice.

I'd frankly say to these men, "You are betraying the very office that you have sworn to uphold, which is to be a teacher of the Catholic Faith, not your own opinions." The same goes for priests who contradict Church teaching. They should reform and recant and understand that they are ambassadors for Christ. They are not the origin and source of Catholic teaching. They are the ones who are to transmit and pass it along, and if they think that Catholic teaching is somehow subject to change, they are misled, mistaken, and they need to recognize that. Nowhere in the *Catechism of the Catholic Church* is there a sentence which says, "Everything contained in this book is subject to further revision based on decisions in the future." It never says that. It can't—because that's not how we understand the Faith.

**Do you think the German bishops want to break from the Catholic Church or pull the world into their vision of things? Some think they've created a monster because they're the second biggest employer in Germany next to the State. If the majority of people become more progressive, the bishops will feel pressured to satisfy the people in order to keep receiving the church tax. What do you think is at play?**
The German situation has several aspects that are very troubling. The first is that some German bishops are following the advice of liberal theologians in denying Catholic teaching and promoting things that are impossible, such as the ordination of women to the priesthood, or immoral, such as the acceptance of homosexual activity as normal and good, and the need for the Church to bless public relationships in which homosexuals declare their intent to commit sin with one another. They are agents of change within the Church who enjoy an outsized influence because of the wealth of the German Church and the fact that the Holy See and many mission countries depend on the generosity of the German bishops to support their activities financially, especially in Africa and Latin America.

A hierarchy that has no money and a lot of faithful, such as we see in various African countries, has much less influence than a hierarchy that has lots of money and very few people, which is the German situation. And it's not because German bishops are necessarily smarter or better educated than African bishops. But some of them are bold and determined to follow the example of Protestantism and have the time and money to promote such ideas.

It's somewhat of a paradox that you have a Church in Germany that depends on a coercive form of support. The German government asks its citizens to declare their religious affiliation to the State and then assesses a church tax that goes to the church one belongs to. The amount one pays is decided by the government. The only way the person gets out of paying the tax is not simply by saying, "Please take my name off the roll." They have to declare before the government that they are leaving the Catholic Church even if that's not necessarily the intent. But, in order to stop paying the church tax, that's what they have to do.

The whole system here produces billions of euros each year for the Church, but it is not based either on voluntary contributions by the faithful or on the fact that those people want to participate in the life of the Church. They are simply taxed, and if they do nothing to stop it, they will continue to be taxed. It's certainly not in line with St. Paul's encouragement to the churches to support the church in Jerusalem by taking up a voluntary collection, for instance. But it's convenient for the German bishops because it gives them a lot of money. But it also puts them into a relationship with the State that can be unhealthy. If they want to maintain this arrangement, they have incentives not to antagonize the State, which could tomorrow turn around and seek to renegotiate the concordat with the Holy See and abolish the church tax.

**Where do you see this going?**
They don't have a lot of faithful, so they don't have a lot of priests. What they do have is a well-paid bureaucracy made up primarily of lay people which views the Church as something that they can shape to their own image. We see that with the German

bishops trying to make lay people pastors of churches, which is wrong, against canon law, and against Church teaching.

It's sad because Pope Francis said he wants a "poor Church for the poor." If the German bishops were serious about that, they would renounce the church tax voluntarily and then appeal to the faithful to give on their own. That would be a more just arrangement because you wouldn't be cooperating with a coercive, state-controlled system that compels people to pay the tax who are not actually participating in the life of the Church, or who, more importantly, would rather determine for themselves how they make their donations to the Church. Now, I know historically the Church enforced tithing for its members so there is a history of saying not only that this duty needs to be fulfilled but that we're going to penalize you if you don't. There's a debate on that. But apart from past practice and obligation, it is just not right that in the German Church you won't be subject to canonical discipline if you go to Communion and are divorced and civilly remarried, but if you renounce your Catholic identity before the German government in order to not pay the church tax, you will be denied ecclesiastical burial.

*In the Sermon on the Mount, Our Lord told his disciples: "No one can serve two masters; for either he will hate the one and love the other, or he will be devoted to the one and despise the other. You cannot serve God and mammon" (Matt 6:24). And in his First Letter to Timothy, St. Paul tells the first bishop of Ephesus, "Those who desire to be rich fall into temptation, into a snare, into many senseless and hurtful desires that plunge men into ruin and destruction. For the love of money is the root of all evils; it is through this craving that some have wandered from the Faith and pierced their hearts with many pangs" (1 Tim 6:9–10). How much do you think the love of money plays into the current crisis in the Church?*

The desire for money needs to be controlled by a firm commitment to not engage in any dishonest activities to enrich oneself or others. Those who exercise stewardship over the Church's money need to be scrupulously honest in all their dealings. Sadly, there are many current instances in which Churchmen have acted irresponsibly and even unethically with the Church's money. Think of Bishop Michael Bransfield's[37] profligate use of his diocesan money for extravagant personal expenses and influence buying. The former Cardinal McCarrick was infamous for his use of monetary gifts to buy influence. Where he got the money from or who were the recipients of his largess has, for the most part, not yet been made public. One of the great deficiencies of the Holy See's McCarrick report was the decision made not to investigate McCarrick's use of church money.

*American Catholics are very generous in tithing. But many don't want to give their hard-earned money to their bishop or diocese due to a loss of trust over the sex-abuse crisis, Vatican financial scandals—including the one involving the use of Papal Foundation money to bail out a mismanaged Vatican-affiliated hospital—and the denial of the sacraments during COVID-19 lockdowns. How can Catholics remain faithful to what they believe is their duty to tithe, in ways that truly promote the Church's mission?*

---

[37] Bishop Bransfield formerly served as Bishop of the Diocese of Wheeling-Charleston, WV.

Catholics have a religious obligation to financially support the Church. The fifth precept of the Church requires that one shall help provide for the material needs of the Church (CCC 2043). That should include making donations to one's parish on a regular basis. But support should also extend beyond the parish to the diocese and to other Catholic institutions. Each one should decide in conscience on what good works and apostolates deserve support. But the work of the Church depends on the offerings of the faithful. Responsible generosity is part of our Christian duty to thank God for our blessings by helping to promote financially the mission of the Church.

***I'd like to follow up regarding the denial of the sacraments during the COVID-19 lockdowns. Is it permissible in canon law for a bishop to forbid his priests from hearing Confessions during such a crisis? And can priests refuse to hear Confessions during a pandemic?***
Canon 986 states, "All to whom the care of souls has been entrusted in virtue of some function are obliged to make provision so that the Confessions of the faithful entrusted to them are heard when they reasonably seek to be heard and that they have the opportunity to approach individual Confession on days and at times established for their convenience. In urgent necessity, any confessor is obliged to hear the Confessions of the Christian faithful, and in danger of death, any priest is so obliged."

Thus, priests need to find ways to hear people's Confessions even in situations such as the COVID-19 pandemic when health precautions require social distancing. It is wrong for a bishop to forbid priests to hear Confessions in his diocese, or for a priest to refuse to hear Confessions. The faithful have a right to receive the means of salvation from their priests, even during the COVID-19 crisis, when that can be done in a way that prevents the spread of the coronavirus. Pastoral charity and obedience to canon law demand that creative ways be employed to allow people to go to Confession. At my parish, we heard Confessions in the parish garden, and we continue to use a portable kneeler with a screen in the spacious sacristy.

**Should priests then continue to hear confessions if their bishop forbids it? How can priests best resist this unjust command?**
Canon 213 states, "The Christian faithful have the right to receive assistance from the sacred pastors out of the spiritual goods of the Church, especially the word of God and the sacraments." So if the bishop were to issue a decree absolutely forbidding the hearing of Confessions in his diocese, he would be acting *ultra vires*, i.e., "beyond his powers." He would be violating the right of the faithful, as set forth in canon 213, to receive the spiritual assistance of their pastors by having their sins sacramentally forgiven. Any priest of his diocese should point this out to him and ask him to withdraw his decree. In the meantime, he should continue to hear the Confessions of those who desire to receive this sacrament. The bishop is within his rights to regulate the place and manner in which Confessions may be heard in a time of a public health emergency, such as the COVID-19 pandemic. Thus, he could legitimately forbid the use of an enclosed space, such as a confessional. But a total ban on the hearing of Confessions violates canon law, which recognizes the duty of priests to hear Confessions and the right of penitents to be sacramentally absolved of their sins.

*Let's turn to the Vatican-China deal. The Pope has not said anything critical about the Chinese Communist Party (CCP) crackdown on Hong Kong, an increased crackdown on religious freedom, not only against Catholics but also persecution against minorities like the Uyghur Muslims. How does the Vatican manage to straddle the fence, championing human rights on the one hand, and on the other, making a secret deal with Communist China? And how is it possible that an institution as committed to religious freedom as the Holy See can do this?*

I believe the Holy See's treatment of the Communist Chinese government is wrong, mistaken, and has caused lots of problems for the faithful in China and elsewhere. It is something that Joseph Cardinal Zen has complained about and condemned but to no avail, in terms of influencing the policy of the Holy See and the pope. I think it's a remarkable lack of consistency to talk about religious freedom and the rights of people to follow their conscience and yet sign an agreement giving a government, which violates the rights of conscience and religious freedom, a role in the selection of Chinese Catholic bishops. The persecution of Uyghur Muslims in China has also been largely uncommented on by the pope or the Holy See.

The Pope is very outspoken about the harmful treatment of migrants and economic inequalities in the Western world. He's called governments to task in this regard, yet the Chinese government is treated as a partner in the affairs of the Catholic Church in China even though the Chinese Communist Party is using its power to destroy the activities of the Catholic Church in China. I think it's a horrifically mistaken approach to ignore the cries and pleas of Chinese Catholics to enjoy the same rights that their brethren in the Western world have to worship freely. I am truly distressed by the Holy See's treatment of Cardinal Zen, which manifests a complete lack of a collegial spirit and a refusal to engage in meaningful dialogue with the Church in China, which is being crushed by the Chinese Communists.

Part of the issue here is: Why hasn't this agreement been made public? To whose advantage is it to keep it secret? And my only response would be that it is mostly likely to the advantage of the Chinese Communists because the Holy See usually takes actions based on agreements which are publicly known, whereas the Chinese government is always secretive in what it does. Who knows why it isn't public? It's certainly because one or both parties don't want it to be public, and I don't like that kind of arrangement, because you're not able to intelligently analyze it and then appropriately critique it and suggest alternative paths of action. When we see results like what we are getting with the selection of bishops who are servants of the Chinese Communist government, we can definitely say this is not a good agreement. But it's regrettable that the Holy See is engaged in a process under which the Chinese Catholic people are themselves suffering increased persecution.

**How do you think that the Vatican should deal with dictatorships and regimes, and do you see parallels between the Vatican's current policy and Ostpolitik?[38]**

---

[38] Ostpolitik was a method used by the Holy See to deal with the Communist countries in Eastern Europe and centered chiefly around the appointment of bishops. Although the policy was aimed at improving the life of Catholics under Communist rule and providing good episcopal appointments, the Holy See sometimes accepted compromise candidates and collaborators with the Communist system.

Certainly, treating Communist governments as potential cooperative partners is always a mistake in my opinion. Because Communism is essentially a criminal enterprise to install people in power who use the rhetoric of "solidarity" and "economic equality" to oppress and terrorize their people, and then use their power to exalt themselves and engage in nefarious activities overseas. Think of Cuba. Witnessing to Christ and his truth is what the Communist governments need, along with the people who live under them. The heroic witness of Pope John Paul II, when he was Archbishop of Krakow, would be the model for me on how you deal with Communist governments. You're aware of who they are and what they are. They do not have a common purpose with Christians; they're not interested in human freedom and fulfillment; they're not interested in coming to a deeper knowledge of God's truth. They're certainly not interested in human rights because they violate them all the time and justify it saying it serves the interests of the Communist Party.

**Can you say more about how John Paul II handled the Communists?**
John Paul II was steadfast in his faith and insisted on the right of the Catholic people of Poland to be able to express their faith in public and in ways that were not according to the plan of the Communist Party. One example was building a church in Nova Huta, which was a new town built by the Communists. There was no church planned there, and then the Catholics went ahead and built a church in the face of opposition. Karol Cardinal Wojtyła went and consecrated the church and prayed there. It's just one example of acting forthrightly and standing firm against Communists.

The mission of the Catholic Church is to proclaim the truth of Christ and to call people into a living relationship with God, so everything has to be focused on accomplishing those ends. When dealing with governments, the Holy See must act in light of the interest of truth and justice in general, and then specific questions regarding the relationship of the Church to a particular government will be dealt with in light of the Church's mission.

Christians have suffered persecution from the beginning, under the Roman Empire, and on and on, so we shouldn't be surprised when this occurs. The Lord told the Apostles, "If the world hates you, know that it has hated me before it hated you" (John 15:18). And so, if we're hated, that's not a sign that we're doing something wrong. If we're a threat to Communists, that's because Communists deserve to be threatened because they cause oppression, mayhem, poverty, and death for the people they allege to help.

**What do Catholics do when prominent pastors and people in authority are making headlines by teaching against the Faith?** Lay people and clergy who hear pastors or others in the Church speak in ways that contradict the Faith or damage the mission of the Church, by making light of traditional ways or doctrines that are clearly taught, should resist them and counter them by appealing to the pastors in general, to the Supreme Pastor and others, to come to the defense of the Faith. This is their right and duty according to canon 212. They can make their own critiques known. The internet is a great way for people to write and get their work diffused widely and quickly.

If someone says something that contradicts Church

teaching, then write an article. But you can also write to the Holy See and the local bishop. You may not get a satisfactory response. But you are doing good for the Church.

**To whom at the Holy See should people write?**
Write to the Pope himself.[39] Say "Holy Father, I'm distressed because I heard the following. . . ." Make sure that what has been reported is accurate and clear and say, "We request your assistance to help the faithful be spared misleading teachings from shepherds."

**What mechanisms are there in the Church for the correction of bishops and priests?**
In terms of what the laity can do, let's look at the German case. If your bishop says that the Church should bless homosexual unions, pseudo-marriages, you can write to him and say: "Reverend Bishop, don't you know that this contradicts the statement that Pope John Paul II issued in 2003 stating that this is immoral and shouldn't be done?" He may or may not answer you, but, based on what happens, the only superior of a bishop is the pope, so you can appeal to Rome and say this bishop is a scandal and needs to be corrected.

**To whom should you address your letter?**
Doctrinal errors are handled by the Congregation for the Doctrine of the Faith (CDF)[40], so you can write and say, "We wish to make you aware that 'Bishop X' has made the following

---

[39] The pope's address: His Holiness Pope Francis, 00120 Vatican City.
[40] The CDF's address: Congregation for the Doctrine of the Faith, 00120 Vatican City.

statements or published the following writings. This needs to be stopped. We beg your intervention."

It's better not to dilute your correspondence by sending it to multiple addresses. Depending on the response you get from the CDF, you might take further steps.

**What about a pastor who isn't prominent (i.e., making national or international headlines) but is in a remote part of a diocese and he's teaching heresy? How should lay people deal with that? What's their responsibility to engage?**
If a priest says things that contradict the doctrine of the Faith and he's amenable to a discussion, then of course one should seek to discuss it with him. But if it's evident that he's not interested in defending what he says, he's simply asserting it, then one should write to the bishop of the diocese and make him aware that this is going on and ask for his intervention.

**I suppose that would go not only for teaching, but also if, for instance, a priest does not allow parishioners to receive Holy Communion kneeling and on the tongue.**
Yes, if the priest violates the rights of the faithful in any way, then he should be reminded that he's doing something wrong, and if he's amenable to change, the matter ends there. If not, one has to appeal to higher authority as indicated. It's an act of charity when you take action to stop something that's wrong in your parish.

**People go online and engage with some of these prominent clergy directly in order to manifest their lack of faith. Do you think that's a valid form of lay apostolate? Is this the "sensus fidelium" (sense of the faithful) at work?**

Fraternal correction in the modern age is done in ways that were never possible or imagined in the past, and people who don't have the chance to meet a priest who is issuing teachings that are problematic, or in fact contradictory to the Faith, have a right to go online and make comments. If a priest is going to use Twitter, for instance, or Facebook to propagate his views, he should not then complain when people criticize him. Now, people should not criticize him in a manner that's un-Christian, but Christianity does include rebuking the sinner as one of the spiritual works of mercy. To teach heresy and error is an objective sin—whether they are subjectively guilty is another matter—but you can certainly say to prominent people, "You're doing damage by what you're teaching." Calling to account people who are supposed to teach the Catholic Faith, but who are actually harming the Faith, is a charitable action. It should be done in a manner that Christ would approve of.

**When is it reasonable for a lay person to put himself on the line in correcting a local pastor or a bishop?**

When the ordinary faithful encounter erroneous teaching, they have a right and a duty to make known to their pastors that they consider what they've heard or read to be in conflict with Catholic doctrine. You have a natural right, recognized in canon law (canon 212) to evaluate, comment, and try to influence people for the good of the Church, based on what you've heard or read. Were a bishop to issue a statement that seemed to contradict Catholic teaching or plainly does, it's no lack of obedience to ask him to explain himself or to say that you're scandalized or upset because what you understand him to be saying is wrong. The bishop should either respond, "That's not what I mean," or say, "I made a mistake, and I'm going to correct it."

The Second Vatican Council highlighted that, in the life of the Church, all the faithful share a fundamental equality as baptized members of the flock. Just as we're all equal in being created by God, we are equal in virtue of being baptized and redeemed. Now, within the Church, Christ appointed a group of men in a hierarchy to guide and shepherd the flock, but that doesn't mean that they somehow no longer have to answer the questions of the ordinary faithful. Sometimes people who haven't studied the Catechism well enough might be confused. But in general, and in my experience, when people are upset about what is being taught by some bishops and priests, they are upset for the right reasons, because in fact what is being taught is wrong.

**Sometimes lay people get upset and angry about this. What's the proper attitude with which to approach your priest or bishop?**
Well, certainly we always say, "Don't express hatred or disdain for people." On the other hand, people get emotional when they hear sacred truths being criticized or cast aside. Try to express, in a dispassionate and docile manner, why you are upset by what's being taught and ask for a remedy. But that doesn't mean we're going to pretend that there's no problem here. Politeness is a useful tool for human relations, but Christ didn't say, "Go out to all the world and be polite" in the sense of making sure no

one gets offended by what you say. You may be subject to revilement for upholding the Church's doctrine against, for instance, the errors being proposed by the German bishops. The Lord said, "For if they do this when the wood is green, what will happen when it is dry?" (Luke 23:31). He said, "'A servant is not greater than his master.' If they persecuted me, they will persecute you" (John 15:20).

**In 2021, lay faithful in a diocese in Australia appealed to the Vatican because they were so upset about their bishop's support for the LGBT agenda. Bishop Vincent Long Văn Nguyễn, O.F.M. Conv. of Parramatta, Australia, was pushing the agenda in schools and opposed local legislation that demanded parents have the right to choose their children's education, especially as regards gender ideology. They drew on canon 212 to make their appeal to the Congregation for the Doctrine of the Faith.[41] They also protested against a newly drafted school curriculum that they said was not grounded in Catholic teaching.[42] In light of the protests and media attention, the diocese moderated its opposition to the legislation and put the new curriculum on hold. Do you think the lay faithful should take similar action more often?**

The case you cite is encouraging for two reasons: the laity made the effort to defend Catholic truth which was being trampled

---

[41] Edward Pentin, "Australian Catholics Petition Vatican to Remove Their Bishop over His Stance on Homosexuality," *National Catholic Register*, May 3, 2021, https://www.ncregister.com/news/australian-catholics-petition-vatican-to-remove-their-bishop-over-his-stance-on-homosexuality.

[42] Edward Pentin, "Australian Bishop Hears Laity's Concerns and Pauses School Curriculum," *National Catholic Register*, August 11, 2021, https://www.ncregister.com/blog/australian-bishop-hears-laity-s-concerns-and-pauses-school-curriculum.

upon by the bishop's endorsement of an immoral agenda, and the bishop then changed his policy. We should pray and work and beg God's assistance when there is a moral duty to oppose a teaching or policy that endangers the Faith.

**What's the best way for a priest to handle it if another priest in his diocese or religious community is teaching heresy?**
Wow, good question. It will depend on the bishop or the religious superior. If the priest is teaching things that contradict Catholic teaching, and if the bishop or superior knows about it and does nothing, there's not much you can do. If the bishop or superior either supports or tolerates what this other priest is doing, in charity for the faithful, if you have a platform, you can critique his teaching and point out how it's inconsistent with Catholicism. It's a plain fact that there's disorder in the house of the Church because people are contradicting Catholic teaching, and it's happening frequently and in a widespread manner. The German bishops are bold in doing it, but they're not the only ones.

**Do you think it's a valid form of ministry for priests to take on other priests directly in the media?**
It is a valid thing to critique other priests and bishops and even the pope in the media, if it is clear that the matter in question involves a serious problem. When a German bishop asserts that it is a Christian duty to bless the rings and vows of homosexuals who are pretending to be marrying each other, it's a duty on the part of a priest to say that bishop is wrong, tell the faithful to ignore what he's saying, and call the bishop to repent. Can you imagine if one of the Apostles went off and did that? Would the other Apostles remain silent out of a false notion of unity

or solidarity? Of course not. It's a sad reality that people who propose changes to Catholic teaching claim to be the advanced guard of progress. They are "bringing the Faith into the twenty-first century" kind of people, so they stigmatize those who critique them as being mired in the past or psychologically attached to previous experience and unwilling to change. The question is not any of that. The question is, "Is this what Christ taught? Is this what the Church teaches?" And if it is, that's what we want to defend. If it is not, that's what we want to condemn.

**Many of the faithful are concerned that celebrity priests can also be a problem, such as Fr. James Martin, S.J., an editor-at-large for** America **magazine. In his talks, books, and interviews, Fr. Martin encourages an LGBT lifestyle. Why is nothing done about him? He seems to receive criticism from lay people but not so much from his fellow priests.**

Fr. Martin, as a speaker and writer, has proposed that the Church should change her teaching about the nature of homosexual attraction and should certainly change her pastoral approach to embrace, for instance, the phenomenon of same-sex civil unions. He also believes that such a thing as "transgenderism" exists and thinks the Church should affirm that a man who claims to be a woman should be supported in that claim and treated accordingly. He believes that homosexual attraction or temptation is the basis of an *identity*, of who a person *is*, whereas the Church teaches that everyone is created by God as male or female and that sexual activity should be engaged in only with a member of the opposite sex within marriage. The Church further teaches that the natural urge of a man for a woman, or a woman for a man, is part of God's plan, and if those urges are diverted into a desire for sexual activity with someone of the same sex, that is *not* an identity and *not* the nature of a person. Rather, it is a problem that these persons have to deal with based on whatever cause is leading to it.

Fr. Martin has done great damage to the life of the Church by his continuing to promote the false notion that there is such a thing as a "homosexual identity" willed and created by God that therefore needs to be respected by God's Church and affirmed. It's quite clear that the Church has never taught that, and never can, and never will, because it goes against both nature and revelation.

***And yet Pope Francis named Fr. Martin a consultant to the Vatican's Dicastery for Communication in 2017.[43]***
I wasn't happy with that and neither were lots of people. Fr. James Martin is not disciplined by his order. He promotes a lifestyle which is immoral and has called for changing the words of the *Catechism of the Catholic Church*. Where homosexual inclination is described as "objectively disordered," he wants it changed to "differently ordered." He basically wants to affirm that humanity is created into two categories: those who are heterosexual and those who are homosexual.

But that was only the starting point because now he wants to say that there are people whose sexuality is such that they are not what they really are. This means that a man can decide that he's a woman even if he's biologically male, and we

---

[43] See https://cruxnow.com/global-church/2017/04/pope-taps-james-martin-ewtn-chief-communications-consultants/.

have an obligation to recognize him as a female, albeit with a man's body. This is a profound mistake and is not an act of charity nor a Christian duty, but rather is an affirmation of a pathological error that the confused person has entered into. There's no benefit for those who have problems with homosexuality to enter into a same-sex relationship of any sort, physical or emotional, because homosexuality is not a natural activity or inclination. It's a deviance from what God has created and should not be encouraged. The idea that homosexual couples who have entered into same-sex "marriages" civilly have to be granted some form of blessing and affirmation in the Church is totally wrong. It's an encouragement for those people to commit sin. It's also an encouragement for them to continue thinking mistakenly that God wants them to engage in homosexuality as a lifestyle, and that's just not the case.

**And what are your thoughts on Pope Francis praising Fr. Martin and his ministry to the LGBT community in a June 2021 letter?**
I was very unhappy to read Pope Francis's endorsement of Fr. James Martin's work with people who have a problem with homosexual temptation because Fr. Martin does not promote chaste living but, rather, wants the Church to see homosexual inclination, and thus logically homosexual acts, as simply different, not disordered. He is a promoter of affirming people in their homosexual desires and seeing those desires as the basis for an identity willed by God for them. This is totally wrong and destructive. It contradicts the clear teaching of both revelation and the natural law. Giving encouragement to this approach that contradicts the Church's teaching is gravely objectionable. I

pray that Pope Francis will come to understand fully—and then reprove and reject—what Fr. Martin is doing to lead souls away from the truth of the Gospel by affirming them in a gravely sinful lifestyle.

***What can the laity do to stop this?***
They can continue to point out to the Church and to others that Fr. Martin does not accurately represent the Church's teaching or true pastoral care for people who are suffering with homosexual attraction or other disorders related to sexuality, such as the mistaken belief that they are not the sex that they were born as.

***Do you recommend that Catholics write to the Congregation for the Doctrine of the Faith to express their concerns about Fr. Martin?***
It can't hurt for lay people to make known to their pastors, even to the Supreme Pastor, their distress that a Catholic priest is engaging in speaking and writing activities that are misinforming people about what it means to treat people with a homosexual problem in a Christian way, demanding that the Church change its teaching and its pastoral approach.

Fr. James Martin has been severely criticized by Archbishop Charles Chaput, OFM, Cap., the retired Archbishop of Philadelphia,[44] and by other American bishops. He has been disinvited from some Church-sponsored venues where he was

---

[44] Archbishop Charles J. Chaput, OFM Cap., "Father James Martin and Catholic Belief," CatholicPhilly.com, September 19, 2019, https://catholicphilly.com/2019/09/archbishop-chaput-column/father-james-martin-and-catholic-belief/.

going to speak. On the other hand, he is affirmed by other bishops and invited to speak by other institutions. It's a sign of the chaos in the Catholic Church when someone who quite clearly is trying to lead the Church in a way that goes against her doctrine and practice on a matter of sexuality is allowed to operate freely and to do so with the blessing of some members of the hierarchy. It's very distressing.

People who are upset can write to Church authorities, asking them to remedy the situation in which a priest in the Church is using his moral authority to promote things contrary to the Faith.

**Why don't bishops discipline priests who undermine morality?**
There's been a hesitancy in the Church to use penalties or legitimate coercive canonical means, meaning that you invoke authority to try to end scandals. There are so many people who have written bad books undermining the Catholic Faith, and yet the Congregation for the Doctrine of the Faith rarely issues corrections of authors. We are in a period in which it's a free-for-all in the world of theology. And then, in the world of Church discipline, liturgical abuses are so rife since the Second Vatican Council that it's almost impossible to see the Mass celebrated in the same way if you were, say, to visit three different parishes on a Sunday. There are so many variations, many of them involving disregard for the rubrics or the rules for celebrating Mass. There's a general lack of vigilance on the part of authorities to uphold discipline and teaching.

**Why do the bishops act like this rather than as good shepherds and good spiritual fathers?**
When John XXIII called the Second Vatican Council, he said there were going to be no anathemas and it was going to be the "medicine of mercy." The idea was that instead of confronting the world, we'll enter into a dialogue, and we'll try to present Catholic teaching and show its truth and benefits through a clear exposition of what it is and why it's good. It is always the first mission and task of the Church to preach the Gospel. But this includes a mission to drive out demons, so to speak, i.e., by confronting evil on its own terms, recognizing it to be evil, and then taking steps to overcome it. If someone is propagating errors, then we identify those errors and tell people not to follow that teaching. And we tell that teacher, "You can't exercise your role in the Church in this way." And if priests are violating the rubrics in celebrating Mass, they need to be corrected and told, "You don't have the authority to do that. The Mass is given to us by the Church. It's not your own creation."

There's a general hesitancy to treat problems as something needing to be corrected by legitimate coercive legal means, meaning that you invoke authority to compel people to act in the right way. Part of that is a certain naiveté that's present in the modern world and unfortunately seeps into the Church, i.e., that exposure to what is good and patience with what is evil will somehow cause people doing evil to stop. It's a form of appeasement to say, "We're going to go slow on correcting these problems." I don't think that's what Christ intended the Apostles to do. He didn't dialogue with the devil. He told the devil the truth and banished him from souls. Not that everybody causing problems is a devil, but the analogy is that, in the face of something that's wrong, our goal is to bring the grace of God to bear, and that's not done by simply saying how wonderful it is to be a faithful Catholic and obey all the rules. You also say, "Catholics are under the obligation to obey the rules, and if they don't, they need to be reminded of it, sometimes in a way that's going to make them unhappy at the moment."

**Some have suggested that bishops do not enforce moral and doctrinal orthodoxy in their flocks because they know Rome won't back them up. For example, a group of nineteen priests who rejected** Humanae Vitae **in 1968 were reinstated at the insistence of Rome when they had been suspended by the Archbishop of Washington, DC.[45] Also, Hans Küng notoriously lost his status as a Catholic theologian, but his attacks on Catholic orthodoxy were extensive, and he suffered no further discipline. The CDF often issues notifications about quite obscure figures for teaching things that much more well-known "Catholic theologians" also hold. How would you answer the claim that the difficulties of which people complain today really stem from a demoralizing and contagious pusillanimity centered on Rome that stretches back decades?** The publication of the *Catechism of the Catholic Church* and the papal encyclical *Veritatis Splendor* on moral questions were clear efforts by St. John Paul II to counteract the wave of dissent from Catholic teaching that overwhelmed the Church in the wake of Vatican II. Those documents are superb and state with precision and clarity the content of Catholic teaching. The problem was

---

[45] George Weigel, "The 'Truce of 1968,' Once Again," Ethics and Public Policy Center, April 26, 2006, https://eppc.org/publications/the-truce-of-1968-once-again/.

that many teachers in the Church ignored or contradicted what was taught in those documents and continue to do so to our day. Many did so without any sanctions by Church authorities, and in some cases, with the active support of some bishops. This meant that many people assumed that there is room in the Church for contradictory teachings. Each can choose what he wants to believe. This, of course, is not a Catholic but rather a Protestant approach.

*A key area of concern in recent years which has heightened with the Biden presidency, is pro-abortion Catholic politicians receiving Holy Communion. Should President Biden, Speaker of the House Nancy Pelosi (D-CA), and other public figures who favor legalized abortion be receiving Holy Communion? And should the US Bishops be united in refusing such persons Communion once they have been given a warning?*

As I wrote in my column at *The Catholic Thing*,

> Should President Joseph Biden be admitted to Holy Communion when he attends Mass? The simple answer is, "No," owing to his public and unwavering support for legalized abortion. Canon 915 of the *Code of Canon Law* states, "Those . . . obstinately persevering in manifest grave sin are not to be admitted to holy communion." Abortion, the killing of innocent unborn children, is a grave sin, as is the legalization and promotion of this heinous practice. It's a criminal violation of an unborn person's right to life. . . .

President Biden obviously promotes the abortion license and has directed that taxpayers' dollars pay for abortions. He's an unapologetic and determined promoter of this immoral attack on human life. This is an indisputable fact. Just ask his supporters at Planned Parenthood and NARAL.[46] . . . [A] Catholic politician who consistently promotes abortion *by that very conduct* actively encourages others to fall into the same sin. In Biden's case, his well-known campaign promises to keep abortion legal and federally funded is clear evidence of his rejection of Catholic moral teaching. He plainly intended to convince other Catholics to join him in gravely sinful behavior. Such conduct renders him publicly unworthy to receive Holy Communion. . . .

The Church has a duty to teach God's law and to sanction members who egregiously and continuously exempt themselves from obedience to that law—and encourage others to do the same. Depriving them of Holy Communion, we may hope, will jar them into reforming their conduct and their opposition to God's binding law for all mankind. . . .

The American bishops should act as a group, and individually in their dioceses, to end the scandal of the continued administration of Our Lord's Most Holy Body and Blood to the highest public official in our

---

[46] NARAL is the National Abortion Rights Action League.

land. To fail to do so amounts to a refusal to uphold the Church's canon law, to the grave harm of souls. It would be a negligent passivity, a failure to defend the sanctity of Christ's greatest gift to his Church.

And it would communicate to all the message that God may be mocked without consequence when an important Catholic public figure decides to support, not God's law, but rather the gruesome linchpin of the sexual revolution, unfettered legal abortion.[47]

**In May 2021, the head of the CDF, the Vatican's doctrinal office, Luis Cardinal Ladaria, S.J., sent a letter to the US bishops offering guidance on how to deal with Catholic politicians who favor legalized abortion.[48] According to reports, US Cardinals Blase Cupich and Joseph Tobin met with Cardinal Ladaria at the Holy Office on April 30, 2021, and are said to have "heavily influenced"[49] the letter. What do you do when**

---

[47] Fr. Gerald E. Murray, "President Biden and Public Scandal," *The Catholic Thing*, May 17, 2021, emphases original, https://www.thecatholicthing.org/2021/05/17/president-biden-and-public-scandal/.

[48] Letter from Cardinal Luis Ladaria, S.J., Prefect of the Congregation for the Doctrine of the Faith, to Archbishop Jose Gomez of Los Angeles, President of the U.S. Conference of Catholic Bishops, May 7, 2021; as posted by Pillar Media, https://www.scribd.com/document/507399449/Pillar-Media-CDF-Letter-5-7-21.

[49] Edward Pentin, "Further confirmation received today that Cardinals Cupich and Tobin 'heavily influenced' Cardinal Ladaria's response to Archbishop Gomez," Twitter, May 17, 2021, 6:35 p.m., https://twitter.com/edwardpentin/status/1394421261254733829; See also Pentin, "Cardinals Cupich and Tobin Met with CDF Prefect in Late April," *National Catholic Register*, May 12, 2021, https://www.ncregister.com/news/cardinals-cupich-and-tobin-met-with-cdf-prefect-in-late-april.

> *you have the Vatican being lobbied by American cardinals who, as Cardinal Müller said, are "members or representatives of the Democratic Party?"*[50]

I am not opposed to American cardinals sharing their observations and thoughts about significant matters with the Holy See. In this case, however, if the reports are accurate, we have a case where two cardinals who are not in favor of denying Holy Communion to President Biden went to Rome to seek a Roman intervention in the internal discussion and debate that the US bishops are currently having in view of coming up with a common approach to deal with this gravely scandalous matter. Cardinal Ladaria's letter is manifestly an attempt to preempt that discussion in ways favorable to the Cupich/Tobin point of view. As I wrote in that same column, Cardinal Ladaria's letter

> is disappointing, even confounding. Remarkably, he never mentions canon 915. He calls for dialogue among the bishops "so that they could agree as a Conference that support of pro-choice legislation is not compatible with Catholic teaching." But the matter is already beyond question. Any bishop who does not agree "that support of pro-choice legislation

---

[50] Raymond Arroyo, "World Over Hot Take: Cardinal Gerhard Mueller reacts to Cards. Tobin and Cupich lobbying the Vatican in advance of their latest letter in denying communion to pro-choice politicians," Twitter, May 14, 2021, 1:58 p.m., https://twitter.com/raymondarroyo/status/1393264446257221632?lang=en; See also "ÖKT: Müller kritisiert wechselseitige Einladung zu Eucharistie und Abendmahl," Die Tagespost, May 14, 2021, https://www.die-tagespost.de/kirche-aktuell/weltkirche/oekt-mueller-kritisiert-wechselseitige-einladung-zu-eucharistie-und-abendmahl-art-218206.

is not compatible with Catholic teaching" should change his mind or his job.

Ladaria then calls for dialogue with Catholic politicians "who adopt a pro-choice position . . . as a means of understanding their positions and their comprehension of Catholic teaching. Really? After almost 50 years of legalized abortion, the "pro-choice" position needs no further study. Let alone "dialogue." It is hard to imagine that President Biden and other Catholic advocates of legalized abortion are unaware of what the Church teaches about the sanctity of human life. They just don't follow it.

Ladaria calls for further dialogue among the bishops, with other episcopal conferences, and further consultation with his office. How long would this process take? It's a needless delay in tackling a major scandal.

**What should the laity do?**
The laity should insist that their bishops follow canon law, which is a reflection of the teaching of the Church. Canon law is the doctrine of the Church translated into the legal and social arrangements in the Church. In other words, the law is not an arbitrary imposition by the authorities. No, it's putting into effect the teaching of what we believe in. So, to safeguard the sacraments, we say that people who are in a state of mortal sin should not receive Communion. But on top of that, for people who publicly in serious matters contradict the Church's teaching, apart from any judgment about whether they are in

a state of mortal sin—which is up to them to judge—we judge that their external behavior is incompatible with the reception of the sacraments.

Canon 915 should be enforced and applied because you are rebuking a sinner, and, in the case of a public sinner, you are identifying to the community that this man or woman's actions are detrimental to the spiritual welfare of his soul and certainly produce grave and irreparable harm to the victim of abortion. It also produces harm in the life of the mother, in the life of the person performing the abortion, and in the wider community because we become desensitized to the evil of abortion when it's so widespread over so long a period.

So, the laity should remind their pastors of their solemn obligation to enforce canon law and make known to people that they should not confuse the passivity of some bishops on this issue with the false idea that the Church no longer considers abortion to be so serious a matter, or just one among many life issues. Bishop Joseph Strickland of Tyler, Texas, is a great example in his bold advocacy. The only thing that an unborn child needs is life, so give the child life. That's the threat that child is imminently facing. So other threats like climate change, economic injustice, or lack of opportunity are plainly of secondary importance and admit of various possible solutions. There is only one solution to the crime of abortion: stop it.

**If a pastor knowingly administers Communion to a notorious public sinner, e.g., a publicly unrepentant politician who has enacted immoral laws, is the priest a participant in the sin of sacrilege and scandal? If his bishop orders him to communicate such persons, should the pastor obey?**

He might be. It depends upon what he knows about the politician and his past actions and also his present intentions. He should seek to verify the politician's history and current stance. He should speak with him, which is usually possible, and verify where he stands. If it is clear that the politician rejects the Church's teaching on abortion and other grave moral questions, he should instruct him to stop coming up for Holy Communion. He should then warn him that if he does present himself, he will be denied the Blessed Sacrament. The bishop does not have the right in canon law to order a pastor to administer Holy Communion to manifest public sinners. The bishop and the pastor must both follow what is laid down in canon 915. If the bishop does not consider the politician to have committed a manifest grave sin by supporting legalized abortion, the pastor has no obligation to join him in that erroneous opinion.

*There was a lot of enthusiasm after the Second Vatican Council for Newman's brief treatise* On Consulting the Faithful in Matters of Doctrine. *Indeed, as reputable Newman scholars have observed, the treatise is called "On Consulting the* Faithful*," not "On Consulting the* Laity*," as some have misreported. So presumably we should only be interested in the opinions, on debatable matters, of those who already accept everything that has been infallibly taught by the Church. Archbishop Samuel Aquila of Denver has made an urgent appeal for a return to Eucharistic coherence and to an understanding that the Eucharist is dangerous for those who do not conform to the Faith of the Church in life or belief (see 1 Cor 11:28–30). Surely without this return to Eucharistic coherence—i.e., not receiving Holy Communion if you are in* *a state of mortal sin and denying Communion to notorious sinners and non-believers—the "synodal path" advocated these days would be vitiated at root?*

The witness of all the baptized faithful who believe in the truths of the Catholic Faith is a beautiful sign of God's active and life-giving presence in his Church. It is a grace that strengthens the pastors of the Church when the faithful resist innovations and strange teachings that contradict their simple and trusting faith in the truths taught by the Church from the beginning. Some theologians and pastors have adopted worldly ways of thinking, seeing the administration of Holy Communion to be a ritualized sign of inclusion and welcoming. They consider it an offense against charity to deny someone the Body and Blood of Christ. Devout Catholic laymen see it, correctly, in the completely opposite way: to deny Holy Communion to someone who rejects the Church's teaching on the right to life of unborn children is the most charitable thing to do. It is the rebuking of a sinner, and a call to repentance, and a defense of the holiness of God's sacred Body and Blood.

*In his letter to the US bishops, CDF prefect Cardinal Ladaria notes that if a national policy is developed regarding the reception of Holy Communion by pro-abortion Catholic politicians, "such a statement would have to express a true consensus of the bishops on the matter." But as George Weigel has pointed out, "The First Council of Nicaea did not wait for the Arian bishops to agree with orthodox bishops before teaching the truth about the divinity of Christ."[51]*

---

[51] EWTN, "World Over—Full Episode with Raymond Arroyo," YouTube video, 59:55, May 13, 2021; https://www.youtube.com/watch?v=ULcYS3J_gFc.

Truth is supreme. If there is a consensus to teach the truth, so much the better. But if a consensus is lacking because some refuse to uphold the constant and universal Catholic teaching and practice concerning the necessary conditions for the worthy reception of Holy Communion, the truth must still be proclaimed. Recalcitrant proponents of giving Holy Communion in violation of canon 915 should not have a veto over those who uphold the Church's canonical discipline, which is a means of teaching and defending the truths of the Faith.

**The letter also notes that such a policy could be a "contentious" issue and cause "disunity" among the US bishops. If the bishops can't defend the most foundational principles and truths on Holy Communion, why should we listen to them on climate change, poverty, or immigration?**

Catholicism is always contentious for those who find its teachings to be onerous or not sufficiently up-to-date. Disunity among the shepherds is a reality in Church history from the beginning. Bishops should overcome that disunity by fully embracing what has been plainly taught from the beginning. If a bishop falls into Modernism, he needs to be called to repentance. If he resists then, as Dietrich von Hildebrand wrote, the charitable anathema should be invoked by the Church's supreme authority, the pope. It is a manifest lack of brotherly love to refuse to offer a fraternal correction when a brother bishop has embraced teachings that go against the Faith of the Church. The unity of the Church is strengthened, not harmed, when his fellow bishops call upon such a wandering shepherd to return to the unity of the Church's Faith.

***It seems that media pressure causes the Vatican to act. One thinks, for example, of the case of former cardinal Theodore McCarrick and the pressure that was put on the Vatican to respond, particularly following Archbishop Carlo Maria Viganò's first testimony in 2018. How much of the present crisis could be averted if the Vatican would act sooner, rather than waiting for media pressure?***

When we speak about media pressure, what we mean is that people outside the Vatican and the hierarchy have a way to influence the pope and the bishops. Public pressure is often the only way to get their attention. That was proven by the clerical sexual abuse scandal. It was the outrage expressed in the media that forced the bishops to stop the cover-ups and remove and discipline criminal priests and bishops. Recall that Theodore McCarrick, having been found credibly accused of sexually abusing a former minor seminarian and placed on leave, only resigned as a cardinal after a second victim came forth in *The New York Times*. Recall that the issuance by the Holy See of the unprecedented McCarrick report was largely in response to public outrage and bewilderment that a man of this sort could have risen so high in the Church's hierarchy, when his nefarious crimes must have been known by many of his fellow bishops and cardinals. It turns out they were, but his immoral actions were never truly investigated or punished for many years.

***Popes used to say a lot less in public and had a much smaller media operation. Now we have many news reporters, commentators, and others claiming to speak for the pope. How could this affect people's perception of the magisterium?***

There will always be people who write books claiming they are conveying the message of the pope, and some will claim insider status. That judgment will be made based on the evidence. In general, popes never gave interviews in the past. John Paul II did the first papal interview book with *Crossing the Threshold of Hope*. That was the beginning of a trend. In general, when you're the pope, you have your own means to speak. You don't need the mediation of an interviewer, so I don't really think it's a good idea to give interviews as a pope. The pope's job is to teach, and he has unique magisterial authority. One doesn't want to diminish that in the eyes of people by having them equate what he says on an airplane with what he writes in an encyclical. But that's inevitably going to happen because people will say, "The pope said [this]." On the other hand, it is true that very few people are going to read encyclicals, and the way you can convey to people the message of Christ and the way the Church responds to current challenges is going to be through television and its equivalents such as YouTube, etc. That's why papal sermons that are given in Rome or on trips have a great significance. But, again, that's all controlled by the pope, so he can be careful with his language. When the Vatican started televising every papal public appearance, I thought that was a good idea because it allows his message to go out. Pope Pius XI built Vatican radio in 1931. The idea of communicating is good, but when you're subject to hostile or neutral interviewers, that can be a clumsy way to get your message across.

**There is oftentimes a tightrope that Catholic media has to walk: one side is to challenge Church authorities during the**

***crisis while at the same time retaining access to those same authorities. How would you recommend they go about this? There's a fine line, isn't there, between cowardice and prudence, and oftentimes one gets the impression that Catholic media falls too often into the former.***

The Catholic media should operate with the assumptions provided by the Faith of the Church. The proclamation of the truth is always primary; thus, the search for truth by journalists is in harmony with the Church's own duty. Reporting on and interacting with those in authority in the Church is meant to promote the mission of the Church by providing information for truthful reporting and analysis. At times, that will involve reporting on disagreements and conflicts. SS. Peter and Paul famously disagreed about certain matters, as chronicled in Galatians 2:11–21. Pretending there are no problems is not only a false way to describe the life of the Church, it is self-defeating as people see through the veneer of "everything's wonderful."

***What is the role of Catholic media in the current crisis? A colleague once suggested that the Catholic media plays the role of the sheepdog in sounding the alarm in order to protect the sheep in the sheepfold. Would you agree with that?***

Yes. Sheepdogs help the shepherds. They sound the alarm when wolves approach the flock. They are very important. A truthful and fearless Catholic media helps the Church to see reality for what it is. It also exposes hirelings, who are not true shepherds. When a false shepherd invites wolves into the flock, the sheepdogs continue to bark, as they should.

*One of the aspects one finds sad is that under this pontificate, and because of the continued and persistent crisis, we've ironically become the self-referential Church that Pope Francis talks about. So, we are constantly caught up in Church-politics instead of being the Church "in uscita" (going forth) that Francis said he wanted in his 2013 apostolic exhortation* **Evangelii Gaudium** *(The Joy of the Gospel).*

Disorder in the house of the Church has increased in ways that I never expected. Rather than discuss ways in which the Church can evangelize the world by answering present challenges to the Faith from outside of the Church, Catholics end up discussing the phenomenon of various attempts to change Church teaching and practice carried out by her own shepherds, as in Germany. This is regrettable.

*Would you like to see a more robust Catholic media? Do we need more of Mother Angelica's spirit these days?*

The more Mother Angelica the better in the life of the Church!

*What do you think Mother Angelica would say about the present crisis? And what do you believe she would say to EWTN?*

Mother Angelica would be horrified reading what the German hierarchy is proposing because it is a complete revolution and upheaval of everything that Catholicism teaches and proposes. Mother Angelica's ardent desire, as we know, was to bring people to Christ in his Catholic Church through the mass media. She understood that that would involve some degree of conflict with the world and forces within the Church that are more worldly and liberalizing, but it didn't matter to her because she knew that promoting the mission of Christ and his Church is the first and only important thing to do.

Catholic media should strive for the highest standards of media excellence and fairness. They should avoid petty and uncharitable characterizations. I do get upset when I read some websites where they are constantly uncharitably upbraiding people who deserve to be criticized but not treated to catcalls and epithets. That part I don't like. It should stop. But I have to say the Church is well served when the media exposes the problems in the life of the Church and highlights voices calling for reform. I think Bishop Schneider is a perfect example, along with Cardinal Sarah, Cardinal Müller, Cardinal Burke—Churchmen who through the Catholic media are able to remind people of what it is we believe in and why we don't believe in other things. It's a great service to the life of the Church.

**In July 2021, The Pillar *published a series of articles exposing alleged clerical sexual misconduct and use of a homosexual "hook-up" app by the general secretary of the US Conference of Catholic Bishops (USCCB) and also discovered the use of such apps within the Vatican.*[52] **The Pillar's** *findings, which relied on commercially available records of app signal data, were presented both to USCCB leadership and to Vatican*

---

[52] "Pillar Investigates: USCCB General Secretary Burrill Resigns after Sexual Misconduct Allegations," *The Pillar*, June 20, 2021, https://www.pillarcatholic.com/p/pillar-investigates-usccb-gen-sec. See also "Location-Based Apps Pose Security Risk for Holy See," *The Pillar*, July 27, 2021, https://www.pillarcatholic.com/p/location-based-apps-pose-security; and "Newark Archdiocese to Investigate App Use Allegations," *The Pillar*, July 23, 2021; https://www.pillarcatholic.com/p/newark-archdiocese-to-investigate.

*Secretary of State Pietro Cardinal Parolin before they were published. The anticipated media spotlight on USCCB General Secretary Msgr. Jeffrey Burrill's alleged activities led to his resignation. The Vatican declined to comment. As a Catholic priest and a canon lawyer, what do you think about the laity using these sorts of methods to exert public pressure and "clean up" the Church, especially at a time when to many it seems that key members of the hierarchy are unwilling to do so?*

The revelations concerning Msgr. Jeffrey Burrill's use of the homosexual hookup app Grindr are a shocking reminder that clerical immorality continues to be a serious problem that reaches even to the highest levels of ecclesiastical life in the United States. *The Pillar* reports that "an analysis of app data signals correlated to Msgr. Burrill's mobile device shows the priest also visited gay bars and private residences while using the location-based hookup app in numerous cities from 2018 to 2020, even while traveling on assignment for the US Bishops' Conference." His mobile device "emitted app data signals from the location-based hookup app Grindr on a near-daily basis during parts of 2018, 2019, and 2020—at both his USCCB office and his USCCB-owned residence, as well as during USCCB meetings and events in other cities."

The use of this app by Msgr. Burrill reveals a reckless pattern of seeking to meet men for homosexual encounters, which are grave sins and constitute a grave scandal for those who come to learn of this. Msgr. Burrill risked his own good name and the good name of the USCCB by engaging in this traceable sinful pursuit of opportunities for sexual gratification with men. He used this app to find men similarly seeking to engage in sodomy, and thus ran the daily risk of this becoming known, as has now happened. He was traced, for instance, to a gay bathhouse in Las Vegas. What in the world is a Catholic priest doing in a gay bathhouse? This pattern of behavior is a horrendous scandal.

The whole purpose of this app is to make oneself known, to put oneself out into the mix of everyone else using the app in pursuit of homosexual activity. There is no privacy when you put yourself out on the "virtual street," which is a high-tech way of "cruising" for sex. Msgr. Burrill should thank the Good Lord that his use of this app was exposed. He can now seek the spiritual and moral help he needs to get out of the gravely immoral homosexual lifestyle, revealed in his case to involve incessantly looking to engage in homosexual sex with strangers. His life was not ruined by these revelations, but rather he was given the opportunity to repent and reform. His resignation was the first step in what can be a hope-filled path of prayer and penance leading to a chaste and holy way of living. That is my prayer.

*The Pillar* is a Catholic news website directed by two lay canon lawyers. Their reporting does not constitute any immoral or unethical form of spying but rather is newsworthy investigative reporting seeking accountability from Churchmen who have significant influence in the Church through their occupying positions of authority. Msgr. Burrill and any other clerics or other Church employees who are identified as living a double life in pursuit of immoral and scandalous behavior should be exposed for their own good and the good of the Church. If a similar investigation had revealed that Msgr. Burrill had been using an app to meet with racist white supremacists to discuss

Nazi racial theories, I doubt that any of *The Pillar's* critics would have criticized the editors for making that publicly known.

The McCarrick scandal did tremendous damage to the Church. Any other clerics who betray their priestly mission through moral turpitude should not be protected from public scrutiny when publicly available and legally obtained information of grossly immoral behavior is unearthed. If I were bishop of a diocese, I would want to know if *The Pillar* discovered any similar situations among the clergy of my diocese.

*In June 2021, one month before* The Pillar *articles, Pope Francis promulgated the apostolic constitution* Pascite Gregem Dei, *reforming Book VI of the Code of Canon Law on penal sanctions in the Church, a process of revision to the 1983 Code begun by Benedict XVI in 2007.[53] The revisions and updates were meant to provide bishops with adequate instruments to prevent and punish crimes perpetrated in the Church.[54] Canon 1395 deals specifically with grave offenses against the Sixth Commandment.[55] Do these revisions apply specifically to the sort of clerical sexual misconduct, app use, and potential cover-up described in* The Pillar *articles?*

---

[53] Pope Francis, Apostolic Constitution Reforming Book VI of the Code of Canon Law *Pascite Gregem Dei* (June 4, 2021), https://www.vatican.va/content/francesco/en/apost_constitutions/documents/papa-francesco_costituzione-ap_20210523_pascite-gregem-dei.html.

[54] Christopher Wells, "Bishop Arrieta: How Book VI of Canon Law Has Changed," Vatican News, June 1, 2021, https://www.vaticannews.va/en/vatican-city/news/2021-06/book-vi-vatican-penal-code-apostolic-constitution.html.

[55] "New Book VI of the Code of Canon Law," Holy See Press Office, June 1, 2021, https://press.vatican.va/content/salastampa/en/bollettino/pubblico/2021/06/01/210601b.html.

***And what would it look like if these reforms to the Code were implemented in this situation?***

Canon 1395 states that a cleric who continues "in other external sin [other than concubinage] against the Sixth Commandment of the Decalogue is to be punished with suspension." If he persists in his misconduct after a warning, "other penalties can gradually be added, including dismissal from the clerical state." The use of a homosexual hookup app should immediately lead to a canonical investigation to determine if the suspected cleric in fact was the user of the app, how often did he use it, and what circumstances can be verified regarding his movements and whereabouts following upon his use of the app. This behavior, if verified, can be punished according to this canon, and likewise according to canon 1399. Such vigilance is required given the tremendous scandals that we have witnessed in the past twenty years following *The Boston Globe's* exposure of the cover-up of sexual abuse of minors in the Archdiocese of Boston in 2002. Lay people need to see that those who are entrusted with the spiritual care of the faithful are held accountable when they give themselves over to immorality while maintaining a public face of normality.

***Aside from bringing these issues to public attention, including that of secular authorities, what else can the laity do to prophetically remind the Church's shepherds to be faithful to their calling, while maintaining a respect for the authority given in the Sacrament of Ordination?***

The type of reporting done in *The Pillar* should be welcomed by the Church's shepherds. The spiritual welfare of any priests involved in moral turpitude, and of the faithful who look to these men for Christ-like guidance and inspiration, requires that once scandalous behavior is revealed, immediate action is taken in pursuit of canonical justice and personal reform. Accountability is rightly demanded when clerics are found to be living scandalous double lives and doing so while continuing to serve as pastors of souls charged with leading the flock by word and example. Hypocrisy is one of the sins that Our Lord most vehemently denounced.

*St. Paul tells the early Christians, "If then you have been raised with Christ, seek the things that are above, where Christ is, seated at the right hand of God. Set your minds on things that are above, not on things that are on earth" (Col 3:1). How much should Catholics be looking at the news? How seriously should we take the temptation to get so caught up in the headlines and flow of bad news that we don't fill our minds with eternal truths?*

We should all spend time in silent meditation each day during which we should converse with Our Lord about everything on our minds, including the difficulties in the life of his Church. We need to develop a supernatural perspective about what is happening, which is just the current manifestation of the perennial battle between the Church and the anti-Church. We need that peaceful serenity that recognizes that the truth does not change, that "Jesus Christ is the same yesterday and today and for ever" (Heb 13:8). We may die while the Church continues in great turmoil, but we should not fret over that prospect. God is sovereign over his Church and asks of us only that we remain faithful even when others fall into infidelity.

*Can reading the news be an occasion of sin for some people? Or an occasion for the devil to lead people into discouragement, especially those who are deeply affected by the crisis in the Church?*

Yes, if the reader does not remember that Our Lord asked, "When the Son of man comes, will he find faith on earth?" (Luke 18:8) That is a warning to us that we must remain faithful and help others to do the same. Being aware of the crisis in the Church should lead us to more fervent prayer and trust in God's goodness. His ways are mysterious. Our response should always be to stay strong in faith, come what may.

*Often one hears that in ordinary parishes, few if any of the faithful have an idea of the crisis in Rome. This seems to be especially the case in developing countries where internet access is limited. Is this ignorance a problem?*

People may not know about the debates and conflicts going on in Rome and elsewhere, but they are surely aware from the mainstream media that things have changed a lot under Pope Francis, and in ways they never expected. The Catholic media should provide explanations that help people see which changes are improvements and which are, in fact, departures from what the Church has always taught and done. In the absence of this information, people may think that Catholicism is an ever-evolving religion that has no fixed or unchangeable teachings or practices, which is not true.

*There are people who are being tempted to leave the Church by what they see in the headlines. As a priest, what do you say to the layman or laywoman who is really struggling to hold on to their faith?*

Keep the faith! Stay faithful to Christ in the Church he founded no matter what troubles are present at any moment. Being a Catholic is the greatest gift you can receive. Do not lose that gift by drifting away with the excuse that things are bad in the Church. That is precisely the moment that our fidelity is being tested. Stay strong!

***To what extent are we experiencing a diabolical disorientation and how can the faithful best navigate it?***
The devil is always at work. Ignore him as much as you can and confront him when you must. The surest way to stay faithful is to frequent the sacraments, pray a lot, study the Bible and Catholic teaching, live a sacrificial life, extend yourself for the benefit of your neighbor, and do not worry inordinately. God is good and helps us at all times.

***In his 2019 book, The Day is Now Far Spent, Robert Cardinal Sarah writes, "Those who make sensational announcements of change and rupture are false prophets. They do not seek the good of the flock. They are mercenaries who have been smuggled into the sheepfold. Our unity will be forged around the truth of Catholic doctrine. There are no other means. Trying to win popularity with the media at the expense of the truth amounts to doing the work of Judas."[56]***
Cardinal Sarah is a gift to the Church in our lifetime. His three interview books should be read by every Catholic who wants to know what is really happening and how to remain faithful

---

[56] Robert Cardinal Sarah, *The Day Is Now Far Spent* (San Francisco: Ignatius Press, 2019), 17.

amidst the crisis of faith in the Church. His writings are full of deep insights that expose and refute false teachings and worldly ways of thinking.

**In the end, is the present crisis in the Church just another fight over who gets to be in charge and impose his will on the rest?**

Abraham Lincoln is quoted as saying that America runs on public opinion. In other words, the life of the nation depends on swaying public opinion in one way or the other in order to try to accomplish social and political ends. That may be true in political life, but the Church is not merely a political body. It has a human element, but it is the Mystical Body of Christ, vivified by the Holy Spirit. God, not the faithful, decides what we are to believe and how we are to live. We are God's instrument to spread his doctrine and his grace. We want to influence people to believe in the doctrine of the Faith. That's not a political choice; that's the response to God's revelation and call to belief. So, we have to make sure that we don't simply view the Church as another arena for victory for one human point of view or another. It's not that. The flock is constituted in such a way that we are to walk together in the green pastures of the Lord. When the faithful shepherds have to yank the sheep away from bad waters or bad pasture by being a little bit tough, that's good. What's harmful is when some pastors say to the flock, "No, we're going in another direction and ignore that other shepherd." And that's what we have in the Church now, which is really distressing. We ask the Lord to give us good shepherds after his own heart (Jer 3:15; see 23:4).

*Chapter 4*

# WINDS OF REVOLUTION

"And they went and woke him, saying, 'Save us, Lord; we are perishing.'" (Matt 8:25)

*Commenting on the Gospel narrative on the calming of the storm (Matt 8:23–27), the fifth-century bishop of Ravenna, St. Peter Chrysologus, writes, "It is not a calm sky, beloved, but the storm which tests a pilot's skill. When the breeze is mild, even the poorest sailor can manage the ship. But in the crosswinds of a tempest, we want the best pilot with all his skill." Fr. Murray, you have served as a Navy chaplain, so such metaphors must have a particular resonance for you. How would you say the captaincy of the present hierarchy, i.e., the bishops in general, is measuring up to the current storm?*

The spiritual health of each diocese depends in no small measure upon decisions made by her shepherds, past and present. The unsettled period following the Second Vatican Council has not come to an end. The storms of dissent, secularization, loss of faith, worldliness, liturgical chaos, immorality, and religious ignorance among the otherwise well-educated continue to batter the Church, the barque of Peter. There are many good and faithful stewards of the mysteries of God among the world's bishops, but there are also some bishops who seek to revolutionize the Church by making accommodations with the very evils that threaten the Church. This out-in-the-open subversion of the Church by those pledged to defend her teachings is a major scandal and a cause of great damage to the life of the Church.

**At the end of the Sermon on the Mount, Our Lord warns of those who hear but do not obey his words as having built their house of faith upon sand, and he contrasts them with the obedient who build upon rock: "[A]nd the rain fell, and the floods came, and the winds blew and beat upon that house, but it did not fall, because it had been founded on the rock" (Matt 7:25). Many voices nowadays within the Church are calling upon us to abandon the rock of obedience to Christ's word in favor of the shifting sands of intellectual fashion. How far will the Lord allow them to prevail?**

Only the Lord knows how long this trial will continue in the Church. The Israelites wandered in the desert for forty years, never knowing when they would reach the Promised Land. What they did know was that God was displeased with their infidelity. We are called to repent of our own infidelities and to encourage our neighbors to return to the Lord through obedience to his words. We must pray that God will raise up saints to inspire and lead the faithful on this path of renewed faithfulness to God.

*Fr. Murray, some people argue that we must maintain the essentials of the Faith, but the non-essentials can be changed. But generally, those who say this move the bar regarding what the essentials are and minimize them as much as possible to allow for as much innovation as possible. How do we tell what things count as essential to the Catholic Faith?*

The Lord entrusted to his Church the Deposit of Faith, which is the body of his teachings to be handed down to each generation in all its purity, uncorrupted by any modifications or omissions. The determination of what teachings are essential as opposed to what are not is fraught with danger. Nothing should be cast aside that would undermine belief in the teachings of the Faith. Our attitude should be that everything taught by the Church has an essential importance in itself, even if some elements of belief take precedence over others. For example, the belief in the Triune nature of God ranks higher than the belief in the existence of angels, but both are true, and we must believe both teachings.

The essential things of the Faith are obviously the Sacred Scriptures, the Creed, the sacraments, the moral teaching, defined dogmas, conciliar teachings, papal teachings.

The essentials of the Faith are then supported, surrounded, and buttressed by all sorts of teachings and practices which are designed to protect those teachings from the corrosive effect of unbelief and heresy. An example of an essential Faith teaching is the Church's Eucharistic doctrine, which proclaims that the bread and wine consecrated by the priest at Mass truly become the Body and Blood of Christ. In turn, this doctrine has been developed and defended over the centuries by the magisterium in response to various heresies. Liturgical practices such as genuflections to and adoration of the Blessed Sacrament—whether exposed in the monstrance upon the altar or reserved in the tabernacle—teach the faithful that this is no mere symbol or reminder of God's presence, but is in reality God present in the Most Holy Eucharist.

To say that we can tinker around with the formulation of dogmatic teachings and rework them to be more intelligible or acceptable is a dangerous business because you can think you are updating the language when, in fact, you are changing it and therefore harming the popular ability to understand its true meaning.

### *How does this relate to Tradition?*

Church Tradition, with a capital "T," is part of divine revelation. We say that the two fonts of revelation are Sacred Scripture and Sacred Tradition, which flow "'from the same divine wellspring' and 'form one sacred deposit of the word of God, committed to the Church'" (*Dei Verbum*, §9, 10). In other words, the gift of revelation includes what the Apostles and the sacred writers wrote down in the Bible, and the unwritten Tradition which is transmitted orally down through the centuries from the Apostles to their successors and is manifest in the way the Church conducts her activities. This includes the liturgical order, the life of prayer, and also the things the Church forbids and discourages. These all tell us what the Apostles received from the Lord for our belief and practice, and not simply for a particular moment but for all time.

This Tradition, since unlike the Scriptures is not written, has to be guarded by having an overall sense of the Faith which is respectful for things that are not immediately understandable but have always been believed or done. This is an area where the Church has gravely failed in its duty in the last fifty to sixty years, by changing so many things that were taken for granted as being part of Catholic Tradition rather than simply human traditions. The Church's discipline of fasting, for instance, was radically altered after the Council. The understanding of fasting and its importance in the life of the Church goes back to the Apostles. The same is true of the liturgical order, that is, how the Mass is celebrated, and the meaning and ordering of the rituals. What was done and how it was done were viewed as a sacred inheritance which goes back to the Apostles in its essential forms and then was developed over time, in such a way as to support what the Apostles themselves did, and what we are supposed to be doing ourselves.

### *Why is Tradition important? What does Church Tradition reveal about our practices, beliefs, and moral life?*

Tradition is important because Christ founded a Church which is the living voice of Tradition. In other words, the things that the Apostles experienced and learned from Christ were not all written down. What was written down was what God intended to be written down, but not everything was written down. As St. John says at the end of his Gospel, "But there are also many other things which Jesus did; were every one of them to be written, I suppose that the world itself could not contain the books that would be written" (21:25).

Just as in a family there are ways of living that are handed on orally and by practice and are essential to the good order of the family and to being faithful to your family's way of doing things, so in the Church that's what the Apostles passed on and their successors understood to be binding and normative. To return to the example of fasting: when you compare the practice of fasting in the Catholic Church to the Greek or Russian Orthodox practice, for instance, you can ask which of them would more resemble what the Apostles and their immediate successors understood to be the will of Christ. It would seem that we have drifted away from that. Most people now have little sense of the Friday fast, undergoing some bodily deprivation each Friday in honor of the Lord's death. And certainly, fasting before receiving Holy Communion has become a mere one hour from the time Communion is distributed, which would almost allow people to bring their coffee and doughnuts right up to the door of the Church. This kind of fasting has little meaning because it requires little sacrifice. The idea that you prepare your body to receive the Body of the Lord by fasting from midnight, as in the old days, or under Pius XII for three hours, is gone. I don't believe that was a good development. I can understand how it would be very difficult to demand fasting from the previous midnight if Sunday Mass were celebrated in the evening, but certainly three hours is a good, conscious attempt to deprive yourself of natural material food in order to receive with recollection and devotion the true Body and Blood of Christ, the Food of our souls.

**What is the pope's role vis-a-vis Tradition?**
One of the primary missions of the pope is to defend the teaching of the Church since he is called to strengthen the brethren, as Peter was commanded by Christ regarding the other Apostles and, in the broader context, anyone else who follows Christ. The pope has the unique roles and charisms of having primacy

in governing and infallibility in teaching so that he can settle any doctrinal disputes. He then has the role of confirming us in all those teachings which are already taught either infallibly or with certitude in the life of the Church. The pope is not above the doctrine of the Faith, and his mission is not to discard doctrines that, for one reason or another, are not found acceptable to some members of the Church. He is the guardian of orthodoxy.

The primary and perhaps most important mission of the pope is to confirm Catholics in the Faith of the Church, in the face of errors, deviations, and plain simple ignorance, so that people can learn, know, and joyfully proclaim their faith together, rather than be subject to different teachers, one teaching one thing, another teaching another thing. He is also to guard the flock "when people will not endure sound teaching, but having itching ears they will accumulate for themselves teachers to suit their own likings" (2 Tim 4:3). That is where you get the collapse of unity in the Church, when heretical teachings are embraced and not rebuked or identified as such.

**Given Christ's promise to Peter that the gates of Hell will not prevail against the Church, does this mean that everything the pope and the bishops do is in accord with Tradition?**
The dual font of revelation is Scripture and Tradition, those things handed down from the apostolic Church. They are inviolable and must be safeguarded. Traditions with a small "t," i.e., ways of doing things that have become part of the Church over many centuries, the popes are entitled to change as they see fit. The whole organization of the Roman Curia, for instance, was largely a development after the Council of Trent that then underwent a major reform after the Second Vatican Council

and is now undergoing another major reform under the current pontificate. The pope is not overstepping his office in doing those things. Now, the wisdom of the arrangements will depend on the prudent judgment of the pope and his associates, enacting changes which they consider to be useful but which may, in fact, prove at a later time not to be useful.

Ordinary governance in the life of the Church is an exercise of human judgment and discretion, and the special assistance that God gives to bishops to guide the flock doesn't mean they can't make mistakes. We should therefore never presume that, because the bishop or the pope occupies a holy office, that everything he decides upon is holy or wise or good. We should presume that they are acting reasonably and with good intentions, but when something is not useful, it can be reformed. The mere fact of canon law being reformed over the centuries shows that laws and rules have to evolve in order to deal with contemporary societal arrangements and developments in the life of the Church. It is not a failing in the Church that they didn't figure it all out from the beginning.

**When does the pope exercise his authentic authority?**
A pope's authority is expressed not only in his teaching but also in his governing. Regarding solemn teaching by the pope alone, the exercise of papal infallibility concerns only solemn *ex cathedra* teaching that is promulgated by just the pope himself as being revealed by God and thus binding upon all Catholics, which means that it must be believed in order to be saved. This particular exercise of papal infallibility has been invoked twice: the dogmas of the Immaculate Conception of the Blessed Virgin

Mary and her bodily Assumption into Heaven.[1] Governance decisions do not involve infallibility. When the pope makes decisions on the appointment of bishops, or on who will work in the Roman Curia, or when a meeting of bishops or cardinals will be convened, those are all part of his authority and are subject to his discretion. Typically, popes seek wide advice in order to make good decisions, but there's no guarantee that a pope will make a good decision. If it becomes known that he is thinking of appointing "Fr. X" to be the bishop of "Diocese Y" and people say that's a huge mistake, making that known to the pope is not disloyalty. On the other hand, when Bishop X shows up, you have to accept that he is the bishop of Diocese Y.

**Or when "Cardinal Z" is appointed as a member of the Congregation for Bishops . . .**
Yes, the pope can do these things. It may not be wise, and we may disagree, but we recognize his authority. There was an African diocese, Ahiara, which refused to accept the bishop appointed by Pope Benedict XVI because he was not from that area or from that ethnic group.[2] That was a case of rebellion on the part of the clergy. That's wrong. On the other hand, in the case of Bishop Juan Barros, when he was made bishop of Osorno Chile, many people criticized Pope Francis for the

---

[1] The pope's infallibility is also exercised in the solemn definitions of ecumenical councils, as well as in preserving and explicating the Church's teaching through the ordinary and universal Magisterium (CCC 891; 2035–36. See CCC 85–90; 882–84. See also CIC, canon 750.2).

[2] Francis D'Emilio, "Pope to Nigerian Priests: You'll Be Fired if You Don't Obey," Associated Press, June 11, 2017, https://apnews.com/article/vatican-city-pope-francis-africa-international-news-europe-ab33dcf7c5c74df2b30330cdf01f8241.

appointment. They kept pressing, and eventually, the Pope recognized he had made a mistake. On the level of the day-to-day governance of the Church, you may for good reasons criticize or question individual decisions as long as you don't rebel or refuse to accept them.

**What are the limits of papal authority? In the secular world, people commonly think that the pope can change the doctrine of the Church.**
The pope does not possess the authority to change the teaching of the Church. The papal office, by its nature, is a guardian of the Faith received from God. In other words, the revelation given by Christ to his Apostles is then handed on to successive generations of the successors to the Apostles to be proclaimed. That faith is embraced by the baptized and is lived and witnessed to by all members of the Church. The pope and the bishops have a unique role because they are the guardians of orthodoxy, and they are the ones who can protect the sheepfold from errors, i.e., teachings that are not true and that contradict revelation. That role in safeguarding the Faith has historically shown the divine wisdom manifested in appointing a vicar of Christ who would guide the faithful and be a bulwark against errors and heresies, because the Church is always under assault by forces and people who reject her teaching and want her to teach something else so as to conform to their way of thinking.

That is a continual problem in the life of the Church. We're seeing it right now, I'm sad to say, from within the Church where the German hierarchy is pushing, among other things, the blessing of homosexual unions, the ordination of women to the priesthood and the episcopate, and other follies which the

Church has never taught and never will teach but which they somehow think they can impose on the Church through the use of their episcopal authority in Germany. That's where the Pope is earnestly called upon by the faithful to call to order the German bishops and, if they fail to withdraw their innovative errors, to discipline them and deprive them of the office that they are so manifestly misusing.

**G. K. Chesterton, in speaking about the English tendency to defend their country no matter what the position is, said, "England, right or wrong, is like my mother drunk or sober." Some Catholics have a tendency to support Catholic prelates or even the pope in much the same way. How might that undermine the authentic authority of the pope?**

The deference that we owe to our parents and, by extension, to spiritual parents such as priests, bishops, and the pope, is a deference based on a divine command, but this deference must be exercised according to divine truth. If your parents are doing something wrong, it's not your duty as a good Christian son or daughter to engage in similar wrong behavior or to not report to the authorities when that wrong veers into dangerous and criminal behavior.

As regards the life of the Church, the presumption is that the pope and the bishops use their authority to promote the good and mission of the Church and, in almost all cases, that's happily been the reality. But there are cases where they have misused their authority and hurt the mission of the Church by trying to change either doctrine or practice. In those cases, there is no filial obligation to remain silent or to agree to support teachings and practices which are manifestly erroneous or manifestly harmful. Even in the pontificate of Pope Francis, and I've talked about it before, the whole Chilean situation with Bishop Juan Barros was not resolved simply by internal Church investigation. It was resolved by public pressure compelling a reinvestigation, which led to the Pope apologizing to the faithful and saying that he had acted wrongly in making Bishop Barros a diocesan bishop. Barros was then compelled to resign, and the entire Chilean hierarchy was put on notice that things identified as wrong in that hierarchy needed to be corrected.

Again, none of those eventual steps would have occurred if the laity had not said something. Therefore, the good of the Church is promoted when people with reason and persistence make known grave errors of judgment on the part of the people in charge in the Church, including the pope. In the case of Bishop Barros, the Pope himself admitted that he'd made an error.

**Fr. Murray, what is the right response when there is pressure from within to change Church teaching and practice?**
My general advice is that when things are happening in the Church that either contradict or seem to contradict Church teaching, or custom, or tradition, or practice, and lay people are stunned or perturbed by it, we should pray for divine guidance to understand properly what's happening so that we don't mistakenly overreact or react in a way that is uncharitable and unchristian. The cause of Christ is not served by sinful treatment of people with whom we have problems. Harsh words, vicious accusations, and imputing bad motives without any evidence is rash judgment and shouldn't happen.

***Has this problem been heightened by the internet?***
Yes. Now within the space of an hour you can review a hundred different media outlets, run a background search on a variety of topics, and have information that in past times would have been unimaginable to obtain so quickly. In such a setting, you find irresponsible criticisms, in the sense that the tone and the word selection reflect anger and even hatred for people, which is certainly not a Christian attitude and also distracts from the matter at hand, which is the objective analysis of what people say and write and do, and the harm or good that's produced by those statements and actions.

Name-calling and imputing bad motives is not a good idea. It is legitimate to analyze a pattern of behavior or the fruit of a line of thinking. For instance, if you're analyzing the Chinese Communist reaction to religious matters in China, you can cite history, Communist doctrine, and eyewitness testimony, and come up with a statement such as, "The Communist government fears and hates Christianity and is using every means possible to suppress it." That's a legitimate statement, and it's basically imputing a destructive motive to Chinese President Xi Jinping and his associates, and they will of course reject it. Then you can say that part of the Communist philosophy is to lie about your actions because lying for the cause of Communism is just another means to victory. In the life of the Church, the presumption is that Churchmen are trying to promote the good and mission of the Church, but they may not see these properly, so you can try to influence their way of evaluating a theory or a practice or a doctrine.

I think that, in the situation we are now facing, the internet helps tremendously in terms of accessing information and being able to interact intelligently with a vast array of people. That's wonderful. But it can also be an opportunity to waste time and engage in gossip and backbiting with strangers about other people, even about the pope, bishops, and priests. Faults against charity have to be avoided.

The general point is, once you come to an understanding of what's actually happening, based on facts and good analysis, the faithful should resist what's wrong and promote what's right. Part of that will mean influencing other people to see that your conclusions are reasonable and based on fact, and to do so in a way that will mobilize public opinion as much as possible in order to resist or criticize something. Such efforts make it more difficult for the Church authority who is proposing the innovation in doctrine or practice to do so, claiming that this is all being pacifically received by the faithful and that the faithful, along with the hierarchy, realizes that this change needed to be made. One needs to make it clear that the opposition is real and is not based on hatred or fear but on the demonstrated incompatibility or unsuitableness of a change in Catholic teaching or practice.

**Let's turn to some specific areas where people think there has been an attempt to change Church teaching. Footnote 351 in Pope Francis's 2016 apostolic exhortation on the family,** Amoris Laetitia,[3] **has been widely interpreted as permitting the administration of Holy Communion to divorced**

---

[3] Pope Francis, Post-Synodal Apostolic Exhortation on Love in the Family *Amoris Laetitia* (March 19, 2016), http://www.vatican.va/content/francesco/en/apost_exhortations/documents/papa-francesco_esortazione-ap_20160319_amoris-laetitia.html.

*and civilly remarried Catholics in some cases. Do you think such a change has been achieved, and if so, how should the faithful react?*

*Amoris Laetitia* says that there are cases when people in an invalid second marriage should be given Holy Communion. That's never been the practice of the Church, based on the teaching that those who have contracted a second, invalid marriage—because they have a prior marital bond—are publicly defiant of the Church's teaching on the indissolubility of marriage and therefore are not living in conformity with the will of Christ in a public way. They therefore are treated as what traditionally we would call a "public sinner," against whom the Church takes public measures as a call to repentance and as a warning to other members of the community not to imitate this behavior. A person's subjective conviction—for instance, that "my first marriage was invalid, and therefore I'm entitled to a second marriage"—is not sufficient to establish that his first marriage was invalid. He certainly has the opportunity to make that claim if he presents a petition to his diocesan marriage tribunal for an examination of his claim of invalidity.

*Amoris Laetitia* also comes to the conclusion, after presenting moral arguments that are extremely deficient, that in some cases the best that God expects from you is that you live in the second marriage. Or, for the good of the children, you may continue cohabiting without refraining from adulterous behavior.

*Amoris Laetitia* is very troubling because, in effect, it ignores the indissolubility of marriage and allows for people to engage in behavior that is condemned by Christ and yet be encouraged to receive the Body of Christ in Holy Communion. That is very troubling.

***Have you dealt with such cases over the years as a parish priest?***
I've certainly dealt with people who are in invalid marriages or are living together without the benefit of marriage and have spoken to them about the fact that they are not allowed to receive Communion.

***How have they responded?***
Most people accept it; they understand. Most people realize that this is not according to what they know Christ wants. We have to face the fact that some people make decisions to engage in sinful behavior and not reform, thinking or even hoping that maybe they'll reform at a later time in life. That's the realism of the Church: not everyone who is at Mass is ready to go to Communion, and therefore we shouldn't give them a false encouragement to disregard what the Church has always taught, by saying, "We're changing this, and now you can go to Communion." Someone might respond, "Wait a minute. If it was wrong yesterday, why isn't it wrong today?" This is why I think that *Amoris Laetitia* is an example of laxism in moral theology.

The reality is that there are very few divorced and remarried people who want to go to Communion. It's just a fact because the reality is that most of those people aren't going to church on Sunday. This innovation is misplaced charity. I don't agree with the idea that, because people can't go to Communion, they are being offended against. The fact that they can't go to Communion is the most charitable thing there can be because it is a call to repent and to not live in an adulterous union.

*Would you say that a similar approach to Communion could be applied to the push for Protestant spouses married to Catholics to receive Holy Communion?*

Yes, this, too, is misplaced charity. The notion that the inability for Protestants to receive Communion is such a serious problem that we have to disregard other aspects of the Faith in order to accomplish this purpose is mistaken. It is also a mistake to say that receiving Communion is the necessary visible sign that someone is considered to be a full member of the Catholic Church. Church membership and lack of reception of the sacraments are categories that go together. You can be a baptized Catholic who never makes your First Communion. It's not supposed to happen, but you don't cease to be a Catholic if you never received Communion. Then there are those who live a life that is in contradiction with the Gospel. They are called to recognize that they shouldn't receive Communion. If they mistakenly think they should, they have to be told they shouldn't. And, if it's a matter of public sinning, then they should definitely not be given Communion after they've been warned about this.

*What would you say to laity who see their own priests distributing Holy Communion in these situations and using* Amoris Laetitia *to justify it? Should they try to correct the practice or simply find another parish?*

If you are aware of situations where people who are in invalid marriages are receiving Communion, the first step would be to speak to the parish priest and discuss whether your concerns are supported by fact. It could be that the person or couple in question had their marriage blessed elsewhere, and we simply don't know about it. Or maybe they are living as brother and sister.

However, in parishes which boast that they have now implemented *Amoris Laetitia*'s liberalizing permission regarding Communion being given to people who are not in valid marriages, then you have to say to the parish priest, "This is not right." He may disagree with you, but then you can say to him, "I'm going to take up my concerns with the bishop because this is a scandal, in addition to being an individual problem for the couple and the priest involved." The bishop may or may not agree with you. This is part of the dilemma that *Amoris Laetitia* has created in the life of the Church: the Pope has supported the interpretation of various bishops that *Amoris Laetitia* allows the priest to make a judgment that "couple X" is able to receive Holy Communion even though they aren't validly married—and that contradicts the universal practice of the Church up to the day *Amoris Laetitia* was issued. I see no way in which *Amoris Laetitia*'s provisions regarding Communion and remarriage can be reconciled with the teaching and practice of the Church.

**In some dioceses, up to 80 percent of people live with their spouse before marriage. How much does this have to do with their formation by Catholic parents over the last forty years? And do you think** Amoris Laetitia **will exacerbate cohabitation?**

Cohabitation was relatively rare in the Catholic world until the last thirty to forty years. Before that, it was extremely rare; it was called "shacking up." And it was not only understood within the Catholic Church to be a mortal sin to be cohabitating, there was a social stigma even in the general society because we still had, at least in the United States and in other places, vigorous opposition to this by the majority Protestant population. That all died out with the sexual revolution, and there is no social stigma attached to cohabitation except in very strict Protestant groups and in the Catholic Church, as well as among Orthodox Christians and Orthodox Jews. But the general culture and the media tolerate and even celebrate this.

*Amoris Laetitia* is a genuflection to the sexual revolution by saying that people who get divorced and remarried should be pitied rather than corrected, that they should be given some slack because God can't expect them not to enjoy the benefits of a second "marital" life even though they're already married to someone else. It doesn't contribute to the support of chastity when the Church basically says that sinful adulterous relationships are not that bad if people have a serious enough reason for entering into them, which is a central message of *Amoris Laetitia* on divorce and remarriage.

Cohabitation is the fruit of poor catechesis in the life of the Church, meaning the decline of Catholic education, the embrace of contraception, and the spreading of a general acquiescence to the sexual-revolution culture, and that's a big problem.

**What are some of the joys for a priest of preparing a couple for marriage?**
I've prepared many couples for marriage. The joy is that you're seeing the divine order, which began with Adam and Eve, who are the pattern of life for everyone else who wants to get married, being affirmed, and embraced. It is beautiful to see the couple come forward and request marriage in the Church because they believe that Jesus Christ is God, and they want his blessing upon their union, and they want his protection and assistance. It's also a sign of their deep Catholic Faith that, even

though it involves some effort and application to get married in the Church, they don't mind doing it because they know this is what marriage is. It's a sacrament, and the Church is taking great care in making sure people don't enter into it without true reflection and understanding of what they're going to do.

I enjoy preparing couples for marriage, and I'm sad that the rate of Church marriage among Catholics has declined precipitously. I've been a priest for thirty-six years and the decline in the number of marriages is statistically notable. I see it as a priest. Cohabitation has become the societal norm, and Catholics are sadly no different than their non-Catholic neighbors in this regard.

But there are sadly many Catholics for whom the idea, for instance, that it's a mortal sin to co-habit without the benefit of marriage is absent from their minds. Or they don't think that God is really troubled by mortal sin, and that is really a problem. They buy into the expression, "God loves me as I am" or "God is unconditional love." Why did Jesus die on the Cross? To obtain the forgiveness of sin. Is sin just simply the equivalent of spilling ketchup? Is it no big deal? No, sin is a rejection of God's law, and it's an entering into a way of life that is, in the end, egotistical and harmful. That's the message that we need to get out to people.

**In discussions over Amoris Laetitia critics say it resembles a self-help book filled with psychological advice, but it doesn't address some of the theological issues regarding the essence of marriage and the necessity of lifelong fidelity.**
There is a lot of pastoral and psychological reflection on how to create a loving and peaceful home and how to deal with the ups

and downs of relationships. The Pope, I think, is reflecting on his experience as a priest in Argentina for so many years. The theological section, particularly in chapter eight, is extremely deficient, and the claim that it is Thomism is unsupported in my opinion. It is not founded in Thomism and, in fact, embraces a theory of human moral agency and responsibility that is at odds with previous teaching. It basically says that there are certain laws of God which some people are not capable of observing, and the Church has never taught that. Sinners who are habituated to sinning can have great difficulty in overcoming their sin. In that sense, they might say, "I can't do this," but they are really just forgetting the power of God's grace or exaggerating for purposes of excusing themselves. To claim that it's metaphysically impossible for someone to observe, "Thou shalt not commit adultery," because of their limited capabilities or previous life experiences, is contradictory to Catholic teaching on human freedom and the power of grace. *Amoris Laetitia* is extremely deficient theologically and should be withdrawn, in my opinion, because it is causing havoc in the life of the Church. If we can't live up to the teaching on adultery, what other teachings can't we live up to? There's a whole line of people at the door waiting to make various claims.

**Do you often come across these claims being made in your life as a parish priest?**
Most Catholics in the pews don't know much about *Amoris Laetitia*. They read headlines, but I would say I have very few conversations with people who ask me about *Amoris Laetitia*. On the other hand, all the priests know about it. And they know there are some priests pushing this new line of moral

reasoning and are applying it to homosexuality and to contraception. They are applying it in ways that are in line with the sexual revolution, and this is troubling to priests who uphold the Church's perennial moral teaching. If the Catholic Church has been wrong about adultery, contraception, and homosexuality, what else is she wrong about? Casting doubt on what has been taught forcefully by popes, most particularly Pope John Paul II and Pope Benedict XVI, by embracing *Amoris Laetitia*'s reasoning and permission for Communion for divorced and remarried people, undermines the whole realm of the Church's moral teaching.

**What effect could this be having on seminary formation?**
Well, seminaries face the challenge of trying to teach what's in the *Catechism of the Catholic Church* and then reconcile that with what's taught in *Amoris Laetitia*. The least controversial solution will be to say, "There are very few cases of this and, as *Amoris Laetitia* says, we have to go on a case-by-case basis, and you're probably not going to find this is a big problem in your life as a priest." But that's dodging the question.

The issue is not how many cases there are and whether you have to judge them individually. Everything has to be judged individually. The question is by what standards and principles are you to judge, and that is what *Amoris Laetitia* has changed. Therefore, if you are going to teach moral theology according to what the Church has taught up to this pontificate, you are definitely going to have to call out *Amoris Laetitia* as being a departure, not a development. And that will cause controversy because people will say, "Popes don't make mistakes." That brings us back to the fact that we don't believe papal infallibility extends beyond limited circumstances, such as solemn declarations. It doesn't extend to every sermon or even to every document that the pope issues.

**Or to papal interviews . . .**
Exactly. As I noted earlier, Pope Francis says there should be civil unions for people of the same sex, as an alternative to marriage. Well, his predecessor John Paul II taught the exact opposite. The reason it's not to happen is because the Catholic Church is not supposed to endorse sinful behavior or legal arrangements that legitimize sinful behavior and are, in fact, stepping-stones to "marriage," i.e., legally recognizing a pseudo-marriage. Pope Francis endorsed civil unions for same-sex couples in a television interview. I saw the video. He did say it, and claimed he'd been saying it for a long time, which is in fact true. He promoted that view in Argentina. So, if you are going to teach moral theology in the seminary, in this pontificate you are going to have to critique what the pope says. That is a controversial thing, but I think it's necessary.

**Given the controversies over** Amoris Laetitia **and other similar examples in this pontificate, when is it appropriate to listen to the pope?**
We should always listen to the pope and seek to gain inspiration and guidance from what he says. When he says something that is in apparent or plain contradiction to something that the Church has previously taught, such as is case with *Amoris Laetitia*, then we have to stand up and say, "No, Holy Father, we think you've got this wrong, and these are the reasons." That's what the "*dubia*" cardinals attempted to do. It's not that

individuals are saying, "My opinion counts more than the pope's opinion," because in the life of the Church opinions are secondary. What counts is Church doctrine, and if we all believe in the doctrine and are living as good Catholics, then we might debate how those doctrines can most effectively be taught or implemented. But we are not going to debate whether the doctrine is true or not because that's not subject to our discretion.

**Staying on the topic of marriage and family, earlier you said the embrace of contraception is at the root of the problem of cohabitation. How much are disputes over Humanae Vitae at the heart of the current revolution?**
The rejection by many, including priests and bishops, of the Church's teaching that the use of contraception is gravely immoral, prepared the way for the rejection of other teachings that go against the sexual revolution. The false appeal to "follow your conscience" so as to exempt oneself from following the Church's moral teaching has had incalculable consequences. Many Catholics consider their own desires, not the Church's teaching, to be the standard for good behavior. The Church becomes a point of reference for selective consultation on matters of morality. She is no longer considered the teacher of universal truths binding upon the consciences of believers. "Cafeteria Catholicism," pick and choose whatever you like, is a widespread reality in the Church today.

**Why have priests and bishops tended not to teach from the pulpit on Humanae Vitae, and how can this be remedied?**
It's essential that we believe in *Humanae Vitae*. It is part of the moral teaching of the Church, and it's non-optional. It is the

truth, and it must be taught. The problem for a parish priest is to be able to teach it well in a Sunday sermon. It's a difficult thing because it depends on being able to explain to people a whole series of teachings regarding the nature of creation, the purpose of marriage, the nature of male and female, and the divine call to be fertile and multiply. Then you have to study individual moral acts. Morality is not simply an attitude or a way of thinking. It governs each specific act that man engages in, and it's a lot of material to cover in a sermon. Most priests are not capable of being able to do that in a ten-to-fifteen-minute time slot.

 I think the solution is for the bishops, each in his diocese or as a national conference, to issue more teaching on *Humanae Vitae* and to do so in a form that they can summarize for priests. Various bishops have done this, such as Bishop James Conley of Lincoln and Bishop John Barres of Rockville Centre. In each diocese, the bishop could essentially tell priests, "This sermon should be given on this day once a year" to cover the moral teaching on the matter. In addition, the bishops should speak about it themselves because in their role as teachers of the Faith, they are not constricted by the time constraints of a sermon at Mass, which is basically the only time that the parish priest is going to be able to communicate with most of his parishioners. The bishops should enunciate and explain the Church's teaching through pastoral letters, pamphlets, videos, and conferences. They could explain the teaching and then draw upon supportive examples from married couples. Moral theologians and medical doctors could also be employed to explain it.

 As a parish priest, I'm not shifting the blame. This is a controverted teaching that doesn't lend itself to an average Sunday homily. But if a bishop speaks and then provides means to communicate with the faithful through the internet and otherwise, he will help us parish priests to deal with this important teaching. Look at the amount of energy the average diocese spends raising money for the bishop's annual appeal. It's well-organized and has a staff. A similar effort could be made for *Humanae Vitae* and other controverted teachings: for example, on so-called same-sex "marriage," "transgenderism," the wrong of sex-change surgery, or on the pastoral approach to dealing with families in which the children have declared to their parents that they want to undergo a transgender surgical procedure—why each one is wrong.

**So why is this not being done?**
The long and the short of it: I think *Humanae Vitae* is not being taught very well because the bishops as a group are not interested in getting into controversy in the Church since so many Catholics have, unfortunately, become convinced that it's a matter of their conscience to choose to use birth control. And that's a disaster because conscience is there to guide you to make good decisions and to obey God's law, not the other way around. The "consult your conscience" trope, which was preached by some priests and bishops as soon as *Humane Vitae* was issued, is a dodge. What we have to say is, "Follow God's truth, and if your conscience doesn't respond to that teaching in the affirmative sense, spend time informing yourself, guiding your conscience to understand why it's true, and praying for light. But do not go and sin because you find his teaching hard to obey."

It's obvious that this was one of the most significant discoveries of the twentieth century: the ability to suppress female fertility through chemical means. That's primarily what we're talking about with birth control. The ability to control fertility changes the nature of sexual relations because there's no longer a necessary connection, through the observance of the natural order, between sexual activity and procreation.

The sin is to take steps to frustrate the natural outcome of sexual relations, thus modifying the divine plan. The divine plan has to be respected because that's integral to creation. If we are here on this planet, we should first rejoice and give thanks to the One who put us here. The next thing we should do is ask: "What am I supposed to do?" And that's God's plan. How do I know God's plan? For this we rely on divine revelation and reason's correct understanding of the natural purposes of God's creation. In college, I remember reading Etienne Gilson's *Reason and Revelation in the Middle Ages*. It's a great short book, in which he says that divine providence is such that God revealed many things that could already be known by natural reason, but which were not easily known because of the condition of humanity after the fall. That's an argument that I find appealing because with many people, if you say, "It's quite clear by examining human nature that this is wrong behavior," they will respond, "Well, I don't see it that way." But if you then add that the Bible prohibits it, many of those same people will say, "In that case, I won't do it."

God has acted to reinforce and supplement man's deficient understanding through divine revelation. That revelation is entrusted to a living magisterium. When new questions arise and the meaning of God's revelation is contested, the authority steps in and says, "This is what it means." Birth control is a perfect example. If you look at chemical birth control by pills, you are rendering a healthy female into a female not enjoying full health by temporary sterilization. To understand what you're supposed to do gives you the ability to cooperate fruitfully with nature, in this case, literally with the fruit of children, but also in other matters to use the body in the ways it was meant to be used. With birth control, that's frustrated. If you look at human sexuality from a classical and Christian perspective, God attaches pleasure to certain activities that people should engage in, in order to propel them to engage in those activities because they're beneficial. If food didn't taste good, many people wouldn't eat. It makes it easier to eat if the food tastes good, but the reason you eat is not just to experience taste. That's the accompanying enticement and reward for doing something good in and of itself, which is eating.

The same thing is true for sexual relations: it may sound strange to some ears, but if there were no pleasure in sex, many people would not engage in it. God knows everything of course, and he knows what humanity needs to flourish and cooperate with creation. That's why pleasure is part of the sexual experience, but it's not the purpose or reason for its existence. Because of fallen nature, man has disordered sexual impulses and the lustful desire for unbridled pleasure, but these tend to be restrained if the natural processes are respected and play out. In other words, if you know you're likely to have a child, you might not engage in sex outside of marriage because you don't want to have illegitimate children.

Birth control changes almost everything as regards the field of sexual morality in Western society, and until Catholics give a prophetic witness of living chastity and avoiding birth control, they are going to suffer the same bitter fruits that are experienced by non-Catholics who have little or no reason, according to their religion or personal outlook, to avoid using birth control.

**Is this an area where lay experts should try to influence the bishops as a body?**
Yes, but the bishops really need to act on their own. The Latin phrase is "*sua sponte,*" i.e., "by his own initiative." I think this is an area where bishops as pastors have to realize that combatting sinfulness is one of the main missions of the preacher and the pastor because sin is the obstacle to salvation. Combatting sinfulness basically means teaching people the difference between right and wrong and then encouraging them to do what's right and warning them to avoid what's wrong.

To do so effectively, one has to explain why it's wrong and encourage people why it's right *not* to use birth control, and to make a big deal out of it. It's noteworthy that, when Pope John Paul II went on foreign trips, he often gave talks against birth control or mentioned it when he spoke about family life. I think he understood that the pontiff has to speak about it. The current Holy Father has said on at least one occasion that the teaching of the Catholic Church on this matter is well-known and doesn't bear repeating. In fact, he's even said there's a fixation on moral teaching by some of the Church's teachers. I disagree with that. With this pontificate, we have also had an undermining of the integrity of the Pontifical Academy for Life and the John Paul II Institute for Family and Marriage, with members and professors saying things that are inimical to Catholic teaching and morality. That's a problem.

***What's the solution?***

The solution, in my opinion, is for lay people and bishops together to come to grips with the fact that we've got a major crisis here. And the major crisis is that Catholics are objectively, and most likely subjectively, sinning when they use birth control, and sin is an offense against God. The result of this sinful behavior is fewer people being born and greater marital unhappiness because when a husband and wife are unwilling to give themselves to each other completely, such that the fruit of their marital union may be a child, a kind of very selfish behavior is being engaged in: the search for physical intimacy and pleasure without the possibility of the natural fruit of the union of husband and wife.

Lots of people come through the parish door, and many were taught erroneous doctrine by false shepherds—priests or others—who said, "Pay no attention to *Humanae Vitae*, you can do whatever you want." Many of those people will be happy to hear the false teaching because if they don't want to have children, they will be affirmed and think they are not offending God. God will judge their subjective culpability, but objectively it is offensive.

Catholics have the obligation to seek out the truth. It's not right to go to a priest who teaches things that are contrary to the Faith and ask him what he thinks. No, if "Fr. X" says it's perfectly fine to use birth control, you have to question yourself, "Do I sincerely believe that he's correct, or do I know that he's a rebel who's telling me something I want to hear?" And that's where we have to be firm in saying, "The fact that a priest says something doesn't make it true." Whatever the priest says has to be compared with what we know to be Catholic teaching.

The same is true for bishops. They are not immune to this. If a bishop makes a statement that sounds like it's heretical or undermines Catholic teaching, you're doing him a favor by making this concern of yours known to him, even in the public sphere—because typically the only way you find out about it is not through a personal conversation with the bishop but because he said it in public or published it. The Catholic ethos of respect for priests and bishops does not include acquiescence in not criticizing bishops and priests when they say things that aren't correct.

**You seem to have a great spirit of freedom in this regard. Where does that come from?**
I would guess my seminary training helped me in this regard, and the Lord said, "The truth will make you free. . . . I am the way, and the truth, and the life" (John 8:32; 14:6). Christian doctrine is not just an interpretation that I find congenial and is subject to private judgment. That's sort of the Protestant mindset. Protestants are not generally upset that Methodists believe one thing, Baptists believe a second thing, and Calvinists believe a third thing. Private judgment allows everyone to interpret the Bible as he sees fit.

Catholics don't think that way because Catholic teaching is not something that I came up with by studying the Bible, or what someone else has told me from their study and that I happen to agree with. The basic teaching is this: Jesus came, he founded a Church, and he gave the Church the mission to bring the truth to the world. I was blessed and fortunate to be introduced to that by my parents, and when I came to understand the teaching, I came to understand it's beauty. But I don't believe in Catholic teaching because it's beautiful. I believe in it because Christ wants me to believe in it, and he wants me to believe in it because he wants me to know the truth, which means he wants me to know God.

When people object to a priest or seminarian questioning or contradicting something that a teacher, or even a bishop, might be saying, I think to myself, "What's the purpose of four or six years of seminary training if men cannot recognize the difference between truth and error at the end of it?" In other words, is it fair to give them an exam about a doctrinal subject and demand that they get all the answers right, and yet when they go out into the parish or listen to a bishop, and the bishop makes basic mistakes, which sometimes happens, we're supposed to say he's right? No, the standard is impersonal. It's not that a human being has a right to tell me what I need to do based on his interpretation. No, Christ gave the authority and the teaching, and they are preserved and transmitted through a human authority. But if that human authority is weak or feeble. . . . We've heard of wandering sheep; we have wandering shepherds at times, and we shouldn't be surprised by that.

**Are the recent changes to the John Paul II Institute in Rome a symptom of this internal revolution, similar to how in the secular world cultural Marxism infiltrated education?[4]**

---

[4] In 2017, Pope Francis refounded the Pontifical John Paul II Institute in Rome and later (2019) gave the institute new statutes, which critics said stripped the academic institution of any true identification with the teaching of John Paul II. The changes included the dismissal of professors known for their fidelity to the teaching of Pope John Paul II. See Diane Montagna, "All Profs Suspended, President Dismissed as Part of 'Destruction' of John Paul II Institute," LifeSiteNews, July 24, 2019, https://www.lifesitenews.com/news/all-profs-suspended-president-dismissed-as-part-of-destruction-of-john-paul-ii-institute.

Yes, the changes in personnel and mission at the John Paul II Institute in Rome reflect a desire to bend to the spirit of the age rather than to confront that spirit with the hard truths of the Gospel. I consider this change to be a tragic repudiation of the Institute's foundational mission, that has the effect of encouraging dissent from the Church's moral teaching.

***Are the changes to the Church's teaching on the death penalty, specifically the changes to the Catechism, part of an internal Church dissent?***

Under Pope Francis's direction, the Prefect of the Congregation for the Doctrine of the Faith, Luis Cardinal Ladaria, S.J., issued a statement explaining the change in the words in the *Catechism of the Catholic Church* on the death penalty.[5] In the statement, he called the change a development of doctrine. I thoroughly disagree with him on that. The Church has always taught that the use of the death penalty is not immoral in and of itself and can be used morally when properly applied. To now say the death penalty is "a violation of human dignity" and may not be morally applied in any circumstance is not a development of the previous teaching. It's a contradiction of the previous teaching.

It is not correct that the change to the Catechism is a genuine development of doctrine. And it is most regrettable that the Holy See engaged in this, that the Holy Father himself has called the death penalty wrong and a form of vengeance. In other words, stigmatizing it as an immoral act. No one is

---

[5] Diane Montagna, "Pope Francis Changes Catechism to Declare Death Penalty 'Inadmissible,'" LifeSiteNews, August 2, 2018, https://www.lifesitenews.com/news/breaking-pope-francis-changes-catechism-to-declare-death-penalty-inadmissib.

compelled to agree that the death penalty ought to be applied in any particular case. But as a Catholic you are compelled to believe that it is not immoral for public authority to use the death penalty in circumstances in which it is appropriate according to the nature of the crime that has been committed. In other words, Catholics cannot say that the death penalty can never be used. The Church has never taught that, and the pope does not have the power and authority to change that teaching.

**I think when the news of the change came out, many people were surprised to hear that the Catholic Church actually does support the use of the death penalty.**
The hostility is among the liberal elites and those who follow them. The average person who is not attuned to the liberal worldview might say, "Don't use the death penalty because it's so harsh and final and you can make mistakes." But I don't think they would believe it can never be used under any circumstances. People who commit grievous, heinous crimes, whether they show repentance or not, have made themselves liable to losing their life in punishment for their crimes. Holding serious offenders accountable is a reaffirmation of their human dignity, for it treats them as free and intelligent persons who are responsible for their bad actions.

**How much do bishops or bishops' conferences have to go along with such changes if they are widely seen as contradicting established Church teaching?**
Once the Holy See has said that the *Catechism of the Catholic Church* will teach that the death penalty should not be used because it's a violation of human dignity, then all the lower

authorities in the Church who agree with that and go along with it are not going to claim that it's against Catholic teaching when, in fact, it is against Catholic teaching. What I'm saying is that the Pope is teaching something that none of his predecessors taught and that is in contradiction with the previous teaching. A successor pope is going to have to reverse this decision. Again, logically, if the death penalty is immoral, then God himself in the Old Testament commanded immoral activity. The Church has justified and explained why the death penalty is a legitimate penalty in law. St. Thomas Aquinas and others have explicated this very well. So, this is a real problem.

**What do you think is at the heart of the push to make the death penalty inadmissible?**
There is a general, but not universal, hostility to the death penalty in the Western world. I think this is partly related to no belief in an afterlife. If this life is all there is, then, for instance, to sentence to death someone age twenty-five, who is convicted of raping and murdering someone and who also killed a witness to the crime, is too harsh a penalty. Some will say, "It's unfair to execute a young man; can't we give him a second chance?" Whereas the Catholic point of view and the common Christian understanding is that this person is given an opportunity, if he doesn't want to go to Hell, to recognize the seriousness of his crime and to repent of it before he dies. The death penalty can therefore be a moment of truth and grace for him because it brings him face to face with the evil he has committed and prompts him to repent of it before his execution.

**What role does papolatry have, if any, in enabling the winds of revolution to blow through the Church?**
"Papolatry" is a word that, if understood as an analogy to "idolatry," would be offering false worship to the pope, i.e., elevating the papacy to the level of the divine, in a way that is forbidden because worship can be offered to God alone. In its common usage, though, papolatry generally means treating everything the pope says and does as obligatory for Catholics to both think and do. The Church has never said that, and certainly it's not coherent with the Scriptures, which tell us that St. Peter was challenged directly by St. Paul regarding arrangements with new converts to the Church. Historically, within the Church, St. Catherine of Siena is honored because she told the pope that he had to leave Avignon, France, and return to Rome, and this was viewed subsequently as a sign of her holiness, that she, in fact, was upholding good order in the life of the Church in the face of political pressures and the like that compelled the pope to be outside of Rome.

It is an unfortunate development from ultramontanism, a nineteenth-century intellectual movement, which was defending the papacy against its enemies, who were basically Enlightenment-inspired revolutionaries who wanted to undermine the authority of the successors of Peter in the Church. In practice, ultramontanism supported centralization efforts of the Church to make the ordinary administration of the Catholic Church throughout the world closely subject to Roman supervision, guidance, and teaching. That is a good thing in itself, but it should never become such that everything the pope says becomes obligatory for Catholics, because that is not what the Church teaches. When papal infallibility was defined by the

First Vatican Council, it was made clear that infallibility concerns not *everything* that the pope says but only those things that are solemnly and clearly defined as being necessary to be believed for salvation.[6]

If the pope thinks, for instance, that it's a good idea for the Vatican to issue a stamp with Martin Luther's image on it, papolatry would say, "Don't criticize the pope because he's the pope; he knows what he's doing." But Pope Francis himself has encouraged critical writing and thinking about what he does. He's talked about a spirit of Gospel frankness. We notice that he's not always receptive to criticism, such as not answering the four "*dubia*" cardinals, or other approaches to him by lay people and scholars. But it's not illegitimate to raise questions and criticisms in the defense of the truth when things that are plainly what the Church has always taught and done up until now are being changed, such as Communion for the divorced and remarried. This is a doctrinal and pastoral problem created by *Amoris Laetitia* that has no precedent in the history of the Church. When this practice was suggested under the pontificates of Pope John Paul II and Pope Benedict XVI, it was strictly and firmly refuted and denied because it is not coherent with the Church's teaching either about marriage or about worthiness for the reception of Holy Communion.

Reverence for the pope—for his person, teaching, and office—is absolutely necessary. But true reverence is always

---

[6] At the same time, the Church's infallibility extends to the solemn definitions and other definitive statements of ecumenical councils, which require the approval of the pope, and also to the definitive teachings of the pope as the head of the ordinary and universal Magisterium (see CCC 891; 2035–36. See also CIC, canon 750.2).

subject to the reverence we owe to God and the truth. When we are reasonably convinced that the pope is doing something wrong or saying something that is wrong, it is not irreverent to point that out. It may not be welcome, and the pope may reject it, but that doesn't matter because you're witnessing to the truth.

**How corrosive do you think papolatry is? Some Catholics and news agencies will simply not allow themselves to criticize or even question many things that the pope is doing, perhaps out of this false sense of reverence, even though well-meaning.**

Papolatry would be a way of characterizing an approach that rejects the notion that it's possible for a Catholic to disagree with the pope, and in practice does not favor people who then engage in reasonable critiques. This is one of the struggles within the Church right now: you are called "anti-papal" because you disagree with *Amoris Laetitia* or the Pope's pronouncements on the death penalty. It is an unfair criticism because simply upholding what prior popes taught is not an anti-papal act, and to tell a pope he's made a mistake is, in fact, a sign of respect and love for him.

The assertion that he has made a mistake in the cases I refer to is not, by the way, a refutable opinion. It's a verifiable matter of Church teaching and practice, which is traceable through the history of the Church right up to this pontificate. And the notion that, until the pope explains things, we really don't know what the Faith consists of is an exaggerated notion. We spend time in the seminary, and we priests continue to read and study precisely so that we know what we're supposed to preach. Therefore, when the pope says something that conflicts with what we've learned previously, it's not for us to say, "I must have been wrong all those years." The burden falls on the pope who is giving a new teaching to say how it is coherent with what we've heard and been taught before. That's where the *Amoris Laetitia* controversy is still a major wound in the life of the Church. Because neither the Pope, nor his supporters have explained how this new teaching on giving Communion to people in invalid adulterous so-called second marriages is, in fact, in line with the Scriptures and the teaching of the Church.

When the "*dubia*"—which were very reasonably formulated based on the teaching of the Church up until this pontificate—are answered by the Pope or his delegate, then we can have a true dialogue in charity, to set forth what is the true teaching in conformity with the Faith and what practices can and cannot be authorized. But the idea that questions and criticisms that arrive at the Vatican shouldn't be answered is not how the Church has operated in the past.

**A characteristic of revolution is political factionalism. Are we seeing this happening through this pontificate? For example, in his Pentecost homily on May 23, 2021,[7] Pope Francis said,**

> Today, if we listen to the Spirit, we will not be concerned with conservatives and progressives, traditionalists and innovators, right and left. When those become our criteria, then the Church has

---

[7] See Pope Francis, Homily on the Solemnity of Pentecost (May 23, 2021), https://www.vatican.va/content/francesco/en/homilies/2021/documents/papa-francesco_20210523_omelia-pentecoste.html.

> *forgotten the Spirit. The Paraclete impels us to unity, to concord, to the harmony of diversity. . . . The enemy wants diversity to become opposition and so he makes them become ideologies. Say no to ideologies, yes to the whole.*

I find that the language Pope Francis uses here is largely imposing a political set of categories on religious doctrine, and I don't think it's appropriate to use such categories. Jesus Christ said, "I am the way, and the truth, and the life" (John 14:6). The Sacred Scriptures record the revelation of God, and the Gospels tell us exactly what Jesus taught. And one of the things he taught to the Apostles was, "He who hears you hears me" (Luke 10:16). So, the Apostles have a solemn role to teach what Jesus taught and then to proclaim that teaching down through the generations. That teaching is clear; that teaching has been developed and explained and explicated by the popes and the councuils over the centuries, so it's not as if we have different versions of the truth. There's one truth, and those who support it, we can definitely say they are conservative because they are trying to conserve what was given by Christ to the Apostles and handed down to us. To formulate two categories: innovators who want to change things, and their polar opposite, conservatives who want to protect the past, and then reject both of them is a mistaken analysis. Cardinal Newman reminded us that Catholicism is by nature a conservative religion, which protects the teaching of the Church against worldliness and unbelief. Remember, we don't exist in a bubble. Left-wing ideology has as one of its main objectives the destruction of Christian truth because it's an obstacle to the accomplishment of its overall goals.

*How does conservatism temper these revolutionary impulses while at the same time retaining the radicality of the Gospel, one that challenges the powerful of this world and worldly ideas?*

The holy struggle to remain faithful to what the Church has handed down to us requires the radicality that Cardinal Sarah wrote about in his 2015 book *God or Nothing*. The powerful of this world often exaggerate their importance and power and try to manipulate people by means of self-serving ideologies that, in fact, deprive the people of their God-given freedoms. In truth, either we believe in God and his truth or we have nothing, not even ourselves. Christ's revelation is the message that frees man, and it is our duty to conserve that message in its entirety and purity.

*Some people say that calling yourself a traditional Catholic is to align yourself with ideologies that create rigidity contrary to what Christ taught.*

Tradition is our living connection through ritual, custom, and law, to the life of our ancestors in the Faith of Christ. The idea that, because something is old, it is obsolete, is a modern mistake. There are some old things that are obsolete: we don't use Model T cars, and the use of "thee" and "thou" has almost completely passed away. But when it comes to approaching God in prayer and sacramental practice, if these ways were good a thousand years ago, they are good now because the nature of God and man does not change. The mere fact that they may be a thousand years old is irrelevant. If, after one or two thousand years, our society is less comfortable with fasting or other penitential practices, that is more a reflection on our society—and it is not complimentary. We can't just say, "People won't tolerate fasting for three hours before receiving Communion." And, by the way, how many Catholics in the pews have been asked or expected to conform themselves to liturgical innovations they find terrible—and there are no worries about their anxiety? To go back to tradition may cause some to be upset, but I think, as Cardinal Sarah has shown in his writings, a return to traditional practices like Mass *ad orientem* would be a blessed rediscovery of something that was mistakenly cast aside.

**At a Sacra Liturgia *conference held in London in 2016, Cardinal Sarah, then-prefect of the Congregation for Divine Worship and the Discipline of the Sacraments, invited all priests to begin celebrating the Mass* ad orientem, *after a proper catechesis of the faithful. The Vatican swiftly issued a correction, emphasizing that the cardinal's invitation was not a directive.[8] You celebrate the Mass* ad orientem *here in the Archdiocese of New York. What should priests do when their bishop is unfavorable to or even prohibits them from offering the Mass* ad orientem?**

There is no prohibition anywhere against celebrating Mass *ad orientem*, either in canon law or liturgical law. Therefore, doing so does not violate a law. If a bishop prohibits priests from celebrating the Mass *ad orientem*, he is acting beyond his powers (*ultra vires*) because he doesn't have the power to eliminate what the general law of the Church permits. This can be pointed

---

[8] Diane Montagna, "Vatican: Cardinal Sarah's Ad Orientem Invitation 'Misinterpreted,'" Aleteia, July 11, 2016, https://aleteia.org/2016/07/11/vatican-cardinal-sarahs-ad-orientem-invitation-misinterpreted/.

out to him. If he still resists, a priest can then have canonical recourse against his decree. You can say to him, "Please communicate this to me in writing because I intend to have canonical recourse against this." The bishop might not be happy about it, but according to canon law, that's how the Church operates. Bishops are not sovereign, without any higher authority. They are answerable to the pope, and the Holy See is the instrument of the pope to manage these questions.

**Do you suggest that priests do this individually or as a group, because sometimes there are several priests in a diocese who want to celebrate the Mass** *ad orientem***, but they are afraid they'll all get shipped off to Siberia.**
Siberia might be a nice place. I would suggest either option because if the bishop is going to insist that the priests of his diocese do not have the right to celebrate the Mass facing East, he is violating canon law. Canon law does not give him that power. To stigmatize a practice which has been the universal practice of the Church for centuries, and which is the continual practice of all the Orthodox churches, and is widespread in the Catholic Church, is baseless. There is no case to be made for why it is wrong or should not be done. What this reveals in part is that the Vatican II permission to celebrate the Mass facing the people became, for many, the primary change that they want to uphold. Part of that comes from the notion of changing worship into a more horizontal experience—we are not just looking up to God and praying to him; now we are looking at each other. But that has led to a de-sacralization of the experience for many, and I know from celebrating the Mass *ad orientem* here in my parish for a number of years that both

the priests and people can be more recollected when they're not looking at one another's facial reactions during the whole Mass.

**People experience the revolution in large part by what they witness at Mass and the liturgical abuses that were rife after Vatican II. How can the faithful resist these abuses and promote tradition within their parishes?**
In the parish it all depends on the parish priest. He will set the tone, and if you have objections to liturgical abuses, if you bring them to the attention of the pastor you'll quickly find out if he agrees with your point of view or is in fact favorable to the liturgical abuses. My whole life as a priest has been spent watching attempts by the previous pontiffs to correct liturgical abuses with multiple documents, but the abuses continue over time.

**Why do they continue?**
Because a document is only valuable if it's enforced. If the pope tells the local bishops that Extraordinary Ministers of Holy Communion should not be standing at the altar or going to the tabernacle, or that you shouldn't have ten Extraordinary Ministers of Holy Communion when you only have one hundred people at Mass, or that priests shouldn't be sitting in the rectory while Extraordinary Ministers of Holy Communion are distributing Communion at Mass, or that priests shouldn't be changing the words of the Missal, these directives will only become operative if the local bishop takes steps to enforce them.

**What do the laity do if they bring their objections to their parish priest in a reasonable way and he says, "Sorry, but this is the way we're doing it."**

Well, they're stuck. You can write to the bishop, but in my experience very few bishops enforce liturgical order in their dioceses, and now with the shortage of priests, there's even less reason to do so for bishops who don't want to get into controversy. Such a bishop will likely think, "Why would I want to get into controversy with that priest? I'm just glad he's there to say Mass." What's happening now, I think, is that people who have the ability are going to a parish where there's liturgical order, or they go to the Old Mass, or they go to an Anglican Ordinariate Mass or to one of the Eastern Rite Catholic churches. But when there are problems, such as terrible music, the misuse of Extraordinary Ministers of Holy Communion, etc.,—there are big problems.

**What effect is this having on the wider Church?**
The sense of correct worship is being lost. As Pope Benedict XVI and Cardinal Sarah have demonstrated convincingly in their writings, much of liturgical practice today is community self-worship. It's the community celebrating itself and its achievements and its particular gifts, as they would say. How often do we see at Mass a beautiful hymn sung by a choir and then people applauding as if it were a performance, not an act of worship. The idea that you have to have liturgical arrangements to make things interesting for people, i.e., changes and additions, leads to the liturgy being conceived of as a product of the human imagination of the particular people in charge, and that is not what the Mass is.

It was nice in the old days when people could go to Mass in any country and it was the same experience. That's basically gone now. The central reality is true: the sacrifice is offered and the faithful can receive the Body of Christ, but things around it become particularistic, and that's not what the Church needs to do.

**Pope Francis's recent motu proprio Traditionis Custodes,[9] which he issued in July 2021, puts severe restrictions on the Traditional Latin Mass.[10] Are these restrictions on Summorum Pontificum[11] a further sign that the liberal revolution within the Church has taken hold?**

Perhaps. The move by Pope Francis to attempt a suppression of the Traditional Latin Mass will meet the steadfast opposition of the many Catholics who find spiritual nourishment and peace in the liturgical prayer of the Church found in the Old Mass. The voices of those who are considered by some to be unacceptably attached to the Church's perennial form of worship are not going to be silenced, particularly when the vast majority of them find themselves unfairly characterized as being causes of disunity through their supposed opposition to the Second Vatican Council and even to the Church herself and her institutions. The vast majority of Mass-goers at the Traditional Latin Mass are faithful Catholics who accept Vatican II to be a legitimate council of the Church and are not opposed to the Church but rather rejoice in the Church's pastoral generosity in

---

[9] "Guardians of Tradition."

[10] Pope Francis, Motu Propio on the Use of the Roman Liturgy Prior to the Reform of 1970 *Traditionis Custodes* (July 16, 2021), https://www.vatican.va/content/francesco/en/motu_proprio/documents/20210716-motu-proprio-traditionis-custodes.html.

[11] Pope Benedict XVI, Motu Propio on the Use of the Roman Liturgy Prior to the Reform of 1970 *Summorum Pontificum* (July 7, 2007), https://www.vatican.va/content/benedict-xvi/en/motu_proprio/documents/hf_ben-xvi_motu-proprio_20070707_summorum-pontificum.html.

responding to their love for the Old Mass. They are a witness to the pastoral wisdom of fostering true unity while recognizing and allowing for a diversity of liturgical expressions, especially when the liturgical form in question is a form of the Roman Rite of the Mass that goes back in its essential elements to the early days of the Church.

**What should we make of Traditionis Custodes *in light of Pope Benedict XVI's statement, "What earlier generations held as sacred, remains sacred and great for us too, and it cannot be all of a sudden entirely forbidden or even considered harmful"?*[12]**

What Pope Benedict said remains true, but sadly Pope Francis does not agree with him. Pope Francis sees the celebration of the Traditional Latin Mass as a cause of disunity that wounds the Church, and he finds that "many" people who are attached to this form of the Mass reject the Church and her institutions. As I wrote[13] at *The Catholic Thing*,

> The Pope's decision is based, in short, upon his evaluation of the motives and actions of "many" people who choose to attend (or celebrate) the EF Mass. They are somehow "exploiting" and "instrumentalizing" that Mass to reinforce divergences in the Church,

---

[12] Pope Benedict XVI, Letter to Bishops on the Occasion of the Publication of the Motu Propio on the Use of the Roman Liturgy Prior to the Reform of 1970 *Summorum Pontificum* (July 7, 2007), https://www.vatican.va/content/benedict-xvi/en/letters/2007/documents/hf_ben-xvi_let_20070707_lettera-vescovi.html.

[13] Fr. Gerald E. Murray, "Is This What the Church Needs Just Now?" *The Catholic Thing*, July 20, 2021, https://www.thecatholicthing.org/2021/07/20/is-this-what-the-church-needs-just-now/.

encouraging disagreements that risk dividing the Church. They reject the liturgical reform, Vatican II, the Church, and her institutions.

Even granting that this is an accurate description—which I do not think is true—is the proper response to the abuse of something good in and of itself the suppression of that good? Isn't the proper response to address those supposed attitudes by engaging in a serene and respectful dialogue that seeks mutual understanding and common commitment to striving for what is good for the Church?

Now, because some people who like the Extraordinary Form Mass do not share an enthusiasm for the new liturgical forms and raise questions about the proper interpretation of Vatican II, *Traditionis Custodes* mandates that no one will be allowed to attend this Mass in their parish church from now on, though the diocesan bishop can dispense from this prohibition (canon 85). Isn't that overkill?

**How convincing is Pope Francis's comparison (in his accompanying letter to bishops) between his new measures and those adopted by Pope St. Pius V in 1570?**
I do not find Pope Francis's comparison to be convincing at all. I agree with Bishop Athanasius Schneider who wrote,

> Throughout history, the true pastoral attitude has been one of tolerance and respect towards a diversity of liturgical forms, provided they express the integrity of the

Catholic Faith, the dignity and sacredness of the ritual forms, and that they bear true spiritual fruit in the lives of the faithful. In the past, the Roman Church acknowledged the diversity of expressions in its *lex orandi*. In the apostolic constitution promulgating the Tridentine Liturgy, *Quo Primum* (1570), Pope Pius V, in approving all those liturgical expressions of the Roman Church that were more than two hundred years old, recognized them as an equally worthy and legitimate expression of the *lex orandi* of the Roman Church. In this bull, Pope Pius V stated that he in no wise rescinds other legitimate liturgical expressions within the Roman Church. The liturgical form of the Roman Church that was valid until the reform of Paul VI did not arise with Pius V, but was substantially unchanged even centuries before the Council of Trent.[14]

Pope Francis's decision is a rejection of the very Mass that Pope Pius V sought to maintain and purify of accretions lacking in antiquity, all the while preserving other venerable Western rites such as, for example, the ancient Ambrosian Rite of Milan.

***How would you explain the importance and magnitude of* Traditionis Custodes *to Catholics who have no particular attachment to the Traditional Latin Mass and who attend the***

---

[14] Diane Montagna, "Tradition Betrayed: Diane Montagna Interviews Bishop Schneider on 'Traditionis Custodes,'" The Remnant, July 23, 2021, https://remnantnewspaper.com/web/index.php/articles/item/5493-tradition-betrayed-diane-montagna-interviews-bishop-schneider-on-traditionis-custodes.

***New Mass? Why should it matter to them?***
Pope John Paul II and Pope Benedict XVI showed great pastoral charity in making room in the Church, the household of faith, for those Catholics who were disappointed with the liturgical reforms following the Second Vatican Council. Those charitable provisions allowed great freedom for priests to respond to requests from the faithful to have the Traditional Latin Mass at their parishes. Now Pope Francis has forbidden the celebration of this Mass in parish churches and has given bishops the power to forbid this Mass to be celebrated at all in their dioceses. Bishops who do this will deprive people of an opportunity for prayerful worship according to the rite of the Mass used so fruitfully for more than a millennium in the Latin Rite Church. This is completely uncalled for and will cause great anguish for faithful Catholics who love the Latin Mass and are not, in my experience, instrumentalizing the Mass for purposes of disunity. Live and let live should apply to the celebration of the ancient form of Catholic worship that plainly has inspired and enriched the lives of so many of the faithful.

It is regrettable that there appears to have been no consultation and dialogue with the priests and faithful attached to the traditional liturgy before the Pope's decision. As I told the *National Catholic Register*:

> Such a dialogue would have allowed Pope Francis to test his conclusions about the thinking and motives of those who love the traditional Latin Mass. I think it would have been demonstrated that the vast majority of such priests and faithful are devoted Catholics who are united to the Church and who respectfully want to

promote reverent worship and are not undermining the unity of the Church when they pose questions about the liturgical reform and other matters decided upon at the Second Vatican Council.[15]

**Faithful Catholics, even those with no particular interest in the Traditional Latin Mass, are dismayed that Francis has wielded his authority so strongly against it, but not against LGBT Masses, or against notorious heretics and immoral priests and bishops. What does the present situation teach us about the respect owed to the pope?**

Catholics owe filial respect and obedience to the pope who is the successor of St. Peter and the Vicar of Christ. One way we show that respect is by always speaking the truth in charity, particularly when we are convinced, with good reason, that the pope has made a mistake. Pope Francis's indulgence of those promoting heretical teachings such as the German hierarchy or those promoting immoral behavior, such as Fr. James Martin, S.J., and others who endorse the homosexual lifestyle, stands in stark contrast with his rather dismissive and harsh treatment of those who love the Traditional Latin Mass. It is only right to beseech him to explain this stark contrast that seems to imply that he considers the Latin Mass to be a greater threat to the unity of the Church than those who would obliterate her dogmatic and

---

[15] Judy Roberts, "U.S. Bishops Weigh Next Steps on Traditional Latin Mass While Others Fear Further Division," *National Catholic Register*, July 19, 2021, https://www.ncregister.com/news/us-bishops-weigh-next-steps-on-traditional-latin-mass-while-others-fear-further-division.

moral teaching. Recall that after receiving sharp and persistent criticism from lay people, Pope Francis himself admitted his error in promoting the Chilean bishop Juan Barros, who was involved in protecting the sexually abusive priest Fr. Fernando Karadima, who was defrocked by Pope Francis and died at age 90 in July 2021. Their complaints led to an investigation that convinced the pope to remove Barros from his diocese.

***Could the pope theoretically impose the same kind of sweeping changes Paul VI introduced in 1969 upon the Byzantine Rite (or another eastern liturgy)?***
He has that power, but it would be extremely unwise to engage in such behavior that would immediately alienate most Byzantine Rite Catholics and would likewise be interpreted as a demonstration of Roman disrespect for the liturgical heritage of the Eastern Churches, both Catholic and Orthodox.

***Let's look at* Traditionis Custodes *in more detail. Pope Francis's document seems to treat the ability to celebrate the Traditional Latin Mass as a "faculty" that needs permission from a bishop, whereas* Summorum Pontificum *indicates that every priest who has faculties to celebrate the New Mass automatically has faculties to celebrate the Old Mass (since they are two forms of the same rite). How should priests act in light of this difference?***
Priests now have to seek "authorization" from the diocesan bishop to celebrate what was called the Extraordinary Form of the Roman Rite by Pope Benedict XVI. Priests could formerly celebrate the Extraordinary Form Mass without such authorization if they knew Latin and had a stable group of the faithful in their parish who desired to worship according to that rite. They

could also celebrate the Mass privately without needing permission. Priests should now in obedience to *Traditionis Custodes* seek permission from their bishop. If such permission is denied, they should ask the bishop to reconsider. If a priest is unable to secure such authorization, he should appeal to the Holy See to overrule the bishop. We should pray the Holy See would act with justice and mercy in receiving such appeals.

**Traditionis Custodes *says that the bishop must consult the Holy See regarding newly ordained priests who wish to celebrate the Traditional Latin Mass.*[16] *Does this mean that the bishop needs permission from the Holy See before granting authorization to a newly ordained priest to offer Mass according to the 1962 Roman Missal?***

No. Consultation means consultation. The document does not say that the bishop needs permission from the Holy See to authorize a newly ordained priest to celebrate the Traditional Latin Mass.

***Does Canon 87§1 of the Code of Canon Law (CIC) allow a diocesan bishop to set aside all the provisions of the document?*[17]**

The diocesan bishop can dispense for the spiritual welfare of the faithful from those disciplinary provisions of *Traditionis*

---

[16] "Priests ordained after the publication of the present Motu Proprio, who wish to celebrate using the *Missale Romanum* of 1962, should submit a formal request to the diocesan Bishop who shall consult the Apostolic See before granting this authorization (Art. 4.)." See https://www.vatican.va/content/francesco/en/motu_proprio/documents/20210716-motu-proprio-traditionis-custodes.html.

[17] Canon 87 § 1 provides, "A diocesan bishop, whenever he judges that it contributes to their spiritual good, is able to dispense the faithful from universal and particular disciplinary laws issued for his territory or his subjects by the supreme authority of

*Custodes* that fall within his competence. This would apply certainly to the forbidding of the celebration of the Traditional Latin Mass in parish churches. He could also erect new personal parishes for the faithful attached to the Latin Mass if that would best respond to the needs of the people of his diocese.

***Why are people who attend the Traditional Latin Mass on a whole so much more faithful to Church teaching and morals?[18]*** Catholics who pay a lot of attention to the liturgical heritage of the Church also usually pay a lot of attention to the doctrines and moral teachings of the Church. They show an appreciation for the patrimony of faith has been handed down to us from Christ by the Apostles and their successors, the popes and the bishops over the centuries.

***In his accompanying letter to* Traditionis Custodes, *Pope Francis accuses Latin Mass-goers of causing division, and yet adherents of the Traditional Latin Mass, perhaps because they tend to know the Faith better, are more likely to push back against a pontificate that appears to be straying from the one true Faith. If that is so, aren't some of the words and actions***

---

the Church. He is not able to dispense, however, from procedural or penal laws nor from those whose dispensation is specially reserved to the Apostolic See or some other authority."

[18] Gregory A. Smith, "Just One-Third of U.S. Catholics Agree with Their Church That Eucharist Is Body, Blood of Christ," Pew Research Center, August 5, 2019, https://www.pewresearch.org/fact-tank/2019/08/05/transubstantiation-eucharist-u-s-catholics/; See also Fr. Donald Kloster, "National Survey Results: What We Learned about Latin Mass Attendees," Liturgy Guy, February 24, 2019, https://liturgyguy.com/2019/02/24/national-survey-results-what-we-learned-about-latin-mass-attendees/.

*coming out of the Vatican under this pontificate the more fundamental cause of division?*

The unity of the Church is a gift from the Lord. The Church is one in her nature as being the Mystical Body of Christ. She is one in her doctrine, her sacraments and her governance. She is one in charity, which is the duty we have to love God and our neighbor. Our union with Christ, "the way, and the truth, and the life" (John 14:6), is the root and source of our unity with all the other baptized members of the Church. So our hope for unity in the Church amidst the divisions produced by doctrinal confusion and a worldly spirit will depend upon Catholics embracing life in Christ through the faithful embrace of the doctrine of the Faith, in obedience to the Church's pastors, but only insofar as they also teach and embrace that doctrine. Any deviations must be pointed out and rejected. False unity would be the result if error and immorality were tolerated for the sake of avoiding confrontations.

*How can Catholics be faithful to Catholic Tradition while avoiding schism?*

By avoiding any break with the hierarchical authority of the Church, which is the pope and the bishops in communion with him. Disappointment and even anguish are part of following Christ and taking up our cross. Faithfulness includes accepting what we would not have chosen to happen but which God in his providence has allowed to happen. This does not imply passivity when the pope has clearly misjudged the situation of those who are attached to the Traditional Latin Mass. They must be like the insistent man seeking bread from his neighbor in the middle of the night (Luke 11:5–8). To speak truthfully about the mistaken premises and the manifestly harsh restrictions of *Traditionis Custodes* is an act of charity directed toward our chief shepherd. It is a call to him to rethink his decision.

**In his first public homily as pope, Benedict XVI said, "Pray for me, that I may not flee for fear of the wolves."[19] Those wolves have not gone away with his resignation. What affect do you think the death of Benedict XVI will have on the current crisis in the Church?**

That is hard to say. Pope Emeritus Benedict deserves our gratitude for his many writings in defense of the Faith of the Church. His liberalizing of the rules for the celebration of the Tridentine Latin Mass accelerated the movement in the Church to promote and cherish the liturgical heritage of Western Christianity. The spiritual fruitfulness of this pastoral decision by Pope Benedict is on display at any parish where many young people and young families come to participate in this ancient form of worship. Any curtailing of this living reality in the Church would be a tragic mistake.

**In March 2021, Pope Francis appointed Joseph Cardinal Tobin of Newark a member of the Congregation for Bishops, giving him an influential role in appointments to the episcopate in the United States and across the world. The Pope seems to be appointing former McCarrick allies to the Congregation for Bishops (Cardinals Tobin and Cupich). How do these two**

---

[19] Pope Benedict XVI, Homily, Mass of Installation, (April 24, 2005), https://www.vatican.va/content/benedict-xvi/en/homilies/2005/documents/hf_ben-xvi_hom_20050424_inizio-pontificato.html.

***cardinals figure into the internal subversion of Catholic doctrine and practice?***
The two new American cardinals on the Congregation for Bishops, Cardinals Tobin and Cupich, are well-known supporters of Fr. James Martin, S.J., and of a homosexualist agenda, meaning they have indicated that the Church needs to change the way she deals with the question of homosexuality. Presumably, now that they are members of the Congregation for Bishops, they are going to take a special interest in promoting to the episcopate priests who share their point of view. And I'm very troubled by that. Fr. James Martin is misleading people and causing people who have a homosexual problem in their life to follow the wrong path of embracing a so-called "homosexual identity." Homosexuality is not an identity. It is an objective disorder (CCC 2357–2358) that leads to sinful activity, which should never be promoted because such behavior is destructive and immoral.

The two new American cardinal members of the Congregation for Bishops do not, in my opinion, represent the majority view of the American hierarchy, but the Pope has decided to choose them, as is his prerogative. I would just hope they don't use their power to promote to the episcopate men who do not understand and embrace the truth of Catholic teaching, but rather embrace Fr. James Martin's thinking.

***Have bishops become too political or too taken up by the temporal as opposed to the eternal?***
One of the most difficult problems we face in the Church, and this is not something new, is that bishops often conceive of their roles as akin to that of politicians, which is that they act firstly

as men with power over others, not as shepherds and ambassadors of Christ. They use that power in a way that is not in line with the mission entrusted to the Apostles, which is to teach, govern, and sanctify the flock of Christ. Sometimes the teaching is erroneous, and the governance is absent, errors are not corrected, and outrages are not dealt with properly. People who are offended by heretical teaching are considered "troublemakers," and a bishop might think, "What do they know? Why are they complaining to me? What can I do?"

The local bishop in a diocese has a lot of power to promote the Faith and protect the sheep, but they often don't use it that way. And when some do, they are unfortunately not supported visibly by many of their brother bishops. Bishops need to conceive of their role not as the religious equivalent of a governor or mayor. They are like the shepherd who has a flock that he has to feed, guard, protect, and instruct. That's what needs to be done, and that's the main role the bishops have to embrace in their own dioceses, and then collectively. Too often we don't see that, and that's a problem.

**Younger priests will one day be bishops. What would be your advice to them?**

Younger priests have an obligation to continue their education and to read and study so that they have a much deeper knowledge of dogma and moral theology than they were able to acquire in their seminary training. And we're so fortunate that, through the internet, they can listen to great lectures. The Thomistic Institute is just one example. The Augustine Institute is another. The St. Paul Center for Biblical Theology is another.

I think priests need to know more. They also need to be more serious about the spiritual life. They need to have a daily plan of life which includes meditation and time dedicated to the Lord: praying the breviary, saying the Rosary, making a visit to the Blessed Sacrament—a whole spiritual program. Because if you're not grounded in a life of prayer, you're in trouble. You've got to go to Confession regularly, and you should get spiritual direction. All the good things they did in the seminary they should continue and even fortify. That will leave plenty of time for other things. The better you manage your daily relationship with God, the better you will manage your everyday life.

**You mentioned the proper identity of the bishop and that bishops need to be shepherds and not politicians. You've also highlighted what you believe priests should do, but what would you say to them about priestly identity?**

This is a good question. Priestly identity basically comes down to spiritual fatherhood, that you are the father of your flock. The analogy is not primarily with human fatherhood and fathering children and having a wife, but the Fatherhood of God. He is the primary model. God the Father sent his Son into the world and the entire life and teaching of Christ is the basis of what priests are supposed to do. But we have to see this as a mission that embodies a fatherly attitude towards the children of God, actual and potential. We care for them with a supernatural outlook focused on Heaven. We also need to be grateful for being priests because we have the opportunity to celebrate the sacraments and preach the Word of God. That brings great joy because you are preparing souls for Heaven and helping them to live a life on earth that is going to be personally fulfilling and consciously directed toward what is good.

Priests can get lonely, they can feel unappreciated, they can think that their bishop doesn't care about what they're doing, and they may be right in that. In other words, they can feel that they're not getting the positive feedback and appreciation that would make them happy, that is, that someone is recognizing what they're doing. That's where the spiritual life comes in. As long as the Lord sees it, which he does of course, that is what really counts. And he will send you many forms of encouragement; we just need to be attentive to those moments of grace.

**And aren't these struggles part of being conformed to Christ as both priest and victim?**
Yes, you have to say, "My suffering in my particular assignment, whether it's difficulties with parishioners or other priests, or the parish has no money, or loneliness: it is all a share in the Cross of Christ and is not to be rejected but embraced." A priest also needs to use human wisdom to say, "If I'm lonely, am I making any effort to go see people? If I feel exhausted, am I exercising, eating right, and getting enough sleep? Am I doing the things that I know are going to enable me to be a good shepherd?" And that's what we have to do. It's not always easy, but neither was Christ's life. Someone might say, "Well that was Jesus. It was easy for him." But Christ in his sacred humanity actually suffered, and when as priests we suffer, and we will, we need to join ourselves to his suffering.

On the human side, though, let's face it, there really are many people out there who do say, "Thank you, Father." We don't do it for the thanks, but it's nice when people say it.

## WINDS OF REVOLUTION

We have to learn to be like Mother Teresa who was praised every day of her life. She thanked the people and realized how their words show their goodness and gratefulness to God. Then just carry on.

**The winds of revolution seem to many to have been blowing through the 2019 Synod of Bishops for the Pan-Amazon Region. One major proposed change during that Synod, especially from the German Church, was to use the pastoral necessity of priests in the Amazon to push for an end to mandatory clerical celibacy.**

The movement to demote celibacy is part of the wave of innovation that we have been experiencing in the last fifty years. I think the Amazon Synod was transparently designed not only to gain married clergy in the jungle but also to extend that to other places in the Church, particularly Germany. I'm glad that Pope Francis upheld the traditional discipline by not even averting to the question in his response to the recommendations that had been given to him by the Synod Fathers.

The effort to eliminate the requirement of a celibate clergy in the Amazon was, I think, quite correctly recognized as a first-step measure by those who don't like celibacy and want to eliminate it from the whole Church. The logic they used was that, because people aren't able to receive the sacraments due to an insufficient number of priests, we need to relax the discipline, and that is not a localized problem only experienced in the Amazon. That's a problem that's experienced in many places.

The value of celibacy as upheld by the Church's Tradition and practice should not be set aside because of either of two things: either the notion that since people need the sacraments, the only way of solving it is by having married clergy, which is not true; or that it's going to be beneficial for the clergy to be married and we'll have a lot more men come forward to offer themselves. The priest is not primarily an administrative officer of the Church who carries out tasks. The priest is the living icon of Christ. The priest is ordained and receives a character that conforms him to Christ, the High Priest. He carries out certain sacred actions *in persona Christi* which other Christians who are not conformed to Christ the High Priest by the sacrament of Holy Orders cannot carry out.

It's a beautiful gift of Christ to his Church and is best embodied in the words of Consecration. The priest does not say, "This is the Body of Christ," but "This is My Body." The priest is acting *in persona Christi*, in the person of Christ, and lending his voice to Christ in order to pronounce these words and consecrate the Holy Eucharist. To make the priest the most effective icon of Christ in the sight of the world and in accomplishment of his tasks, he should present a living image of Christ. That is why holiness among the clergy is a first obligation, why priests should be educated—because Christ is supreme Wisdom. He knew all things, so we have to know as many things as possible in order to preach well.

We should also embody Christ, who is the Bridegroom, whose Bride is the Church. For Holy Mother Church, the priest, and even more so the bishop, stands in the place of the Bridegroom. Having a married priesthood is not essentially incompatible because the Church does authorize married clergy in the East and, by exception, in the West for ministers converting from Anglicanism and Lutheranism who petition the Holy See to be ordained to the Catholic priesthood. But priestly celibacy most fully represents the image of Christ, who was not married, to a world which is never going to see Christ until the Second Coming, but will see priests and will see that these men have a unique relationship to Christ for the accomplishment of tasks that Christ has given only to his priests.

**How do you respond to those often-dissenting prelates in the German Church who say the sex-abuse crisis shows that the Church should let priests be married?[20]**
The sex-abuse crisis is primarily a crisis of homosexuality in the clergy. A married clergy does not solve that problem. There is also the phenomenon of so many priests leaving the priesthood to marry. This crisis was definitely experienced acutely after the Council and continues to this day. This problem is related to an inability to live out celibacy, which many factors feed into. The Holy See, in its mercy and in its law, allows for the dispensation from the promise of celibacy for the welfare of the priest and, in the case of a priest who has already fathered children, for the welfare of the mother and the offspring of the priest, who will now assume full and public responsibility for raising them.

**Is the allowance of such dispensations a change to canon law?**
We've always had dispensations, but there is a crisis that is related to human frailty and also imprudence, often of priests who develop friendships with unmarried, and even married women, for emotional support. There are also some priests who

---

[20] Christoph Strack, "Sex Abuse Scandal in German Catholic Church Sparks Celibacy Debate," DW, September 24, 2018, https://www.dw.com/en/sex-abuse-scandal-in-german-catholic-church-sparks-celibacy-debate/a-45609846.

were never really convinced of the value of celibacy but wanted to be a priest anyway. Some live a double life and come to the point when they say they can't do it anymore.

**Statistically, most abuse happens in the home . . .**
Yes. Marriage is not a crime prevention measure in the sense of preventing all child abuse. The Church's crisis involves unmarried priests, and most cases involve homosexual behavior with someone who is already sexually mature. Certainly, it's an abuse of authority, it's an abuse of God's law, it's a gross abuse of the victim.

The problem is homosexual activity involving two sexually mature people, one of whom is an immoral and predatory priest and the other is an imposed-upon legally minor male who is sexually mature, meaning that he is capable of engaging in normal sexual relations and impregnating a woman.

Married clergy would introduce all the aspects of marital life into the clergy as a whole, and there are some benefits but also some significant deficits. The issue is: what does the Church consider to be the best way for her ordained ministers to serve as living icons of Christ among the sheep?

**Women deacons and women's ordination is yet another example of internal dissent which we've touched on briefly. Should women deacons be regarded as a camel's nose under the tent, eventually leading to what the dissenters hope will be women's ordination?**
A female diaconate, meaning women ordained to the first degree of the sacrament of Holy Orders, is unknown in the history of the Church. This fact reflects the Church's understanding

that Christ did not intend to confer the sacrament of Holy Orders upon women. The movement to ordain women deacons ignores this plain fact and claims—without support—that the completely separate historical category of deaconesses were, in reality, deacons. This is simply not the case. And I do believe that it is being used to lead the way to priestly ordination for women, something which is impossible.

**Why do you think Pope Francis authorized another commission on women deacons?**
The results of the first commission were never made public, which is disappointing. If the results were made public, people would have the ability to judge the strength of the arguments raised and whether there's a necessity for further historical research or theological argument over the matter. Previously the Holy See and the International Theological Commission had looked at the female diaconate and issued a negative judgment on it.

Why is there another commission? I don't know. In the political order, commissions are a way to park issues on the back burner. I hope that's the case because women deacons are an impossibility.

**Some argue that there's a sort of Hegelian spirit at work in the Church, especially with this pontificate, the idea that we've always got to progress to a point of self-realization. Do you agree with this?**
Hegelianism is at the root of so many modern errors because it treats what is true as simply a temporary attempt to know the truth and that what is true today is subject to further revision.

According to Hegel, there is a thesis (A), antithesis (B), then a combination of A and B gives rise to a new synthesis, and that synthesis then becomes a new thesis (A) waiting for a new antithesis (B). It's an ongoing process of auto-destruction and doesn't reflect the nature of reality. Hegelianism is a philosophical error that's been adopted by some who want to do away with absolute truth, with dogmas that don't change. But the Catholic Church has always said that truth does not change because Jesus Christ said, "I am the way, and the truth, and the life" (John 14:6). He is the eternal Word, the only Son sent from the eternal Father, and what he says is true, authoritative, and is meant for all ages.

Martin Luther engaged in a selective process of changing doctrines he wasn't comfortable with and claimed it was a reversion to early Christianity. The claim of almost every heretic is that he is not inventing anything new but merely bringing back to the surface something that had been buried "under the dead weight of tradition." This is a gross error because it involves projecting your own thought onto the past and claiming it as a source of authority. This then becomes an obstacle to an accurate understanding of how, in the providence of God, what is revealed and understood becomes better known and understood but does not change, as Cardinal Newman taught in his *Essay on the Development of Christian Doctrine*. Luther wanted to change things, whereas the Catholic Church wants to make things better known and understood by revealing their essence and nature more fully, not contradicting what was taught before but making it plainer and more evident.

*This brings us back to the German bishops. Some people think that the German bishops are an isolated case of radicalization in Europe, but it seems they might have much more effect than people realize. You have studied the "Fundamental Text" of the Synodal Way.[21] What knock-on effect is the Synodal path already having on the rest of the Church, and what effect could it have in the future?*

The German bishops are a perfect example of what Marshall McLuhan meant when he said, "The medium is the message." This means that what counts is not the product but the process. It's not so much that the "Fundamental Text" says this or that strange teaching, but that they are willing to produce a document that says those things. That is, they are engaging in a process of undermining the teachings of the Church while relying on *one* of those teachings to do that work, namely, that Catholics should pay attention to what bishops say. In other words, they are refusing to fulfill the obligations of their episcopal office in order to undermine teachings that they don't agree with, and at the same time, they continue to occupy an office that confers authority upon them, which is one of the teachings they do agree with. Therefore, the process that they're engaging in is heretical. It's a selective embrace of some teachings of the Faith while at the same time selectively rejecting other teachings.

The product is horrible. The German Synodal Path's "Fundamental Text" is, in fact, contradictory of Catholic teaching and would destroy the Catholic Church wherever it was

---

[21] Fr. Gerald E. Murray, "German's Schismatic Synodal Way," *The Catholic Thing*, February 22, 2021, https://www.thecatholicthing.org/2021/02/22/germanys-schismatic-synodal-way/.

adopted. It would make it a Protestant church, which is essentially a community which decides for itself what the Bible and Tradition mean. The mere fact that the bishops engage in this while still remaining Catholic bishops is indicative that this is an open subversion which is poisonous, because it's telling people to *ignore* the Church when it teaches some things but *believe* in the Church when "we" as representatives teach you new doctrines.

**The logic of Luther's principle of private judgment would seem to imply that doctrinal questions should be determined by popular vote. Do you feel this idea lies behind the proposed German Synodal Way?**
The German bishops, I think, are unduly influenced by their Protestant neighbors, not only by the fact that a large portion of the German population is Protestant, but that they as Catholic leaders pay a lot of attention to Protestant theologians and their understanding of the meaning of Christianity. And there is a lot of what we would call "me-tooism": "You teach this? Me too. You teach that? Me too." In other words, desiring to imitate them because they think this is the enlightened, rational, and progressive way that the Church must follow to interact properly with the modern world. And that is simply a renewal of Modernism, the heresy condemned in the late nineteenth and early twentieth centuries by the popes, especially by Pope Pius X.

What we have here is a basic refusal on the part of a large part of the German episcopate to fulfill their duties because they want to *change* what they're supposed to teach.

**The German lay committee is said to be very powerful and to be pulling the strings behind the bishops to some extent. In**

*the words of one German commentator, "The bishops have dwarfed themselves in front of the ZdK (Central Committee of German Catholics)." How can the ship be corrected when we have these opaque but powerful lobby groups working behind the scenes?*

Any group in the Church that does not support and defend the authentic teachings of the Church should be disbanded. The toleration of subversion of the Faith by officially sanctioned groups of dissenters does tremendous damage to the Faith of ordinary Catholics who come to assume that they too no longer have to believe what they were once taught to be unchanging truths of Catholicism.

*Many of these groups seem to be calling for a more democratic form of governance in order to push forward their agenda. Is democracy ever compatible with the hierarchical order of the Church founded by Christ?*

Democracy as a political institution is not the way the Church is organized. The Church is organized hierarchically, and sovereignty does not derive from the people. Christ willed to found the Church on Peter and the Apostles. It was set up such that the shepherds of the Church were first appointed by Christ, and then they were given the task of passing on to their successors that *authority* and *power* that they had received from Christ. They are, therefore, not elected officials who represent the flock. They are, in fact, men who have authority, as a shepherd does over the flock, for the guidance and feeding of the flock. Just as Christ is the prime Shepherd, so the bishops are shepherds under him, and priests assist the bishops.

On the other hand, we can say that, within the Church,

there is a spirit of *shared responsibility* for her mission. The fact that the laity do not elect the bishops doesn't mean that the laity are simply in a position where they listen to the bishops and that is all. They have the right and duty to make known their concerns about problems that they're experiencing or that they notice in the world or in the Church. It's not an offense for the sheep to turn to the shepherd and say, "We think you're leading us into bad pastures, and we're not happy about it."

Within the Church, ecumenical councils and other meetings of bishops *do* involve voting and discussions but, in the end, all of those discussions and votes only have value if the decisions are confirmed by the pope. And again, even though the pope is elected by the College of Cardinals, they *do not* confer his authority on him. The process of election is essentially a nomination of someone to the chair of Peter. When the man accepts their nomination, the Church teaches that he receives the authority that St. Peter had from Christ, as a successor of Peter. And it is not dependent on the continuing consent of the College of Cardinals. You can't recall a pope. And so, there are elements of consultation and voting in the Church—we have priests councils that advise diocesan bishops and take votes on questions before them. But the essential idea of democracy is that the people are sovereign, and once they have determined the governmental arrangements they want, then they get to vote on which people will occupy the posts of authority that they have established. That's not what the Church is.

**The pressure to change the Catechism on homosexual acts and the teaching that they are "intrinsically disordered" (CCC 2357) is something certain German prelates and priests have**

*been pushing for, including Bishop Georg Bätzing, president of the German Bishops' Conference.[22] This is clearly another part of the revolutionary storm the Church is facing. How should she deal with it?*

In openly stating that he wants to eliminate from the *Catechism of the Catholic Church* the teaching that homosexual activity is inherently immoral, Bishop Bätzing obviously violates Catholic doctrine. It's intolerable, and for a bishop to propose it is horrendous. If he really believes that, he needs to resign as a Catholic bishop because he is no longer faithfully discharging an office that he certainly accepted with awareness of the requirements of canon law, and according to his own sworn oath, i.e., that he would uphold the teachings of the Church about homosexuality and all other matters. This is a prime example of subversion from within by those who are meant to safeguard orthodoxy.

*Some in the Church in Germany were very powerful in promoting eco-theology and women's ordination and directly promoted having a pagan idol in the Vatican during the Synod on the Amazon. How should the laity and hierarchy be responding to this existential threat in the Church?*

The laity should make known to their bishops and to the pope that they reject these attempts to revolutionize the Church through changing doctrine and practice. It is, in fact, an obligation on the part of the faithful to defend the Faith inasmuch as it is in their power to do so. They will explain the Faith to those

---

[22] Edward Pentin, "Pressure Intensifies on Catholic Church to Change Teaching that Homosexuality is 'Intrinsically Disordered,'" *National Catholic Register*, April 20, 2021, https://www.ncregister.com/news/pressure-intensifies-on-catholic-church-to-change-teaching-that-homosexuality-is-intrinsically-disordered.

for whom they have responsibility, such as their children and family members. They will share that in the community. But they should also make known to bishops and to the pope when they think things are problematic—and there are a lot of problematic things right now. The Pachamama idol being brought into the Vatican was a horrendous aberration, and it should never have happened. The ceremony that was performed with it in the Vatican gardens was horrendous because the exterior appearance was that of an act of worship given to a pagan idol. People who kneel and bow to a statue are doing what pagans do to their idols. This is not right. This was *not* a Catholic icon. This was *not* an example of someone praying to the Virgin Mary, or to a saint, or to Jesus. It is horrible and should not have happened, and making known opposition to that sort of thing is a noble and praiseworthy act by Catholics.

**Scripture talks about the erection of the abomination of desolation within the sacred altar (cf. Matt 24:15). Some have suggested that the Pachamama was one instance of this. Others have suggested it's an example of the smoke of Satan entering the Church of God. How serious do you think the ceremony with the Pachamama was? And what do you think should be done in response? Some have suggested that St. Peter's Basilica needs to be reconsecrated.**

I would say this: the Pachamama incident, which had different aspects, was a horrendous imposition upon the Catholic faithful and the Catholic Church by people who are doctrinally confused. The act of prostration that occurred in the Vatican gardens and the procession of the statue into St. Peter's Basilica were unholy outrages. Pagan symbols should not be brought into Catholic churches unless brought there as an example to be preached against. The fact that the Pachamama statue was brought in and shown respect and included with items intended to represent the faith-lives of people from South America was, in my opinion, patronizing and outrageous. Having the statue at the Carmelite Church of Santa Maria in Traspontina was also an outrage because, as was done at the Vatican gardens ceremony, the statue was placed in the center of the main aisle of the church and people sat around it as it if were an icon of the Virgin Mary or a statue of the Sacred Heart of Jesus.

***In fact, several copies were placed at side altars as well.***
Yes, it was brought in and displayed in a way that the Catholic Church has only done with images of Christ or the saints. That was horrendous. The best thing that happened was when the images were tossed into the Tiber River by the Austrian layman, Alexander Tschugguel, because it was a bold statement and a prophetic action that the Catholic laity will not passively stand by while paganism is being promoted. The whole idea that somehow Latin American Catholicism is promoted by bringing into churches pre-Columbian pagan ritual items is a grave error and it should never have been tolerated by the Pope and his associates, and it was. It was a terrible mistake and the laity made that point. It was somewhat like St. Paul confronting St. Peter as related in Galatians 2, which is a holy way of acting even if it does risk causing some emotional bitterness on the part of those being rebuked. But it is still useful and good.

*Why are so few bishops standing up against the German Synodal Path?*

There are individual German bishops, such as Rainer Cardinal Woelki of Cologne and Bishop Rudolf Voderholzer of Regensburg, who have objected, but they are in a small minority. Gerhard Cardinal Müller, who is not part of the German hierarchy and is in Rome, has objected strenuously to it.

*And other bishops around the world?*

I don't think that most bishops are paying attention to the German situation to the degree they would if it were in their own country or a neighboring country. Some bishops probably agree with the German bishops. I think they're a small minority. The German bishops have, for various reasons, the most radical profile in the world's hierarchy, and the fact that the majority of their bishops are either radical or passive means that the leadership of their episcopal conference is radical and has no intention to desist on their own from their radical proposals. They are going to go as far as they can. The German Synodal Way is really a revolutionary assembly and they make no bones about it: they want to change the doctrine of the Church and the structure of the Church. And that should be of concern to everybody because it's dangerous.

*Do you think the bishops around the world should be paying closer attention to this situation?*

Yes, I think they should, and I think the Vatican should pay more attention to it. Tolerating people airing their proposals may be nice in an academic setting, where discussion in the faculty lounge allows for speculation on "how we would run the university if we were in charge." But the Church is not the faculty lounge. These are the shepherds who are supposed to be leading the sheep into good pastures beside restful waters; in fact, they are giving them bitter weeds and poisoned water, and are not giving them the true teaching of Christ. St. Paul says, "Jesus Christ is the same yesterday and today and forever" (Heb 13:8). Jesus's doctrine is not like a political platform that changes with administrations.

**One bishop who has spoken out forcefully is Archbishop Samuel Aquila of Denver, who took the unique and bold step of writing an open letter to the bishops of the world, warning them about the German Synodal Path.[23]**
God bless Archbishop Aquila! May his fellow bishops follow his good example.

**Will the German Synodal Path lead to schism? And do you think schism is a natural consequence of these revolutionary tides?**
I don't think the German bishops are going to announce that they no longer recognize the pope as the head of the Church or announce that they no longer will obey him. I don't think they are schismatically going to declare, "We no longer owe obedience to the Roman pontiff. We are the ultimate deciders here."

---

[23] Archbishop Samuel J. Aquila, "A Response to 'Forum I' of the German Catholic Synodal Path: An Open Letter to the Catholic Bishops of the World," May 13, 2021, https://mk0archdentacevyxl7k.kinstacdn.com/wp-content/uploads/2021/05/Archbishop-Aquila-A-Response-to-Forum-I-of-the-German-Catholic-Synodal-Path.pdf?fbclid=IwAR0_9mAYXDhMSxYKu8Dcq--zvvHiBaubOwJSjlpI9AwGG4MQJpPtQ0efy7s.

Because there you're getting into a heretical notion of rejecting papal supremacy in the Church. I think that like most agents of revolution who occupy positions of power, they will try to use the authority that their position offers them to undermine and subvert the organization that they lead, and they will hold on to the reins of power as long as they can in the hope that the higher authority will relent and let them do what they want. I think that will be their strategy. The reality is that if all the German bishops who reject Catholic teaching on sexual morality were to leave and say the Catholic Church is wrong, we're going to start our own Church, they would immediately become marginalized and trivial figures because they would no longer have authority over the Catholic flock and no longer be operating as Catholic bishops.

**Or have access to the money . . .**
Yes, they would lose the financing that goes to Catholic bishops through the church-tax system in Germany. I call this "subversion in plain sight." In other words, they're not operating in the shadows trying to undermine the organization. They're doing it in the newspaper and in front of the TV cameras. It's a disgraceful way for them to act given the oath of fidelity that they have sworn to uphold Catholic teaching. And they have a canonical responsibility to be in communion with the Roman pontiff and obey his teaching and commands as regards practice.

We're definitely in a very serious moment in the life of the Church, and we have to pray for the conversion of those who embrace anti-Catholic doctrines, that they will reject them. And if they don't, we have to pray that Church authority will remove them so that they won't be able to render harm from an official position.

*Are we living in an age of apostasy?*

We're certainly in an age of lots of people rejecting the teaching of the Church and losing interest in religion, and in prayer, and in the question of salvation. We live in an age of sentimentality in religion, where people think everyone gets to Heaven so that all that matters is how we arrange our political and social life here below, such that everyone gets the maximum degree of pleasure and enjoyment out of their limited time on planet earth. Part of the universal salvation error that we discussed earlier is to say, "Well, if everyone is going to Heaven, why insist too strongly on rules? Because these rules don't really have anything to do with whether you get to Heaven or not." That's a grave error. Not everyone gets to Heaven. The Lord warned about those who will be sent to the place of "weeping and gnashing of teeth" (Matt 25:30) because of their own culpable behavior.

**John Paul II often talked about a "silent apostasy" in Europe. Speaking at the 2017 Fatima Centennial Summit held at Buckfast Abbey in England, on October 12–13, exactly one century after the Miracle of the Sun, Cardinal Burke said there are diabolical forces working to draw souls away from the Faith into a widespread apostasy. Such forces have entered even into the ranks of the priesthood, he said, leading some pastors to offer "poisonous fruits" to "the very souls for whom they have been consecrated to care spiritually." Do you think the extent of the apostasy is now coming into focus, and how can it be stopped?**

Apostasy means a total abandonment of the Catholic Faith (CCC 2089), and it's quite clear that many priests and even bishops no longer teach and uphold in their teaching important elements of Catholic truth. That is undeniable because they themselves maintain that the Church should change certain teachings, particularly in the realm of sexual morality. The innovators indict themselves by their own words. They have created a mindset in which the Church's claim that her teaching is unchanged and unchangeable is treated as an illegitimate claim and is rejected by them. They maintain that their innovations are simply a new and welcome discovery of the true meaning of Christianity.

This is part of what Pope Benedict XVI called the "dictatorship of relativism," because truth is basically consigned to the realm of the dominant popular opinion of the moment. So if everybody unhesitatingly believed a certain teaching at one point in the past, and now they've rejected it, that teaching no longer has any force. It's also called "historicism," according to which truth is historically conditioned, i.e., what was true yesterday can be false tomorrow, but that doesn't involve any crisis because that evolution is, in fact, part of God's intent. The Church rejects all of that.

You also have the apostasy of people abandoning the practice of the Faith, not even engaging in any serious thought about her teachings, just simply confining religion to the realm of folklore and to being a spiritual coping mechanism for living in a difficult world; and now that the world is more modern and there's more freedom and people have fewer social constraints because traditional ways of life are disappearing, they would say, "Why would I bother with religion? If I need to find a coping mechanism, I'm smart enough to do it in other less constraining ways."

That's the apostasy of turning away from God and worshiping oneself, pleasure, money, and power.

***How do you think it can be overcome or stopped, if it can be? Or does it just need to play out?***

Everyone has their freedom, so they will determine what they're going to do. The mission of the Church is to try to influence people to do the right thing, and so, for believers, meaning baptized people who have been given some education in the Faith, the mission of the Church is to further that education and to try to help them to understand that the teaching of the Church is not subject to revision or modification in order to suit popular tastes of any age, and certainly not of our own which has devolved back into pagan practices in so many ways.

Regarding Catholics who are positively rejecting Church teaching, be they members of the clergy, or theologians, or teachers in Catholic schools, the Church has to clearly restate her teaching and then call these people back to order.

***And Catholics in the media . . .***

Yes, Catholics in the media who are using it to promote what they allege is updated Catholicism, but which is, in fact, contrary to Church teaching, need to be called to task. It's an act of charity to someone who is erring and leading other people into error or sin to call on him to stop that behavior and embrace the truth because that is what *God* wants him to do, not simply what a Church leader, such as a bishop or the pope, is telling him to do. That's fraternal correction in the Gospel.

The authorities of the Church, i.e., the pope and the bishops, enjoy in canon law the power to issue sanctions for people who are recalcitrant or disobedient, and those sanctions are designed to call them back to repent and to believe—and it's a matter of the good of their soul. Salvation depends on fidelity to Christ, and we are not the ones who invent the meaning of fidelity to Christ. Christ gave that task to the Apostles and instructed them to teach the brethren and to go out to the whole world.

This is why it's so serious when a bishop uses his authority to teach error, as in the matter of the blessing of same-sex couples. This is not a small matter of a difference of opinion. This is an abandonment of one of his responsibilities and a matter of particular urgency, given the promotion of homosexual "marriage" in the Western world. As the recent document of Congregation for the Doctrine of the Faith said, the Church has neither the ability nor the power to bless something which God has condemned.[24] Sinful behavior is not going to be approved of in any way, given any status, any positive recognition as such, or any form of blessing. Because if you bless something, you are indicating that it's good. Since the Church says it's not good, we're never going to bless it. For bishops to say the opposite means they have abandoned belief in what the Church teaches to be good and evil as regards human sexuality.

**How much did Vatican II formalize or help establish these revolutionary tides? And is the post-Conciliar Church on a trajectory of, to quote Leon Trotsky, "permanent revolution"?** The dynamic of change in the Church that was introduced by Vatican II was not intended to be a revolutionary rejection of all that came before the Council. However, as you indicate,

---

[24] See CDF, "Responsum of the Congregation for the Doctrine of the Faith to a *Dubium* Regarding the Blessing of the Unions of Persons of the Same Sex," Holy See Press Office, March 15, 2021, https://press.vatican.va/content/salastampa/it/bollettino/pubblico/2021/03/15/0157/00330.html#ing.

proponents of revolution seized upon the moment to illegitimately claim that Vatican II was the beginning of a new Church freed from old ways and teachings. The Holy See has fought back against these specious claims since the end of the Council, but without success in many areas. The German Synodal Way is a perfect example that some dissidents in the Church never take "no" for an answer. They keep trying to bend the Church to their mistaken way of thinking. The Church is not in a state of permanent revolution, but she is continually being attacked from within by those who reject her teachings.

**In his 1907 encyclical,** Pascendi Dominici Gregis, **Pope St. Pius X asked:**

> **But how the Modernists make the transition from agnosticism, which is a state of pure nescience, to scientific and historic atheism, which is a doctrine of positive denial; and consequently, by what legitimate process of reasoning, starting from ignorance as to whether God has in fact intervened in the history of the human race or not, they proceed, in their explanation of this history, to ignore God altogether, as if he really had not intervened, let him answer who can.**[25]

---

[25] Pope Pius X, Encyclical on the Doctrines of the Modernists *Pascendi Dominici Gregis* (September 8, 1907), § 6, https://www.vatican.va/content/pius-x/en/encyclicals/documents/hf_p-x_enc_19070908_pascendi-dominici-gregis.html.

*Are these revolutionary tides essentially Modernism proceeding towards Protestantism, which would eventually lead to agnosticism and eventually outright apostasy?*

We are witnessing a revival of Modernism in the Church today. It is essentially a rejection of God and his revelation and a worship of human intelligence and achievement in search of self-affirmation. Man, not God, is the measure of all things. It is spiritual self-destruction.

*In May 2021, the Vatican announced a "new method" for the next synod, titled "For a Synodal Church: Communion, Participation and Mission." Initially set for October 2022, it now comprises three phases (between October 2021 and October 2023 inclusive), involves two different* instrumentum laboris,[26] *and culminates in an October 2023 Synod of Bishops at the Vatican. What do you think the underlying purpose is of having a two-year synodal process? Is it, as the Vatican says, to obtain a comprehensive account of the* sensus fidelium *(sense of the faithful), or do you believe something else is at work here?*

The process announced for the next synod on synodality amounts to a two-year popular referendum on Catholicism. The pressure groups that worked with the German hierarchy to produce the revolutionary proposals in Germany will now have the world for their stage. Rather than bishops speaking together to find ways to promote the mission of the Church in our day, we will have a repeat of the "Call to Action" Detroit Conference in October 1976, which imposed itself on the

---

[26] Latin for "working document" for a particular synod or other gathering.

Church in America.[27] Radical ideas will be promoted and called the will of the people. Defenders of Catholic truth will be cast as self-interested and fearful protectors of their comfortable certainties who are unwilling to listen to the Holy Spirit speaking through the people. Revolutionaries in the Church have long desired a "Vatican Council III" to complete, what they call, the unfinished work of Vatican II. I fear that the two-year synodal process will be an alternative version of a general council, conducted in slow motion and guided not by the need to defend the Faith against modern errors, but rather aiming to incorporate those errors into a new, anti-Catholic creed.

**The announcement of a two-year process for the 2023 synod appears to reflect the ideas of Jesuit cardinal Carlo Maria Martini, who viewed synodality as a vehicle for questioning Church teaching.[28] Fr. Murray, is this the climax of the revolution?**

We shall see. It will certainly be manipulated by those who find Catholic teaching in many areas to be intolerable. Two years is a long time. And the object of discussion, synodality, is a vague and unclear concept, thus subject to widely contradictory interpretations. Simply speaking, a synod is a meeting of bishops. Synodality thus refers to things related to meetings of bishops. The whole idea of meeting for two years to discuss

---

[27] See Fr. Vincent P. Miceli, S.J., "Detroit: A Call to Revolution in the Church," *Homiletic and Pastoral Review*, March 1977. As reprinted at https://www.catholicculture.org/culture/library/view.cfm?recnum=4544.

[28] Edward Pentin, "Permanent Synodal Church—A Progressive Jesuit Cardinal's 'Dream' Come True," *National Catholic Register*, May 21, 2021, https://www.ncregister.com/blog/permanent-synodal-church-martini-dream.

what it means for the bishops of the Church to meet seems to be overkill. The unstated agenda must be a focus not on meetings, but rather on what is discussed at meetings. Thus, Catholic teaching will be called into question. Get ready for much unpleasantness when the spokesmen for the grievance lobbies line up for their turn at the microphones.

**In an interview with Vatican News after the announcement, the general secretary of the Synod of Bishops, Mario Cardinal Grech, said,**

> **For Pope Francis the** sensus fidei *[sense of the faith]* **best characterizes this people that makes them infallible** in credendo. **This traditional aspect of doctrine throughout the history of the Church professes that "the entire body of the faithful . . . cannot err in matters of belief" by virtue of the light that comes from the Holy Spirit given in Baptism. . . . Therefore, we must listen to the People of God.**[29]

**How much are certain figures in the current pontificate using uncatechized faithful to ultimately push through their heterodoxy and revolutionary ideals?**
The *sensus fidelium* (sense of the faithful) does not equal the results of surveys or opinion polls. The Church's duty is to listen to Christ. The duty of her shepherds is to faithfully transmit

---

[29] Andrew Tornielli, "Cardinal Grech: Transformation of Synod to create space for People of God," Vatican News, May 21, 2021, https://www.vaticannews.va/en/vatican-city/news/2021-05/cardinal-grech-interview-synod-secretariat-changes.html.

Christ's teaching. It is true that the entire body of the faithful cannot err in matters of belief, but history shows that in many times and places, a significant number of the faithful have fallen into error, and that a small remnant remains to give faithful witness to Catholic truth.

**What do you say to the lay people who are disheartened or feel abandoned by the shepherds for all the reasons we've discussed here and more? What do you say to the scattered sheep?**

The sheep should follow the shepherds when the shepherds are leading them into green pastures. If the shepherds are leading them into rocky soil, meaning teaching that is either deficient or contrary to clearly known and defined Catholic dogma, then the sheep should rebuke the shepherds and not agree with them on those matters. The duty of a loyal Catholic is to be submissive to the shepherds, to pray for them, to inform them of one's concerns if you think they are erring. If they actually propose things that are immoral, as in the case of the German bishops, who have proposed the blessing of homosexual unions, then we rebuke them forcefully and condemn that kind of grave infidelity.

**In terms of trying to quell the storm, critics often say that all we seem to hear are words and more words, but we see little action. Is it now time for concrete action to be taken to try to stop this ever-growing internal dissent, or should we stay on the ship and weather the storm? Or is it a genuine both/and for the Catholic faithful? As St. Thomas More said, "You wouldn't abandon ship in a storm just because you couldn't control the winds."**

God's providence is guiding all things, including the day-to-day life of the Church. When things devolve into major crises, we should remember this wise advice: "The main thing is to keep the main thing the main thing." Our unwavering union with God in his Church is the main thing we need to focus on. From that will flow any good efforts we can make to influence the course of events in the Church. Our fidelity must be absolute. God will reward our faithfulness with blessings that will overflow for the good of the Church and the world. A Jesuit priest friend of mine always ended his letters with these words: "Courage and confidence!" Amen to that!

*Chapter 5*

# STANDING UP FOR TRUTH IN A HOSTILE CULTURE

"Why are you afraid, O men of little faith?"
(Matt 8:26)

*At the climactic moment of Jesus's trial before Pilate, the question of truth is placed in the center by Our Lord himself. "For this I was born and for this I came into the world, to bear witness to the truth. Everyone who is of the truth hears my voice" (John 18:37). To which Pilate responds, "What is truth?" (John 18:38). Increasingly the very idea of objective truth is becoming seen as offensive and socially unacceptable. Educational institutions have become tools of ideological purification and the texts of the Western canon and the very idea of informed debate have become unacceptable. How do Christians respond to this weaponized relativism?*

Keep proclaiming Christ's truth as taught by his Church, with complete confidence and conviction that the truth sets us free from error and fear. The self-contradictory claim, "It is true that there is no truth," is made by opponents of Catholicism to preemptively disarm believers by putting them on the defensive. Relativism is an attempt to evade reality, creating an imaginary "reality" in which those with social and political power impose their ideas—coercively and even violently—on the rest of us. By remaining true to our Faith, we give witness to reality in its fullness. God's designing hand is found in his creation. His Word spoke to us two thousand years ago and continues to speak to us today through his Church. There is found our source of confidence and peace when the world attacks us.

*In recent years, this weaponized relativism has taken on increasing potency in that even once conservative governments, public figures, and institutions have succumbed to secular ideology or what many today call "wokeness." How can Catholics possibly withstand or resist this when those whom we once considered allies have now deserted the battlefield?[1]*

The collapse of the Western world's cultural and legal Christian inheritance marks the reentry into pagan brutality. The legal recognition and promotion of previously unspeakable moral

---

[1] An example is Boris Johnson, the prime minister of the United Kingdom and a once-conservative politician, who has more recently been adopting distinctly unconservative policies. In the June 2021 G7 meeting in Cornwall, England, Johnson said we need to "build back better, in a greener, fairer, gender-neutral way." As cited in Lucy Fisher, "Boris Johnson Vows to Build Back in 'Greener, Fairer, Gender Neutral' Way," *The Telegraph*, June 11, 2021, https://www.telegraph.co.uk/politics/2021/06/11/boris-johnson-vows-build-back-greener-fairer-gender-neutral/. Another example is the adoption in many Western countries of the same-sex agenda.

turpitude and vice is now undermining all aspects of moral and family order in the West. Children are propagandized in school, and powerful corporations use their influence to promote disordered and harmful behaviors. Those who resist this social and legal revolution are gleefully stigmatized as haters who must not be allowed a voice in the public square. In the West we will soon be in the same position in which believing Christians found themselves in Nazi Germany and Soviet Russia, and in which they still find themselves in Communist China. Fidelity to Christ carries a heavier price each day.

**As Christians, would you say this hostile culture can best be viewed as "enemy-occupied territory," as C. S. Lewis once wrote?[2]**

In part it is enemy-occupied territory, but there are people who continue to live and defend a Christian way of life in their countries, families, and social ways of life. They defend the inheritance of Faith in many places such as the Philippines, Africa, Latin America, and Eastern Europe. In the United States, the divide between red and blue states largely mirrors the level of religious belief and fervor of the different regions of the country. A hopeful sign for our nation is that most immigrants to this country arrive with and affirm traditional social mores and are largely supportive of our country's Judeo-Christian laws and heritage.

---

[2] "Enemy-occupied territory—that is what this world is. Christianity is the story of how the rightful king has landed, you might say landed in disguise, and is calling us to take part in a great campaign of sabotage." C. S. Lewis, *Mere Christianity* (New York: HarperCollins, 2001), 46.

**What are some of the causes of the loss of confidence in objective truth and people's doubt that truth exists at all?**
The anti-authoritarian wave of the 1960s has gone from questioning the authority of political and educational leaders to now questioning the authority of religious leaders and religion itself. At its root, it's an attempt to destroy what those leaders represent and, in the case of the Catholic Church, it's an attempt to undermine the ability of people to accept the Catholic Faith calmly and to believe it in a way that will give them confidence that they're doing something good. The idea is to say that religion is a bad thing and people don't realize it, but now we're making you realize it, so if you keep believing in religion, you're causing harm to others.

It's not a new idea; it's been around for a long time. But many people now in the Catholic Church are genuinely questioning the value and truth of Catholic teaching when they are told that it's producing cruelty and harm and bigotry against people. It's a destructive error to say that no one has authority to speak on behalf of God and that anyone who says that is deluded. And so we Catholics are considered the most deluded of all because we claim to possess God's revelation in its fullness, and so we're confident we can answer all modern questions that come up with reference to divine Revelation. The new authoritarians of the cultural left basically want to say everything is relative, and yet, at the same time, these enlightened and woke people claim to know better than we do on everything important. And so they are going to make us cower in the corner if we continue to insist that our religion is true.

*How has decadence and hedonism exacerbated the loss of truth?*

The unrestrained pursuit of pleasure is destructive of the natural order of things and the God-given purpose of human life. Hedonistic ways of life are selfish and lead to conflicts and hatred of one's fellow man. We are made to love and serve one another, not to use and exploit others in pursuit of self-aggrandizement and a misguided notion of satisfaction. Pleasure detached from morally good action is a diabolical trap that ensnares us in sadness and isolation. Lying about all this is the common tactic of those enslaved to sin. Truthful recognition of one's sins, followed by repentance, is the path to freedom and peace.

*What do you think are the greatest obstacles that the Catholic laity have to overcome in order to stand up for truth?*

Standing up for the truth will generally occur in the circle of their family, friends, and associates. There are some Catholic laity who will become public figures because of their positions in the world of media, academia, or culture. But the greatest witness you give is to those with whom you have the most contact, because you have the most opportunity to influence them. Those are also the people who are going to see your failures and the inconsistencies in your own life, and so you have to be able to ask forgiveness when you fail to live up to what you're encouraging others to follow. But that's part of being a Christian disciple. We learn even from our own failures.

I would say to the laity, have confidence that the teaching of the Church *is* true. If it is denied by everyone in the room, that doesn't mean it's any less true. It's just not appreciated and loved by those people. But the saints in Heaven are a witness to the truth of the Faith, as are believers on earth. The Lord warned us that times would get bad. He said, "When the Son of man comes, will he find faith on earth?" (Luke 18:8). He wouldn't ask that question if he wasn't giving us a warning that such an eventuality is a distinct possibility.

My attitude is this: religion as a sociological experience—in which everybody belongs to the same group and has the same expectations—is not what religion really is. At the current point in the life of the Church, there are lots of people who don't believe in the same thing. So one says to oneself, "My duty before God is to save my soul through his grace." That means obeying his will so that he will lift me up to heavenly life, and, in the meantime, having the best possible influence on the people he places in my path. To do that, I need to be educated, and disciplined, and willing to extend myself in charity for others.

***In classic Catholic theology, it is said that sin darkens the mind to truth. It might seem that many people are blind to the truth because of widespread sin. What sins do you think most contribute to this inability to recognize the truth and have confidence in it?***

The first sin would be a lack of faithfulness to the First Commandment, the failure to acknowledge and worship God as the source of our existence and the ongoing sustainer of our lives. This is not so much on the theoretical level but on the practical level, when people don't think about God, pray, or go to Mass. That leads to a completely human-centered view of the world. It fosters a mindset that, in human affairs, the best way to get along with your fellow man is to not antagonize him or to give him what he wants as long as it's something that doesn't affect you. But that just falls into complete relativism. Because no one makes any truth claims, no one tries to enforce through law and custom a way of living, everything is up for grabs. But in that case, it basically comes down to a soft or hard dictatorship. Whoever has the most authority and power will force his way on others.

The sin of not referring everything to God in the first place is an obstacle to humility, which says: "God speaks the truth, I'm not the source of truth, I need to submit myself to it and try to convince my fellow man to do the same."

The problem begins first with individuals, but it is part of an ongoing dynamic within societal norms. As more individuals drift away from religion, societal forces emerge to encourage that movement and stigmatize those who remain faithful. As that continues and more individuals depart, the educational system becomes corrupted, such that religious people are not even debated with anymore but simply told, "You're out of the picture. Your ideas don't fit in the modern world." So that sin of failing to honor God, to not recognize his sovereignty and truth, causes societal chaos, which is manifest in individual chaotic living and thinking. This failure to honor God is now also manifest in "cancel culture." It's a very coercive movement to try to stop people from thinking and believing.

**What other sins do you believe most contribute to this problem?**
Greed and lust are main sources of problems in human affairs, and they are less restrained in modern societies than they were in times of greater religious faith. There used to be societal agreements about sanctifying sex and honoring it, and not

making it into a debased commercialized program, which is what we have now.

Regarding greed: in the Christian dispensation we are taught not to love mammon but to love God. We are also taught that we have to be generous with our neighbor. But what images do we encounter in our popular culture? Ostentatious wealth to highlight your own so-called "acquired value" in the world, i.e., the "I'm rich, I'm famous" boast of the rapper with a couple of pounds of gold hanging from his neck and wads of hundred-dollar bills in his hands saying, "I've got it made."

The point is that that kind of self-parody might have been part of a comedy routine in the past. But now it's commonplace in the entertainment world, where the idea is, "If you've got it, flaunt it," and that human success measured by material possessions is the highest goal to which one should aspire. That's become a big problem, because greediness causes people to engage in selfish and stingy and sometimes criminal behavior, and it causes people to miss the real point of life, and so we see people sacrificing family life for the sake of acquiring possessions, or making envy the subject of entertainment. People have always been interested in how rich people live, but it's gone from a curiosity in some people to an absolute "be all and end all" of their being. Greed is a very serious problem.

The glorification of celebrity culture is also a big problem. It really wasn't possible before television but now, with the visual streaming that is possible on televisions, computers, smartphones, etc., people can now do all kinds of things that are disgusting and self-abasing and really horrible on camera, in order to convince the world that they're famous because they've "been on TV," so to speak. It's idiotic. You have people committing crimes and filming it, and then putting it on the internet. Some of the people who rioted in the US Capitol Building on January 6, 2021, recorded their criminal behavior. This kind of exhibitionism and desire for publicity and fame is a real problem in modern society. This is particularly seen with children who get the wrong ideas. Then they record things they're going to regret for the rest of their lives, because it's out there in the public domain on the internet.

**Standing up for the truths of the Faith in Western culture is very challenging for many Catholics, who seem afraid to profess and defend the Faith they know and love. Why do you think this is?**
Some people do not want to have fights with their friends or family members who disagree with Catholic teaching on certain things, usually morality. Other people are confused because they aren't sure what the Catholic Church teaches anymore, following post-Vatican II disorientation. It's not that amazing that sometimes people will hear something said in a sermon and they'll say, "Father, I haven't heard that in forty years." It's all in the Catechism, but it's just simply not been taught or has been contradicted by some preachers.

We are in the midst of a long period of defective education and poor religious catechesis. People often don't know how to answer questions about the Faith because they were not properly taught or because they want to avoid a fight. Sometimes they are frustrated because they hear authorities in the Church contradicting what they thought they had learned earlier in life and which, in fact, remains Catholic truth, and that is most discouraging. For instance, when you hear a few German bishops say they want to bless homosexual couples, people say, "What's wrong with these people and why are they in charge?" It's a time of confusion, it's not surprising that people are not as assertive or calm or confident in defending the teaching of the Church. That's why Pope John Paul II wanted to embark on a New Evangelization, to get the doctrine out there, to get people to know and love the Faith and to have confidence in it.

***How significant (or not) do you think inroads into the New Evangelization have been?***
There are various movements, apostolates, and educational enterprises that are tremendous sources of strength for the Church. I would put Catholic media at the top of that list. My own experience at EWTN shows me how powerful that is for reassuring and educating people that Catholicism has not changed. It's the same yesterday, today, and forever (cf. Heb 13:8), and momentary problems are just that—momentary. I think men such as Cardinal Burke and Cardinal Sarah have a tremendous influence, as do the small groups that have developed media apostolates, educational apostolates, and prayer apostolates.

The sad part of the story is that, in the United States, the Catholic higher educational system, primarily Catholic colleges and universities, are grievously deficient by and large in communicating Catholic truth and a love for it, communicating an apostolic spirit to go out and spread it. It's a sad reality, I believe, that most Catholic undergraduates at Catholic universities and colleges end up as non-practicing Catholics upon graduation, and that is an indictment of those schools, which are firstly apostolates in the Church. They probably don't see themselves as such anymore, but that is what they are since they were created to promote the life of faith.

**I assume you are referring to some of the Jesuit-run universities in the United States, rather than newer Catholic colleges such as Thomas Aquinas College, Wyoming Catholic College, etc. How much do you believe the Jesuits are responsible for the decline of Catholic education?**

Yes, we would call them the "legacy" colleges as opposed to the newer colleges. It was very sad when Georgetown University chose not to put crucifixes in new buildings following Vatican II. That policy changed in 1998, due to the involvement of lay people, although the crucifixes are not front-and-center in various classrooms, and plaques accompany them to explain their "historic or aesthetic importance."[3]

In any event, when Catholic colleges have no problem with pro-homosexual clubs, abortion counseling, or involvement in various aspects of the abortion culture among students—and other horrible things that were previously unthinkable—these universities don't produce confident, believing, practicing Catholics. They produce worldlings who are more dedicated to worldliness. It's not right, and it's sad.

**Some lay men and women feel they need to tune out Church news in order to concentrate on family life and raising their children. That seems to be a very reasonable attitude for some people.**

---

[3] Laura Engshuber, "At a Crossroads," *The Hoya*, March 29, 2012, https://thehoya.com/at-a-crossroads/.

It is, and the primary responsibility of a mother and father is to raise their children with a profoundly Christian formation and education. But there is a role to be played by concerned lay men and women. People with money can finance other people to carry out activities. They can finance conferences, speeches, books, articles, and Catholic periodicals that are faithful to the Church's magisterium and Tradition. One can certainly always learn one's Faith better, studying Catholic theology and philosophy based on Christian principles. To learn those well will equip you well to do better whatever you are doing to promote the true, the good, and the beautiful. Think about a mom with several children. She's very busy but has a particular interest in art. She can study Christian art from the early Church and Middle Ages to try to turn that knowledge into a way of expressing to people the beauty and truth of Catholicism; and she can do that through personal influence or publications.

Prayer and penance are not easy but are available to everyone and should be done. The contemplative sisters praying for the Church and the pope and the bishops and the priests gain so many graces. We'll never know the good that's been done by them until the next world, but we know it to be true. For lay people, in their own way, to enter into a similar Christian way of life is very important.

**What would you say to the layperson whose Catholic apostolate involves demands and sacrifices that they think are justified but which put undue pressure on family life or disrupt it?**
When you work for a good cause, you should make sacrifices yourself but not impose sacrifices on your family that are

unreasonable or cause harm. This is the great dilemma, for instance, of Catholic writers and journalists and people like that, because the way the media works now, you don't write an article, mail it, and expect to see it published in three weeks. You write it now, and it can easily be published in five minutes on this or that platform, and they want it published in five minutes because they want to be ahead of the story. You have to learn to set limits. Workaholism is a form of escapism. It looks like you're dedicated, and in a certain way you're producing output, but you're doing it at the cost of your higher duties, which is to take care of your family and to put your own spiritual life ahead of your work. Prayer comes before work because prayer prepares you for your work, and prayer is your lifeline to Heaven.

*You don't buy the idea that "my work is my prayer"?*
No, *ora et labora* is the motto of the Benedictines. Pray *and* work. You can turn work into prayer by offering it up and by trying to do it with a recollected spirit for a higher purpose. Those things I believe in. But you can't say, "Since I worked all day, I don't have to pray." No, that's escapism. It's like a married man saying, "I was in the presence of my wife all day, but I never uttered a word to her. But she understands because I was busy." It doesn't work that way.

*What does the average lay person do when facing challenges to the Church's teaching in the workplace or in other situations? What does a Catholic office worker say, for instance, when the teaching that they hold dear is being assaulted by their colleagues and perhaps even their boss around the water cooler?*

Each person has to make a considered judgment as to how to deal with hostile co-workers. While we want to help others see the truth and beauty of Catholic teaching, we go to work to earn money to support our families. Anything that unduly interferes with or puts that at risk *must* be avoided. Silent and calm witness to one's belief may be the best witness when faced with hostility.

**How much does adherence to traditional practices and disciplines, such as abstaining from meat on Fridays or a more rigorous prayer life, help strengthen one's resistance to these secular pressures to conform?**

Giving glory to God always draws us closer to him and prepares us to live our faith in the midst of a generalized religious laxism and culture of unbelief. Taking Christ's example and putting it into practice in concrete ways is a means to becoming more Christlike and makes us receptive to the motions of grace in our soul. It makes us more solicitous for those who do not know Christ or who ignore his teachings.

**In one of his final talks before his death in 2017, Carlo Cardinal Caffarra said at a conference in Rome that Satan is hurling at God "the ultimate and terrible challenge" to show that he is capable of constructing an "anti-creation" which mankind will be deceived into thinking is better than what God has created.[4] Cardinal Caffarra helped found the Pontifical John**

---

[4] Edward Pentin, "Cardinal Caffarra: Satan Is Hurling at God the 'Ultimate and Terrible Challenge,'" *National Catholic Register*, May 20, 2017, https://www.ncregister.com/blog/cardinal-caffarra-satan-is-hurling-at-god-the-ultimate-and-terrible-challenge.

*Paul II Institute for Studies on Marriage and the Family in 1981 and was one of the four "dubia" cardinals. He also said that Sr. Lucia's[5] prophetic words—that "the decisive battle" between the Lord and Satan would be over marriage and the family— "is being fulfilled today."[6] How do Catholics witness to the truth in a world that has largely accepted what Cardinal Caffarra called in this talk "the culture of the lie," i.e., "the ennoblement of homosexuality," abortion, and gender fluidity, and which views faithful Catholics and others who oppose this agenda as intolerant or hateful?*

The Catholic Church has a clear teaching about the nature of the creation of man and woman, and that has come under attack, particularly in my lifetime, through the attempt to normalize homosexuality, and now the attempt to take further categories of sexual and psychological deviancy and make them into identities. Instead of just male and female, for which the identity corresponds to the body—which is something we never talked about in the past—we now have people who claim to be female with a male body, and male with a female body. There are those who then undergo cosmetic surgery in order to give the impression that they are not what they are. But that is window dressing, and it doesn't achieve anything but the mutilation of one's own body.

People who support that ideology tend precisely to attack faithful Catholics as being hateful, instead of engaging in reasoned discussion about their objections to "transgenderism"

---

[5] Sister Lucia was the oldest of the three children to whom the Blessed Mother appeared in Fatima, Portugal, in 1917.

[6] Diane Montagna, "(Exclusive) Cardinal Caffarra: 'What Sr. Lucia Wrote to Me Is Being Fulfilled Today," Aleteia, May 19, 2017, https://aleteia.org/2017/05/19/exclusive-cardinal-caffarra-what-sr-lucia-wrote-to-me-is-being-fulfilled-today/.

and surgery to remove or reconfigure sexual organs. The goal is to cower us into submission by claiming that we are hateful. Anyone who is doing something hateful is doing something displeasing to God. They are therefore claiming that we are being unfaithful to God by allegedly hating people who consider themselves to be "transgender." The only answer to this is to say, "You're wrong. I'm not a hater, and I may not convince you of that fact, but that's just the way it is."

**To what extent is it a serious hindrance in standing up for doctrine and morals when liberalism, which is the prevailing culture, seems intent on affirming people in their sin rather than lifting them out of it?**

The liberal mind largely rejects natural law thinking and allegedly proposes that everyone should be allowed to do as they please, as long as they do not infringe upon another's right to do as he pleases. What is not clearly stated is that anyone who disagrees with this view of life must be silenced and ostracized. It is permitted to tear down almost every moral and ethical norm of Western civilization, but it is not permitted to object to the ideological justifications given for this destructive behavior. The cancel culture is the transformation of liberalism into the vindictive enemy of all those who disagree.

**What do you say when a mother comes to you saying, "My son is 'gay,' but I love him all the same. Why can't the Church accept him like I accept him, i.e., for who he is? Why isn't the Church more like a truly loving mother?"**

To love one's son is to wish the best for him, which includes encouragement of obedience to God's law and the avoidance of whatever leads to sin. Those who choose to identify themselves as homosexuals and who embrace a lifestyle that includes the committing of the mortal sin of sodomy have fallen into a terrible error. They wrongly conceive that their inclination and decision to engage in sexual acts with persons of the same sex give them a personal identity that differentiates them from people who are heterosexual. This is the source of great confusion in their lives. The categorization of people as either being constitutionally heterosexual or homosexual, based on their sexual proclivities, is simply false. We are all heterosexuals. Some people have a problem with an attraction or addiction to homosexual acts. God created man male and female, with differentiated sexual faculties that are designed for the procreation of children. The inborn natural sexual attraction of men for women and women for men is designed by God to realize the purpose of the propagation of the species within a committed marital union. Any other use of the sexual faculties is disordered and sinful. Any inclination to seek sexual acts apart from natural relations in marriage is a disordered inclination and must be resisted. So the mother in question is mistaken if she believes that the Church should endorse behavior by her son that constitutes a grave offense against God's law in a matter of fundamental importance. She should rather encourage her son to renounce sinful ways and seek God's help to live chastity. She would do very well to encourage her son to seek fellowship and guidance from the Catholic apostolate Courage.[7]

---

[7] To learn more about Courage, visit their website at https://couragerc.org/.

**Fr. Murray, society is so different today than it was, say, in the 1950s. We now have so many broken homes, so many children damaged by divorce and broken marriages, and so many people lacking parental love and the formation that comes from that. Is it fair to apply a pre-conciliar doctrinal and pastoral approach to people who are essentially victims of the collapse of the family and seemingly not so receptive to traditional Catholic moral teaching?**

The proclamation of the truth is always necessary, in season and out of season, and becomes even more urgent when societal breakdown obscures the value of Catholic moral teaching and promotes the spread of immoral lifestyles, with the consequent unhappiness and disorder that result from turning away from God. People who have suffered because of the social prevalence of divorce, and now the acceptance of the homosexual lifestyle, need to hear a clear presentation of the truth that sets all men free from their sins and gives them the grace and wisdom to learn to live at peace with the crosses they have to bear in life. Catholics are called to witness to the truth of the Gospel, confident that their fidelity does great good for those seeking true happiness and peace in their lives.

**The greatest proponents of Pope Francis's pastoral approach, especially of going to the peripheries and his field-hospital analogy, would argue that Francis specifically caters to these kinds of people, for whom the language of traditional Catholic moral teaching fails to resonate. What do you say to this claim?**

I do not agree with this approach. It is not the mission of the Church to hide any part of the truth of the Gospel in the vain expectation that people will come closer to God when they are only told the uplifting and inspiring parts of the Gospel and left with the impression that the Church no longer insists on upholding the hard teachings. It causes great confusion when Pope Francis and others indiscriminately accuse those who defend the fullness of Catholic morality of being rigid rigorists whose zeal for God's law is really a mask hiding emotional problems. That is simply not true in the vast majority of cases. Catholic moral teaching is demanding because God made it so.

***How much does the transgender phenomenon derive from the problem of epidemic family breakdown?***
The mistaken idea that a boy who considers himself to be, or wants to be, a girl is really a girl is just that, a mistake. The origins of these mistaken ideas are multiple, and I am not a psychologist qualified to speak with knowledge and authority on that topic. But it is clear to me that before the sexual revolution and the greater prevalence of divorce in this country, the instances of so-called transgenderism were few and far between. Confusion about the purpose of sex leads to confusion about what it means to be either male or female. The dehumanizing of sex leads to dehumanized males and females who feel alienated from their own bodies. We are living in a time of profound social disorder that results from not honoring and respecting the natural order created by God who made our first parents male and female, plain and simple (see Gen 1:26–27).

***What should a parish priest do when confronted by a culture that is trying to normalize and ennoble homosexuality, such as when a homosexual couple comes seeking Baptism for a child in their care?***

That's a good question. There is no guidance from the Holy See so far about this specific question. There is guidance in the 1980 *Instruction on Infant Baptism*,[8] which was issued under Pope John Paul II, about baptizing the children of non-practicing Catholics. It states that if there is no reason to believe that the child will be raised Catholic by its parents, the child can nonetheless be baptized if someone else can supply a Catholic upbringing, such as a grandparent.[9]

The question here, however, is not simply about someone who is neglecting the practice of the Faith, but someone who has positively embraced something that is contrary to the Faith, which is scandalous behavior and which will daily be a counter-witness to the child. The traditional understanding is that sins against nature have a special gravity that doesn't attach to sins that are according to nature. Homosexual activity is worse than fornication because, in the latter case, you are violating God's law but within the created order. Homosexual activity is not only a sin against God's law but also a sin against God's order of creation.

By way of background, part of the dynamic of homosexual couples who adopt children—or when a child of one of

---

[8] Congregation for the Doctrine of the Faith, Instruction on Infant Baptism *Pastoralis Actio* (October 20, 1980), https://www.vatican.va/roman_curia/congregations/cfaith/documents/rc_con_cfaith_doc_19801020_pastoralis_actio_en.html.

[9] Instruction on Infant Baptism, § 30.

them is conceived with the aid of a surrogate father[10] or mother—is to create the appearance of normalcy for their relationship. They acquire one of the most important aspects of an authentic marriage, while nevertheless *not* being truly married. That is, children are a sign—or normally give the impression—that two people are married, because that's what married people do: they procreate and raise children. In many ways, they are using children, and their desire for children, to justify bad behavior and make it appear normal.

If a homosexual couple brings a child to the parish priest, saying they are civilly married and that this is their child and they would like to have the child baptized, in my opinion the priest should say, "What witness are you giving to this child by virtue of your gravely sinful misbehavior and counter-witness? Why would you ask the Church to baptize this child when you reject what the Church teaches about marriage and sexual sin?" Then I would engage in a discussion with them on that. I would be very hesitant to baptize such a child, but I haven't yet been confronted with this personally.

**If such a homosexual couple both profess to be baptized and practicing Catholics, won't this cause the child confusion not only about marriage and family but about what the Catholic Church teaches? And isn't it possible that the child will end up resenting the Church for allowing him to be raised in a way that contravenes not only the Church's doctrine but natural law, asking, "Why did the Catholic Church allow this to happen to me?"**

---

[10] Including through in vitro fertilization (IVF) and artificial insemination.

The Fr. Martins of the world say, "Well, in the case of a man and woman who aren't married, you will baptize their children, and they are giving a counter-witness." But in this case, their situation can be remedied if the couple decides to get married, if they are in fact free to marry in the Church. Or one can say, "The relationship is contrary to the doctrine of the Church because it's adulterous or fornication, but it is a relationship in which children can be born in the course of nature. Therefore, it is not a rejection of the divine creative plan but of the proper and Godly manner in which that plan is to be carried out. It is therefore less offensive than those who not only reject God's plan but also reject the truths on which that very plan is based, i.e., that sexual activity is never to be engaged in between people of the same sex, and that utilizing surrogate parents or adopting a child who has no physical relationship to either of the two men or women involved, is not a good thing. It's a form of child abuse, and I know that is going to be an unwelcome message with the pro-homosexual crowd who will respond, "But how can you say it is child abuse for two people who love each other to raise a child?" The answer is: people who lead each other into what the Catechism calls "acts of grave depravity" (CCC 2357) do not really love each other, because they lead each other into mortal sins that gravely offend God and his law. And people who teach a child by word and action that sins against nature are, in fact, good and wholesome, are communicating an anti-Gospel message.

**And for a child, growing up and seeing chaste affection between their mother and father is normal and good.**
Yes, and this is an encouragement and education to follow that example. But in the case of a homosexual couple, it would be

teaching a child to imitate their behavior, misinforming him and confusing him. The child doesn't have the psychological ability to handle the crisis that will beset him when he encounters other children with a mother and a father, and then asks who his mother or father is and why she or he is not there for him. The Christian education of children in aspects of human affectivity, and the nature of their bodies, and the difference between male and female—all this is taught and learned. But it's short-circuited and sabotaged when it's done in an immoral way.

I think the pastorally prudent thing is to say to a homosexual couple, "As long as you are living in a sinful relationship that is a caricature of marriage, you're not capable of raising this child in the Faith, which is the obligation incumbent on Catholic parents and that, as long as this relationship continues, the counter-witness you're giving doesn't qualify you to receive a positive answer to your request to baptize this child. If anything changes, please come back." By denying the request, you are also compelling them to question the imagined wholesomeness of their relationship. They are already aware that it's not blessed by the Catholic Church because they can't have it blessed by the Church. The Church won't and can't bless such a relationship. The Holy See recently reaffirmed that, even if some priests and bishops in Germany ostentatiously reject that teaching, thereby contradicting the Gospel and confirming people in gravely sinful relationships.

***Moving from the parish to the classroom, should a Catholic schoolteacher use a pronoun or name adopted by a "transgender" student?***

No, and the Catholic school should not admit students who claim to be transgender and insist on wearing the clothing of the opposite sex because that's completely false and disruptive, and it's in plain contradiction to the doctrine of the Faith regarding God's creation and his plan for creation. To admit such a student and then to go along with the pathology that he or she is now of a different sex—so that Billy, who now wants to be called "Barbie," is as much a real girl as Nancy who is sitting next to Billy—would be a disaster and would undermine the Catholic nature of the school.

Catholic schools should not admit students who are experiencing this difficulty and insist on dressing as members of the opposite sex. It is disruptive and unacceptable behavior that is in violation of the norms governing Catholic schools, which is that boys wear boys' uniforms and girls wear girls' uniforms, because boys alone are boys and girls alone are girls. The Faith teaches that boys and girls are what and who they are by God's design, and that's not subject to reworking by anyone.

***And the schoolteacher who is Catholic but working in a public school?***

If you are working in a public school, and it's a condition for your employment that you have to use an inaccurate pronoun to identify someone who claims to be of the opposite sex, you have to make the decision. Is it necessary for me to continue to work here for a serious reason? If I engage in this behavior, is it clear and evident to people that this is simply a matter of following the rules and not an endorsement of the rules? You could easily conceive of a situation where a teacher is one year away from qualifying for a pension and is presented with this case, and is told, "Any teacher who feels uncomfortable with engaging in this behavior will be subject to sanction, including loss of job." If the teachers' union isn't willing to defend the teacher and uphold his or her right in what is a religious liberty issue (but also a human nature issue), I could conceive of a case where you'd go along with this in an institution which is not representative of the Catholic Church, and at which it is necessary to maintain your employment in order to support your family and to receive the benefits that you worked for, for all these years.[11] You might also adopt the expediency of only referring to all the students by their first names, thus avoiding a fight over pronouns.

*How is that not compromising? How is it different than burning incense to today's idols?*
The burning of incense to an idol is an act of false worship. No matter what anyone may say, calling a man by a female pronoun is game-playing enforced by propagandists who want to make you believe that this is true, that you're talking about a woman when you're really talking about a man pretending to be a woman. Game-playing is not on the same level as false worship.

---

[11] Given the religious liberties guaranteed by the US Constitution's First Amendment, Catholic teachers and other employees should consider contacting, as needed re: workplace issues, organizations like the Thomas More Law Center (https://www.thomasmore.org/); the Becket Fund for Religious Liberty (https://www.becketlaw.org/); and the American Freedom Law Center (https://www.americanfreedomlawcenter.org/).

***But would it be lying?***
Lying is to speak against your mind. Using a pronoun that is inaccurate, but doing so on the command of the employer, is a bit like instructions to a sales clerk to smile and not argue with clients at a department store. In other words, if someone is obstreperous and abusive, your natural response is to say: "Stop it or get out of here." But your employer tells you that you have to say, "How can I be of further assistance? Can I get another salesperson to help you?"

***Although none of that is an untrue reflection of the situation. Aren't you simply continuing to be kind and polite?***
Yes, but we have to consider the corruption of language. The vast majority of people, and certainly Catholics, would maintain that only a woman or girl should be referred to as "she" and therefore you use "she" to refer to women, not to people pretending to be women. The reason why the school has to *instruct* you to obey the wishes of the individual person who wants to be called by the pronoun of the opposite sex, is because they know this is a change in the use of language that they are now compelling you to go along with. In that institutional context, the word "she" no longer means only women. It means women, plus men who claim to be women. So, the ordinary sense of the language has been changed, not because you agree that it can be changed or should be changed but because the authority figure is compelling you to use a specific word in a new way. This is coercive newspeak that is indicative of the totalitarian nature of the cultural revolutionaries who attempt to rewrite both history and nature. Our resistance to this may have to give way at times to the need to hold our job through formalistic cooperation without any internal agreement.

***Cultural Gramsci-ism?*[12]**

Yes, it's what the moral theologian Msgr. William B. Smith of St. Joseph's Seminary at Dunwoodie was wont to say: "Verbal engineering always precedes social engineering." In what I've said above, I've been looking at it from a legal point of view: How could I spare teachers who need twenty years to get a pension from losing their job at year nineteen because they don't want to call Billy "she," but must do so or be fired? Little William does not become "she" because he dresses up in a skirt.

**What should parents do if their child attends a school with an episcopally sanctioned sex-ed program that parents believe to be immoral or at least an occasion of sin? Should they defer to the diocesan bishop's judgment?**

No. If the parents become aware of a sex-ed program that is, in fact, an offense against chastity and modesty, they should ask the school to withdraw it. If the school says, "we can't" or "we won't," they should ask for their child to be exempted from the class. And if they say that's not possible, then you remove the child from the school.[13]

**And what do parents do if the local bishop or a group of bishops support little Bobby's being told that he can one day grow up and marry a man?**

---

[12] Antonio Gramsci was a twentieth-century Italian Marxist philosopher who viewed churches, charities, the media, and schools as organizations that needed to be invaded by Socialist thinkers.

[13] As noted above re: Catholic employees, parents should consider contacting, as needed re: employment situations, organizations like the Thomas More Law Center, the Becket Fund for Religious Liberty, and the American Freedom Law Center.

If Catholic schools are teaching immorality in the realm of sexuality, then you rebuke them by writing a letter to the bishop or making a public comment based on your definite experience, not your suspicions. Parents need to be actively aware of what books and other resources are being used to educate their children. Ask the school for the list of books being used in your child's education. If your child brings home a textbook which says, "the Catholic Church understands that not everyone agrees with her position on marriage. Therefore, the Catholic Church, while it does not perform same-sex marriages, understands that other people don't agree with us and will therefore support people in whatever decision they make"—no, you can't agree with that.

**In 2015, Cardinal Sarah referred to gender ideology and Islamic fundamentalism as "like apocalyptic beasts" similar to Nazism and Communism.[14] Since then, the beast of gender ideology has become a behemoth, and now, under the Biden administration, it's highly likely that gender ideology will become a normal part of the curriculum in public schools. What should parents do to protect their children from being indoctrinated with such sexually deviant social engineering?** Parents should find out what the curriculum is for each grade they have their children in, and specifically inquire as to whether theories that are in stark conflict with the Catholic Faith are being taught. If they are, they have to request that the school let their children opt out of those classes and go

---

[14] Edward Pentin, "Cardinal Sarah: ISIS and Gender Ideology Are Like 'Apocalyptic Beasts,'" *National Catholic Register*, October 12, 2015, https://www.ncregister.com/blog/cardinal-sarah-isis-and-gender-ideology-are-like-apocalyptic-beasts.

to separate rooms for other learning activities. The state has no right to propagandize children with ideas that contradict their religion. To claim that there are more than two sexes, or that one can become the other, is to contradict the Bible, and Catholic teaching, and human biology. Children should not be used as pawns in social engineering to try to convince people that there's such a thing as what used to be called a "trans-sexual" person and is now called a "transgender" person. By the way, this is a propagandistic use of language, taking a grammatical category of Romance languages (such as the French *la montagne* [mountain-feminine] and *le ciel* [sky-masculine]), which is arbitrary and conventional, and deviantly making it a designator for what is natural, that is, being male or female.

**Is it enough to request that your child be put into a separate room? Couldn't he or she still be exposed to the propaganda through other children? Would you encourage parents to fight to have such curricula banned from schools?**
My presumption is that these "transgender studies" will only be enforced in liberal jurisdictions where there's little chance of overturning it at the school level, certainly at the public-school level. I certainly encourage people to fight this, but, as we've seen, when the government wants to stamp something out, they use lots of means to accomplish it. When they want to promote something, in this case "transgenderism," they are going to use the same force and may have a certain amount of success, only because they have a captive audience.

***Would you encourage parents to take their children out of school and homeschool them if they can't get their children exempted from these classes?***

I do. I encourage homeschooling and co-op learning, where homeschooling families get together and then teach children as part of a homeschool program. The internet and modern communications make possible sharing resources and ways of communication that weren't possible in the past.

The Catholic school system was started because we didn't want children being educated in what was then a Protestant-dominated system that was manifestly anti-Catholic. Now, we're falling into a new era of manifestly anti-Catholic sexual immorality and gender studies, so the remedy may be building more Catholic schools, private schools, home schooling co-ops and whatever else is possible. For example, the US Supreme Court's 2020 ruling in *Espinoza v. Montana Department of Revenue* gives hope that parents can use their educational tax dollars, at least in part, to pay for their children's tuition at Catholic schools.[15]

***In recent years, in the United States, drag-queen story hours have increasingly been held for young children in public libraries. Would you go so far as to say that teaching young children gender theory in this way is child abuse?***

It is manipulative to take children and introduce them to theories that conflict with common sense and the religious

---

[15] See Andrea Picciotti-Bayer, "'Espinoza v. Montana' Is a Victory for Religious Freedom," *National Catholic Register*, July 1, 2020, https://www.ncregister.com/news/espinoza-v-montana-is-a-victory-for-religious-freedom.

teachings held by the families. There is probably more concern for not offending Muslim students in public schools by offering meals that conform with Muslim dietary regulations and avoiding history classes that would in any way cast a negative light on Mohammed's war-like behavior, than there is for shielding Christian students from being taught the absurd notion that God made Adam and Eve but didn't quite get it right in every case thereafter. That's probably a safe bet.

**In today's internet age, the scourge of pornography has affected so many young people. How might that relate to the rise of transgenderism and the normalization of homosexuality?**
Historically Christian societies have rightly banned the publication and distribution of pornographic materials because they undermine public morals and the innocence and purity of youth, and they are a destructive form of entertainment for adults. The sexual revolution of the 60s led to the attempt to normalize what is an abnormal use of human sexuality. Pornography is dehumanizing, victimizing, and is something that mocks, deprecates, and debases the natural instinct of sexual union of man and woman within marriage, a natural instinct which is sanctified by God through the Sacrament of Marriage. Christian moral teaching totally rejects pornography and insists on respect, modesty, and purity.

The modern world is dedicated to denying the proposition that reproductive behavior has something to do with reproduction. I don't like the word "reproduction" because it undervalues the procreation of new life by its analogy with industrial production. Nonetheless, it does highlight that sex between human parents results—by divine design—in new human beings. The natural purpose of the union of a man and a woman in marriage is the procreation of offspring, the natural fruit of their mutual human love. Everything about the way God made man and woman capable of transmitting the gift of life needs to be treated with respect, privacy, and reserve, because that contributes to the proper ordering and civilizing of the sexual urge.

The opposite is the case with pornography. It is a diabolical way of undermining the proper ordering of society where sexual relations are within marriage, and it's a private matter. It's not on public display and it should never be used as a form of entertainment through images and the like. But the devil works on human weakness. Women have a civilizing influence on men when they uphold standards of purity and modesty. When they surrender those to try to become more acceptable to ravenous men, we have a breakdown in all fields. Hence the need of a licentious society for abortion and contraception to keep this horrendous descent into chaos going. Selfie pornography is now the way to become a self-made celebrity. The idea that people record themselves in pornographic videos and share them is just horrendous, but that's what the culture has led to. It is horrid and disgusting.

### What do parents do?

First, if you believe in Christian morality, know that you'll be criticized by many other people. So stop paying attention to the criticisms. Don't worry if you're called a prude, and behind the times, and medieval. Ignore all of those criticisms. You want your children to be as happy as possible by living a good life.

*And what advice would you give teenagers?*
For teenagers, be independent thinkers, not obsessively worried about what anyone else thinks about your decision to follow Christ. For females, dress modestly and like a lady. Males should also dress with self-respect. Young men and women should look respectable at all times, such that their grandparents would be happy to have them come in the house and engage in a nice conversation. Don't bring disgrace on yourself by thinking that you'll become more popular by looking like the various entertainers we see on videos. Sexual pleasure is an attraction, but it's put there by God in the first place to make sure that the human race continues through lifelong marital unions. Food tastes good so that we want to eat, but you don't eat just in order to have the experience of taste, and you shouldn't eat in a disordered way. Sexual relations between man and woman is about bringing children into the world, and that's done within an expression of committed love in marriage. Certainly, the pleasure aspect is good and desirable, but it's for married couples and not for others.

**Parents have voiced concern that the Chinese-owned company TikTok is encouraging young people to experiment with bisexuality and promoting girls planning and carrying out at-home abortions. Do you have any particular advice for teens (and their parents) on guarding their minds and hearts from the deluge of filth on social media?**
Yes, know what your children are seeing on their smart phones and tablets and computers. Control their devices as you control other important aspects of their lives. Be the adult in their lives who spares them the agony, embarrassment, and

trauma of degrading themselves in the name of popularity, celebrity, or fame.

***As a parish priest, what three aspects of the culture affecting children and young people particularly concern you?***
I am concerned about teenagers and electronic devices. Socializing through electronic devices has become a substitute, and an inadequate one, for true socialization through friendship and actual proximity and time shared together in person. The specter of three college roommates sitting on their couch, each on their screen, texting each other in place of talking, is somewhat of a caricature, but it happens. The benefits to be gained through electronic media are undeniable. Pope Francis has a Twitter account that allows him to communicate globally and instantaneously with many people. That's all to the good. But electronic media can easily become an obstacle to proper socialization.

***Intellectual formation is somewhat compromised as well. We have grown so accustomed to getting immediate responses and having access to so much information that the whole process of critical thinking can be undermined by excessive use of phones and computers.***
That's a good point. The second thing would be that—through the internet—televised entertainment is available in quantities and diversities that was never the case in the past. So, you can waste a lot of time watching a much wider range of movies and cartoons and videos, crowding out the necessary time to read books, to see live performances, and to even develop an interest in those things. You end up with a group of people whose

reference points are shaped not so much by reading and direct life experiences of music, theatre, and public speeches, but by movies or music videos and the like—which are not going to allow you to understand the world in the sense that is communicated through traditional education.

The third thing I'd point to is overweight children. We have the paradox of a culture dominated by a fascination with sports, but children are not necessarily engaging in sports and receiving proper nutrition. At least from what I see in New York City.

**What particular dangers do you see for girls and young women, and for boys and young men?**
On the female side of the house, i.e., in the world of young teenage girls today, the twentieth century in the United States saw a great development in women's educational opportunities, which produced lots of important advances in various fields, such as science, literature and art, law, religion, and these are all to the good. Or you think of how many women were of great assistance during the Second World War because of their education and newly acquired skills. There are all sorts of aspects of modernity that, by giving women the opportunity to develop their intellect and abilities, are very good. But that's countered by the culture which teenagers are encouraged to get into, which is to pursue celebrity for its own sake and not to take learning seriously. People are talking more than ever with a wider range of people, but the content of the conversation is more vacuous than ever before. We're faced with the liberal paradox: we have the #MeToo movement to protect females and guarantee women's rights, and the same liberals are trying to

legalize prostitution by calling it "sex-work" and saying it needs to be regulated. Where's the common good here? The same people who say that the man who acts like an immoral beast at work should be fired, then say he should have the right to pay a woman to engage in the exact same immoral beastly behavior he was seeking at work, and that the government shouldn't get involved to stop this. This is crazy.

When it comes to boys and young men these days, there's little expectation of honor, and manliness, and responsibility. At least from my point of view, that's not being communicated as it was in the past. One of the starkest realities is the contrast between military recruits and their peer group outside the military, and the different ways those two groups speak, act, and think. Part of it is that the military has a clear notion of what it needs to do to protect the nation, and so they demand high standards. But even that is now under assault from the forces of political correctness and the like, much to our peril as a nation.

**You can't be sitting in your parents' house playing video games for hours.**
The video-game culture, the expectation that society owes you a living, and things of this sort all contribute to the problem. People say older folks always criticize the younger generation, but I don't think that's the essence of this critique. It's not simply a difference of age. There is just not the same level of responsibility demanded of young men in the 2020s as there was in the 1930s and 1940s. That's part of a cultural decline.

***What should a parish priest do about a cohabiting heterosexual couple who intends to get married in the Church but wants to continue living together right up to the wedding day?***

One of the things I've noted clearly since I was ordained is that the majority of the couples whom I prepared for marriage when I was first ordained in 1984 were not cohabiting. Now the overwhelming majority are. The explanation for this is largely that there is no social stigma attached to cohabitation, as there was before the sexual revolution and was still present in the immediate decade that followed, so let's say between 1968 and 1980. The social stigma lessened and lessened, and now it's almost entirely non-existent. So young Catholics preparing for marriage, or a Catholic preparing for marriage to a non-Catholic, are very likely to be cohabiting because that's what everybody does. And it's wrong.

When couples come to see me, and I've done a lot of marriage prep, I ask them, "Do you think this is right, or do you know that the Church doesn't agree with this?" Every one of them, without exception, understands that cohabitation before marriage is not in accord with Catholic teaching. Nonetheless, they want to be married in the Church because they understand the difference between cohabitation and marriage, and they want the benefit of the blessing of their marriage.

We are here to help sinners find God, including helping them to fulfill God's will as regards marriage for those who are engaging in behavior that goes against God's law. So I tell them, "You need to live separately in separate apartments, and if that's not possible, you need to live as brother and sister and refrain from sexual activity, sleeping in separate beds." Because typically, in high-rent Manhattan, couples are living together partially with a desire to save money because rents are so high. That's not the case with every couple, but with the majority it is. You tell them, "The sin in cohabitation is not being in the same apartment; it's giving in to the temptation to fornicate. So living together is a near occasion of grave sin. You need to get out of that near occasion of grave sin in whatever way you can" (see CCC 2353).

Another thing I tell couples is, "You're asking God to bless your marriage, but you can't ask him to bless your marriage if, at the same time, you're not willing to obey his law regarding what marriage consists of, by anticipating what marriage is before getting married. Live as you are supposed to while engaged, in holiness of body and mind, and then have your wedding blessed by God and his Church."

**How do couples generally respond to this?**
Most of them agree to it. I remember one couple saying they found it too onerous, but most of them agree to it. The Good Lord knows whether they are telling me the truth or not. When someone tells me they are going to consider what I said, or better, that they are going to put it into practice, I have fulfilled my duty to call them to repentance and conversion. The question remains, "What about scandal?" Because the problem is not only the personal sin of the two people involved but the scandal given to the community. Right now, in a big city, where cohabitation is a nearly universal practice in that age group, there's not much scandal being given on that level. There is certainly scandal being given to their parents and relatives who are Catholic and aware of God's law. We hope they speak with their family about what they are doing to prepare well for marriage.

One thing you realize as a priest is that Christianity demands a common affirmation of the good and the stigmatization of what is bad, and that the community has to support both of those aspects. When people join religious orders, we praise them or when young men enter seminary we praise them, because we realize that their sacrifice and dedication is valuable. When people live together without the benefit of marriage, we need to stigmatize that behavior. It seems nowadays the opposite is happening. People get the notion in their head that it's better for them to live together first because, in this way, they get to know each other better. Statistically, it's been shown that that's a disaster because you seek to enter into married life that is based on total commitment without time limits, but you're living in a relationship in which there is no commitment at all, and each person has a right to set the time limit by saying, "I'm outta here." Cohabitation before marriage does not make divorce statistically less likely. Whereas in marriage in the Church, even if someone abandons husband or wife, they are still married, and they know that getting into it. Observing God's law before marriage is good training to live God's law within marriage with the help of God's grace.

### *How is the law of graduality relevant here?*

This expression was used by Pope John Paul II in his 1981 apostolic exhortation *Familiaris Consortio*. He wrote:

> Married people too are called upon to progress unceasingly in their moral life, with the support of a sincere and active desire to gain ever better knowledge of the values enshrined in and fostered by the law of

God. They must also be supported by an upright and generous willingness to embody these values in their concrete decisions. They cannot however look on the law as merely an ideal to be achieved in the future: they must consider it as a command of Christ the Lord to overcome difficulties with constancy. And so what is known as "the law of gradualness" or step-by-step advance cannot be identified with "gradualness of the law," as if there were different degrees or forms of precept in God's law for different individuals and situations.[16]

The idea is that when the laws of God are difficult to observe, we don't bend the law. We teach people God's law and patiently encourage them to observe it.

Psychologically, there has to be a definite moment when we break with sin, in which we say we reject it and then we fulfill the Lord's command. The idea that people gradually work up to conversion: yes and no. Once someone becomes aware of the law, he is bound to observe it whether he feels capable of doing so or not. If he claims he is incapable of observing God's law, that's not a correct analysis. It may be that the force of habit compromises his willingness to observe the law because he is so habituated to the bad behavior. We need to keep encouraging him and, hopefully, he will arrive at a point where he breaks the bad habits through mortification, discipline, and

---

[16] Pope John Paul II, Apostolic Exhortation on the Role of the Christian Family in the Modern World *Familiaris Consortio* (November 22, 1981), § 34, https://www.vatican.va/content/john-paul-ii/en/apost_exhortations/documents/hf_jp-ii_exh_19811122_familiaris-consortio.html.

gaining more grace through other practices that help to us to grow in God's grace.

**And more light to see how it offends God.**
And to have a greater hatred for sin, which is the *only* legitimate hatred. That's something we need to cultivate. We're not supposed to dialogue with sin and try to find reasons why it's reasonable. It's not reasonable and it's ugly and it *does* lead to damnation and produces social and personal chaos.

**Radical feminism has led to many social ills, the worst being a seemingly insatiable worldwide demand for legalized abortion, the first anti-creation pillar mentioned by Cardinal Caffarra. How did we reach such a level of barbarity?**
The great error is to basically consider that the road to success in life for a woman is to become like a man, and as a result, to become convinced that you cannot be burdened with pregnancies because pregnancies sideline you and then they create an emotional and legal obligation to the child. You can see why radical feminism is based on the assertion of the right to contraception and abortion, and then on the right to divorce.

**It can put women on a path to being like men but often ignoring their virtues while imitating their worst vices, i.e., being brutish and promiscuous without consequences.**
Yes, sex without consequences, the reality that a man can have sex with an unknown woman, walk away, and that's it. A female can do that, but she may end up having a child, which changes everything in that woman's life. But some women don't see their unborn child as a gift from God. They want

to be like the man who walks away, so abortion is the escape mechanism. One of the worst aspects of rap and hip-hop culture is its degradation into sexual anarchy, with women trying to outdo men in the disgusting lyrics their "songs" contain. It's horrible, and it gets transmitted to teenage girls who often idolize pop stars and hip-hop musicians who are in fact sowing a mindset of self-destructive behavior. The hip-hop stars walk away with the money, but the teenage girls (and boys) walk away with what? Nothing, except their minds corrupted and their lives trashed. Thanks be to God that he forgives and restores us to his grace when we turn to him in sorrow for our sins.

Pornography and its associated evils are things that Christian cultures try to eliminate from the public square, but which "liberated" Western feminism and its allies want all over the place. One of the encouraging signs has always been groups of feminists who are against pornography, but of course while feminist leaders generally may sympathize privately with these women, they will do nothing to promote that vision because it contradicts their sexual libertinism.

Divorce is something that God doesn't want. We know that from the Scriptures. The union of Adam and Eve is exclusive and lifelong, and that's what marriage is by its nature. The Church can tolerate the separation of spouses for grave reasons. The culture now basically treats marriage as a temporary arrangement, celebrated as if it were going to be permanent but with no real expectation of that. If one spouse decides he or she wants out, they have the right to do that. The ones who suffer most are generally women and children.

The key to happiness for married couples is to embrace the truth that the union of man and wife, physically and emotionally, reaches its highest fulfillment, God willing, in the conception and birth of children. As priests, we say that in marriage instruction, and I believe it's absolutely true. But some young people, because of our social environment, say, "But what about leaving my options open?" And you have to say to them, "Close the options. There are no options. When you're eighty-five years old at the dining room table at Thanksgiving, that's the wrong time to say, 'Gee, I wonder why we didn't have any kids. Why didn't I listen to the lesson of two thousand years of Christian civilization in which childbearing is not a chore or a penalty but rather a blessed fulfillment of the divine commandment to be fertile and multiply?'"

**"Toxic masculinity" is often used as a term to deride traditional male characteristics that were once considered virtues, such as being a leader, protector, and provider. Is this loss of male virtue just another casualty of radical feminism?**
Those who promote the slogan of "toxic masculinity" are usually seeking to revolutionize societal norms so as to seize power from what they deride as "the patriarchy." This is a recipe for social breakdown and chaotic relations between men and women. The best rebuttal is to study and imitate the way Our Lord Jesus Christ lived, laying down his life for his Mystical Bride, the Church (see Eph 5:24–25, 32), and to learn from the great male saints who exemplified how men should treat women and children.

**Is there such a thing as Catholic feminism?**
The Church has always taught the fundamental equality of men and women as revealed in the account in Genesis of the creation of Adam and Eve. She who is "bone of my bones" (Gen 2:23) is

in no way inferior to Adam. So the Church affirms rights and duties incumbent upon both men and women. For women to seek to vindicate those rights might be called Catholic feminism, but that expression is very problematic as most people will reasonably associate anything called "feminist" with a whole series of demands that are rejected outright by the Catholic Church, such as the "right" to an abortion.

***What elements of a healthy feminism do you think are legitimate, if a healthy feminism exists? And what elements of feminism do you think have wreaked havoc on human relationships, the family, and society?***

The Christian vision of womanhood and the resulting cultural developments over time are a fruit of the revelation of God in the Book of Genesis, i.e., that in creation man and woman are created equal and for each other, and within marriage each person has to freely agree to marry the other. In other words, the woman is not an acquisition by man of something that is useful to him. No.

You come together and make your vows, and each has the exact same right to say yes or no. Flowing from that is a hierarchical relationship in which the man is the head of the household and the woman is the heart of the household, and is meant to support and aid her husband and her children. But by being the prime educator of the children and the prime civilizer of men, she has a vital and equal role and is in no way at the level of a slave. Not in a Christian household. In a true Christian household, women are not treated as slaves.

In society, as developed by the Church, the Christian education of woman has been noted since the beginning, and it developed greatly in Europe since the time of the Counter-Reformation. But even before that, the growth and development of female monasteries and associations of women in the Church to promote good works, which they direct themselves and are in charge of, is a sign that women are not mere accessories to men. They have the ability to promote the mission of the Church under their own guidance. Of course, we're all under the guidance of the hierarchy, because the Church is not an association of the sort where people decide what they want to do without answering to a superior authority.

In my case, my grandmother was a lawyer, my mother is a lawyer, my sister went to graduate school, and I think the education of women is very important and is one of the glories of Christian civilization.

The raising of children and the care given to orphans, primarily by women religious, is a sign that in the Church people accept responsibilities and develop talents given by God to promote the common good.

And I know that most men would be helpless without the aid of women. That's just a fact.

**How should the laity best prepare for the expected battle against secularism as it takes a deeper hold, and society as we know it possibly collapses?**
As a law-and-order man, I would say elect people who will appoint justices to the US Supreme Court who will interpret the Constitution of the United States according to the plain and natural sense of the words. Everything is subject to overthrow in human affairs, but the US Constitution is written in such a way that we have been able to preserve our union and freedom

and prosperity. And in areas where freedom didn't exist, such as slavery, we were able to remedy that. The hope for the United States of America is that the constitutional order will be upheld by the ultimate legal authority, which is the Supreme Court. It is a plain fact that voters in federal elections now are heavily focused on electing the right people to the US Senate and the presidency, precisely because they will get to decide who goes on the Supreme Court. We are ruled by justices, and not by elected representatives, in most important matters concerning societal arrangements that depend on law.

**Let's move to cultural Marxism. When Marx formulated his vision of the world, he saw it as a fight between the rich, the bourgeoise, and the workers, and for him the world is known in economic terms. However, with Antonio Gramsci came the idea that the world is not divided between economic levels but between the oppressor and the culturally oppressed. So Gramsci formulated the principle of "cultural Marxism," which is a culture of victimhood fighting against whomever they see as their oppressor. Ultimately, though, whatever is disordered or unnatural sees itself as oppressed because it will always be in the minority, although a coalition of social forces have come together in recent decades to mainstream various disorders and related sins, all in an attempt to undermine objective truth and therefore the Judeo-Christian foundation of the West. How should people respond to this cultural movement that we now see in all sectors of society?** My general advice, again, is to teach your kids to be independent thinkers, which is exactly the opposite of the cancel-culture mob of so-called "independent thinkers" who are straightjacketed into a group-think mentality that affirms that reality is whatever we decide it is, and everybody who disagrees is evil. We should never fall into that pattern of thinking. We should rather develop independent critiques based on perennial teaching about philosophy, Catholic theology, history, et al. The world of science refutes so much of these claims about bias and such: How can you have a "white mathematics" versus a "black mathematics"? Claiming that whites are oppressing blacks in mathematics is absurd. It has no meaning. There is no "white biology" versus "black biology."

One of the great advances of modernity is the increase in scientific knowledge and accomplishment, and the Church rejoices in that. Because to understand God's creation and put it to good use is part of the divine command to "subdue" the earth and cultivate it (Gen 1:28). It has to be put to good use of course, but to know better how God created the world and man is a good thing.

Cultural Marxists say that science is an oppressive element because it will not affirm, for instance, the false claim that there are not two sexes but rather multiple gender identities. If we say to people, "You're male or female depending on your DNA," then the cancel culture says, "Each person has the right to determine who and what they are." And you say to yourself, "Really? I don't believe that. To try to make me believe that is anti-scientific, and it's also coercive in the realm of thought." So, we've got to be independent thinkers and reject that. It's somewhat like the Chestertonian point of view, that the absurdities that we encounter have their origin in the first absurd one, which is the devil. Normality may appear to some to be boring, staid, and uninteresting. But, in fact, it is the most thrilling thing in the world. Discovering the way God made things and finding out how it all works, that's where we find meaning and purpose in life.

**The Soviet newspaper Pravda, a word which means "truth," was known by everyone to be propaganda and a lie. This was satirized by George Orwell in his book 1984. How is cultural Marxism fomenting propaganda and what people in Communist cultures would often describe as a "culture of lies"?**
The project to destroy objective truth and morality lies at the heart of cultural Marxism because it's their path to seizing power. Right now, in the West, the legal system, which is rooted in the classical Roman and Greek heritage as refined and developed in the Christian world of European life, is an obstacle to what the cultural Marxists would say are not crimes, but "necessary means" to restore their sense of justice. This basically means, "We're in charge of everything. We'll take all your money and property, and you have nothing to say about it." The obstacle to that is law, and custom, and ultimately the Christian Faith, which teaches us, "Thou shalt not steal" (Exod 20:15) and that we all enjoy "the glorious liberty of the children of God" (Rom 8:21), meaning we are created free to use our abilities and talents to learn the truth and live by it.

The radicals on the other side basically want to take over and make everybody into zombies who will do the will of the cultural Marxists. Their goal is that everyone marches lockstep behind them saying, "Take us to where you want us to go."

The everyday struggle you read about in the news to undo the accomplishments of Western civilization reflects this effort. They are very conscious of this. Why are they trying to burn down courthouses? They hate the idea that there are any rules that they don't make and that they have to obey. Most people like a legal order that affirms, "What belongs to me belongs to me and not to you, and you have no right to seize my property or coerce me into doing what you want." Cultural Marxists don't like that idea. It's a new form of Communist thinking and makes North Korea look like a boring version of what they are trying to accomplish. But it will have the same result.

Cultural Marxism will be resisted as long as free citizens, who love God, understand that they have to resist something which would destroy the good aspects of our civilization that need to be maintained and defended: law, freedom, true justice, and in the end, a society dominated by love of neighbor, not envy and hatred.

***How does the average Catholic resist the tide of Cultural Marxism in society?***
The best way to fight against bad ideas is to fill your head with good ideas, and then to share them with others. That's the long march in the good sense. If we embody in our own thinking and living the Gospel and just forms of social organization, that will radiate out toward others. One has to admire any citizenry that is serious about hard work, education, being a good member of society, and contributing to the welfare of those who are poor and sick. If we have all those things in mind, then we can carve out and maintain in our own personal lives a very balanced, wholesome, and joyful way of living, and that will radiate out towards others. One of the great contrasts in the United States is between the immigrants who want to get here, not so that they might riot and burn down buildings, but so that they can

get a job and support their family and make a better life for themselves and those back at home, and the typically well fed and clothed home-grown radicals with no apparent cash problems who want to ruin everything they find unacceptable for whatever reason. The needy and oppressed of the world are not coming here in order to tear down the US but to build it up, and that's what the people who are already here should be doing. Those dissatisfied sectors of society need to be resisted and not coddled. That is, don't agree with them in order to shut them up, because they'll never stop demanding. Dr. Seuss is only the beginning of the ones they want to cancel.

The cultural Marxist will also claim that any depiction of living styles, clothing styles, or other ways of life that accurately depict a foreign country is a racist act of "cultural appropriation," which implies theft and not admiration. Again, it's just another attempt to produce doubt and guilt in the minds of those who live good and ordinary lives, getting people to ask themselves, "Am I not really a racist?" Not because they are racist but because, if you can get them to question if they're a racist, perhaps you can get them to question whether they should be a Christian or a loyal American. It's an effort to break down their self-confidence.

**Antonio Gramsci, who as we noted was one of the chief protagonists of cultural Marxism, believed that one of the chief instruments to achieve his goal was education. Are we now reaping, particularly in the West, the fruits of a sort of Gramscian educational takeover by Socialist thinkers in schools, universities, and academia?**

I think we are. Certainly at the college level, most faculty members do not teach in the way that their predecessors taught a hundred years ago, meaning being grateful for living in a free society where they had benefactors who could build universities to teach young men and women the truths distilled over the centuries, not only in Western civilization but elsewhere, in order to build a better society. Large numbers of faculty members are now involved in grievance studies, which is a way to co-opt power by stigmatizing anyone who's done anything meaningful or been financially successful as somehow being privileged and illegitimately in possession of the fruits of his labor. That is a terrible, destructive way of thinking. It's an irony that, in a fabulous and expensive building donated by, say, an Irish-American millionaire who started out selling newspapers as a young boy, won a scholarship to that school, graduated and then made his fortune and donated a building, it's ironic that the professors and deans now sitting in the offices he paid for would put him on trial figuratively, and even literally, because he was an example of "white privilege" who "oppressed" others through his success.

This is nonsense. It's basically a racket and a scheme to take problems in American or European history and identify them as the source of everything that ever was done in those societies, rather than as things inconsistent with the basic values that those societies embody in their laws and customs. Those societies did have fundamental contradictions which they overcame over time, such as slavery in the United States, or a lack of equal opportunity for women in education and work, or anti-immigrant bias—things that don't reflect the Christian values of our country or the core principles of the US Constitution. Those glaring contradictions that were wrongly enshrined in law and custom we've eliminated, for the most part, with slavery and its Jim Crow aftereffects being the most serious example.

To say that because slavery existed in the United States means everything in America is illegitimate and that our society needs to be destroyed and recreated is wrong. Because our society itself extirpated slavery through a war that produced a tremendous number of casualties. To this day, our society is conscious of the need to enshrine in law and custom the equality of all Americans. The Civil Rights Movement was meant to get rid of the remaining legal and social attachment, especially in the South, to the slave-society arrangements. A country that has elected a black president and now has a black vice-president can't be a fundamentally racist society. It makes no sense to claim that.

**What would you say to young university students who are dipping their toes into Communist and Socialist thought?**
Know your enemy, but know your own convictions even better. Exposure to bad ideas is part of educational development, but the goal is to learn those ideas so as to better refute them through rational argumentation. When I was in college in the late 1970s, one of my friends remarked that the only author that every single Dartmouth student had read was Karl Marx. I think he was right. It is not bad to know what Marx wrote, but it is more important to understand why Marxist thought is so wrong and led to the murderous dictatorial regimes of the Communist world. The challenge is to learn the ideas that created Western civilization so we can appreciate more what has been bequeathed to us and pass that on to the next generation.

*How else is this hostile culture manifesting itself in America?* In the civil order, we face a leftist reworking of America. The prelude to that was the riots in the summer of 2020, and related attempts to rewrite history by eliminating symbols of that history. But I believe that we still have a free country where there are free elections and legal remedies to resolve disputes in the courts. Even as the constitutional order faces constant threats, American Catholics should continue to be forceful advocates for what is good, and true, and just in our country.

America, in its foundation and for most of its history, is a Protestant country, dominated by government leaders who are Protestant and share a general vision of Christianity which resulted in the maintenance of social and legal standards that were in accord with Catholic teaching by and large. Those standards are all coming under assault now because the traditional Protestant establishment became very liberal after the Second World War, if not before. The Evangelical wing in the Reagan era gained influence and then declined because it hasn't been able to establish itself as a replacement for the Protestant establishment in terms of its presence in the national experience. But it is important. The paradox is that the future presidential administrations most friendly to Catholic interests and concerns will be ones elected primarily because of the votes of Baptists and Evangelicals in rust belt, southern, and western states.

*A Chinese emigrant in Virginia who endured Mao Zedong's brutal Chinese dictatorship said that "critical race theory" being taught in schools is an "American version of the Chinese Cultural Revolution," and that the only difference is that they used class rather than race to turn people against*

**one another, denounce their heritage, and destroy all that was not Communist.**[17] **Many already recognize this as simply an old Marxist tactic, adopted by Saul Alinsky and others, to fan artificial hostilities and agitate to the point of conflict to achieve a specific goal. But what exactly is the goal here?**

The goal is, as always, the illegitimate seizure of power and money, in this case by browbeating a nation into denouncing its own basic goodness and surrendering itself into the hands of the enlightened leftist elite, who alone can absolve the people of their implicit and systemic racism. It is a con job, a massive fraud that has the support of influential sectors of society that seek to avoid their own condemnation by appeasing the woke mob. It is pathetic, but it is the reality of the situation.

**People are concerned about the rise of China as they see its increasing global dominance bringing seemingly unstoppable totalitarian threats to security, liberty, and human rights. How should the Church respond to this?**

The Holy See's secret agreement with the Chinese Communist government is one of the most ill-advised decisions I've seen in my lifetime in the realm of the Church-state dealings. Because it essentially surrendered the independence of the Catholic

---

[17] During the Chinese Cultural Revolution, Xi Van Fleet said she witnessed students and teachers "turn against each other" and schools change names "to be politically correct. We were taught to denounce our heritage and Red Guards destroyed anything that is not Communist: statues, books, and anything else," she said. "We were also encouraged to report on each other, just like the 'Student Equity Ambassador Program' and the 'bias reporting system.'" As cited in Michael Ruiz, "Virginia Mom Who Survived Maoist China Eviscerates School Board's Critical Race Theory Push," Fox News, June 10, 2021, https://www.foxnews.com/us/virginia-xi-van-fleet-critical-race-theory-china-cultural-revolution-loudoun.

Church into the hands of the Communist Party of China in the hope that this will somehow produce goodwill and better relations between Catholicism and the Chinese government. But, as is always the case when dealing with Communists, concessions are viewed as admissions of weakness or a refusal to resist, so they steamroll those who come to them hat in hand and seek their favor. The most recent example is the document the Chinese Communists issued on the Catholic Church in China and the selection of bishops. It makes no mention of the Holy See or of any agreement. That's not an accident.

The Chinese Communist Party, which seeks to control everybody in the country, realizes that the Catholic faithful are being confused by the Holy See's decision to enter into an agreement with the CCP concerning the selection of bishops. Perhaps they think those Catholics will become demoralized, and that may in fact happen. They also realize that when the Holy See concedes to the Communist government a significant say in determining who governs the Church, the temptation for their "partner" will be to mute criticism of the Communists when they do, in fact, violate rights, which is already happening, in order not to jeopardize the agreement.

For the broader world, the contradiction of capitalists financing the most brutal Communist dictatorship through purchase and production of goods in China is an example of the famous statement often attributed to Vladimir Lenin:[18] "The capitalists will sell us the rope with which to hang them." By nature, totalitarian states are aggressive, and if they have

---

[18] Lenin led the 1917 Russian Revolution and then served as the first head of Soviet Russia.

the ability, they will attack their neighbors. We are therefore in a difficult position where, rather than affirming the witness of faithful Chinese Catholics by supporting the independence of the Church, the Holy See has more or less trusted the Communists and said, "Let's make a deal." But no one I know thinks the Church has achieved any benefit from this deal worth speaking about.

**You mentioned that if they have the capability, they will attack their neighbors. We've seen that in Hong Kong. People are now standing trial for alleged violations for what are basically free-speech activities. In addition to prayer, what can Catholics in the West do for our brothers and sisters whose freedoms are being taken away?**
I think that Catholics in the free world have to remind the Holy See that the reason this deal was entered into was to gain results for the Catholic Church. No results are visible. The claim that we should be satisfied that we are now jointly naming bishops is a diplomatic pretense, because the Chinese Communist Party leaders have final approval on any nominated bishop. So it doesn't mean we are naming good bishops or that we are naming bishops who are doing the work of the Church rather than the work of the Communist Party. It certainly doesn't mean that the Catholics in China feel that they are being allowed to practice their faith in the way that Catholics in the rest of the world are able to, and they wonder why the Holy See would ever be part of any kind of arrangement to allow this to happen.

The Communist Party forbids the catechesis of youth. So how in the world could we say naming the bishop of a diocese means anything when that bishop is not allowed to teach the young people in his diocese the Catholic Faith, provided teaching young people is even one of his goals in accepting his nomination as a bishop?

**Generally, in Communist systems, young people are not allowed to attend Mass or enter Church buildings.**
Yes, if this were happening elsewhere, such as in a Western country, and the political leadership approached the Vatican saying, "We want control over the naming of bishops," they would be rebuked and told the Holy See safeguards its independence, as this is part of the gift which Christ gave to St. Peter to lead the flock. The fact that the Communist government is a dictatorship and won't be persuaded, means we ought to bide our time and wait for freedom to arrive there, rather than cooperate with an oppressive system in the name of paper gains, of having certain dioceses governed by bishops who, again, are almost certainly unreliable since they have to be approved by the Communist Party, and also know that they face arrest if they go against the will of the Communist Party.

**How do you view the more hardline approach of figures such as Joseph Cardinal Zen, who believes an appeasement of the Chinese Communist Party is useless? Shouldn't the Vatican be more seriously engaging with him?**
People are usually eager to defend what they think is defensible and explainable. That's what politicians do all the time. That's what professors do in the classroom all day. Churchmen have to be eager to promote the welfare of the Church, but they also have to be humble and wise enough to realize that the perspective offered by other people, particularly those on the

local scene, needs to be heard, analyzed, and perhaps implemented. To ignore or shun Cardinal Zen or others like him who say the Vatican-China deal is a disaster is not a sign of confidence in the arguments that can be marshaled by the Holy See. Therefore, humility and wisdom would demand that Cardinal Zen be brought in, consulted, and taken seriously, because it's not just the good of the Holy See's diplomatic efforts that is involved here. We also have to keep very much in mind the ordinary faithful and clergy of China, who are already suffering under a Communist dictatorship and do not want to see their Communist oppressors being given any form of unstated acquiescence in continuing on that route by a Holy See eager to maintain a deal.

**A deal which is secret . . .**
Yes, a deal which the Holy See has not—and apparently will not—make public. One has to ask oneself: did the Chinese Communists only agree to the deal on the condition that the Vatican keep it secret? We don't know the answer to that, but it's a reasonable speculation. It could also be that the Holy See desired not to make known the provisions because they are not ready to defend them from a hostile critique. The style of Church governance hoped for by many after the Second Vatican Council was that the mission of the Church would be the concern not simply of the hierarchy, but that their decisions would be informed by broader consultation with the affected faithful. The idea is to consult and listen to the voices of those who can offer, in a Christian perspective, varying points of view about matters dealing with the world and the Church. I think that's a reasonable way of looking at the idea of "opening the

windows," as John XXIII said, one that would allow the fresh air of different perspectives to come in.

One thinks back to the concordat with Germany under Hitler. The Holy See viewed it as a wise decision, but it was critiqued by others. Looking back, it was just another opportunity for Hitler to consolidate power, and it did not protect the interests of the Church in any significant way. In fact, it marginalized the Catholic critique of Hitler and made Catholics who were hostile to Hitler's government wonder why the Holy See would adopt such a position.

**Are Catholics today particularly disadvantaged in resisting this hostile culture because of widespread ignorance due to years of neglect in educating the faithful about our great history, our rich cultural heritage, and the Church's central role in the creation of Western civilization?**

A professor of mine at college said that students know where they are in space but not in time. People travel widely from America to visit European countries with rich historical monuments. How often, though, are those visitors largely unaware of the history of the countries they are visiting? Unfamiliarity with history and literature means that too many people walk through magnificent cathedrals with very little idea of why they were built or what is the meaning of the religious art found therein. We need to promote the study of our Christian heritage in order to appreciate how divine providence has been at work in our world.

*Cancel culture is becoming a buzzword of today, but the Church also has a history of this, i.e., censoring books and movies, e.g., placing books on the Index. More recently, we've seen such Christian censorship when, for example, Russia censored Elton John's biopic,* Rocketman. *When is cancel culture right and when is it wrong?[19]*

Society has always, and I think reasonably, judged that it needs to exercise censorship over certain publications and entertainments in the public sphere for the common good and for moral order. So, we do not have X-rated movies on broadcast television, depictions of gory violence are not shown as part of cartoons for children. Certain language restrictions are used. We do not tolerate the use of obscene language in certain settings, such as courtrooms or the halls of Congress. There are rules for decorum, how one can speak and act, and what one can display. In other words, government enforced restrictions on speech and video presentations do exist. The question is, are they in the cause of good order and justice and what is right and holy? Or is their aim to suppress free speech and ideas that would question the cancel-culture premises? The Left by and large is not against censorship. They are just against censorship that they don't control.

---

[19] In 2019, Italian media reported that €1 million of the Catholic faithful's offerings to Peter's Pence, a Vatican fund used "for the many different needs of the Universal Church and for the relief of those most in need," was invested in the biographical musical film on the life of Sir Elton John, *Rocketman*. See Diane Montagna, "Pope's Charity Helped Finance Sexually Explicit Pro-LGBT Elton John Biopic," LifeSiteNews, December 6, 2019, https://www.lifesitenews.com/news/vatican-uses-peters-pence-to-finance-elton-johns-rocketman/.

### Is unlimited free speech good?

No, unlimited free speech is not good, and Catholics have never believed it is, because certain things have to be kept secret. For instance, there's an absolute necessity in the Church for the priest not to reveal what he's learned in Confession. He should also not reveal the things he learns in confidential conversations. The cardinals take a pledge not to reveal what happens in conclaves. Restrictions are placed on speech for good reason and should be enforced.

As regards the debate of ideas in the public realm, this is where you get into prudential judgments. Typically, in Catholic societies in the past, the propagation of non-Catholic religions was restricted, and they were not given the same rights to promote their religious teachings as the Catholic Church was given. In the context of a society that is Catholic, where the vast majority of the population is Catholic and the system of government recognizes Catholicism as the official religion of the society, it's not unjust to restrict the expression of ideas that would undermine the Catholic Faith of the citizenry. That is a classical position of Catholic moral theology, but prudential judgments about how far that should be exerted and how it is employed in the course of governing a society must be made. Contemporary Catholic societies have to account for maintaining law and order and the common good in situations that may require relaxation of formerly stricter rules.

In a society where Catholics exist as a minority, the best thing that Catholics can enjoy in that society is to have freedom of speech and religious liberty, and that is something we would desire in Muslim majority countries, where they almost always have a very restrictive notion of what other religions can teach.

We would disagree of course and say, "God commands us to preach the Gospel." As a general proposition, free speech in a Western democratic society is one of the means for the Church to defend herself and propagate the Faith, and that's very important.

**What action, if any, should be taken, and by whom, seeing that most of the mainstream media is essentially propaganda for secularist values and the woke Left?**
I'm generally in favor of free speech and letting people sell their ideas and see who wants to buy them. The less government involvement the better because the government is allegedly a neutral arbiter, but we experience that that's not the case. The people in charge are trying to use government power to suppress opinions and even hide truths that they don't like. One of the best correctives of corrupt government is a free press because it can expose the corruption. I think that's part of the genius of Western Christian civilization: by stating that there is a truth not subject to the authority of man, the authority of man is first and foremost dependent upon what is true. Therefore, those who speak the truth in the face of human authority are, in fact, fulfilling a divine purpose.

**Even when the media itself becomes corrupt, then, you believe it's just better to let it self-destruct?**
Yes, because if there is freedom of the press and freedom of speech, people who are dissatisfied with the corrupt media will form their own. That's one of the great advances of the internet world, that you don't need the concentration of wealth you once did to be able to establish an effective means of mass communication. It's seen in trivial matters, such as influencers

on TikTok and Instagram who are selling fashion and beauty products at a pace and volume that used to take an enormous advertising budget. They can sell the same amount of product at a minimal cost. That means that, by analogy in the realm of ideas, Catholic media outlets with restricted budgets can put a platform out there and influence a lot of people in a way they never could previously.

**Cancel culture tends to foster polarization of opinions. How does this tendency affect people's ability to form friendships and dialogue with people with whom they disagree?**
Public shaming for holding opinions contrary to the leftist worldview of the cancel culture is shameful because it doesn't uphold what the Left allegedly wants to uphold, which is the little guy being treated fairly in society. And the "little guy" doesn't just mean people with no money in their pockets or those who belong to a racial minority or have immigrant status. The little guy is someone with an idea that he thinks is important and wants to get out there, but he has a lot of enemies or encounters a lot of apathy.

The Catholic Church's teaching on homosexuality is treated as bigotry. That teaching is based on the Bible.[20] Therefore, the Bible is a book that produces bigotry, and therefore anyone who believes in the Bible is a bigot. That's how the logic goes, and it is now being used in order to tell people to ignore the Catholic Church and not to read the Bible. That is a betrayal of what the Left is allegedly out there to do, which is to free people from oppression. They are actually oppressing people for exercising their freedom.

---

[20] It's also based on the logic of the natural moral law (see Rom 1:18–32; 2:14–16).

**What would you say to Catholics or other Christians who hear those arguments and become confused about what to believe? How would you reconfirm them in their faith?**

Number one, God is not a bigot, and God's Word is not bigotry. The question is, how do we know who God is and what his Word is? We say that we believe that God first revealed himself to the people of Israel and then to the whole world through Jesus Christ. So if you believe in Jesus Christ—which is what I want everybody to do—then you'll come to understand the importance and necessity of being a believer and of learning what God has revealed.

There is no contradiction between God's truth and justice, so if God's truth is that homosexual activity is wrong, it's not unjust for me to claim that homosexual activity is wrong. I'm not a bigot. I'm speaking a truth and acting justly. People will then ask, "Why do you say that homosexual activity is wrong?" The answer is, "Because God said so." They might then ask: "But why did God say that?" To which one can respond: "Because God did not make the human person to engage in homosexual activity and, therefore, he forbade it in the Scriptures, and the Church has, therefore, always taught that this truth has to be lived. It's not just words on paper to be thought about. It will cause many people who want to engage in homosexual activity to feel bad when they are told that the Church contradicts their desires. But that's good, because normally we feel guilty because we've done something wrong and need to repent. As God said through the prophet Isaiah, "For my thoughts are not your thoughts, neither are your ways my ways" (Isa 55:8).

We also know that God's ways are reasonable. It's self-evident that sodomy is a disordered use of the body.

Indeed, such acts are clearly contrary to the natural purpose of our sexual faculties.

**How can you help people to have constructive conversations with one another rather than simply writing others off because they have a different view?**
You need to embody in your own life the command of God to love your neighbor. We have to show people that we love them. As regards strangers, the way we show them love is through respect, listening, politeness, and kindness—an attitude of benevolence. In other words, we treat people as valuable and interesting in and of themselves because they are made by God in his image and likeness (Gen 1:26–27). We are therefore interested in what they have to say. On the other hand, we're not patronizing by agreeing with everything they say or smiling and nodding our heads and saying nothing. We try to engage in a conversation about why, while we appreciate them as a son or daughter of God, we think they're mistaken about some of their ideas, and if they care to hear why, we'll be happy to explain it. If not, we'll just leave the matter at that and perhaps renew the conversation at a later date.

**Many of the secularist policies diametrically opposed to Church teaching are being advanced by the current US administration and Congress led by Catholics such as President Joe Biden and Speaker of the House Nancy Pelosi (D-CA). Is this a sign of the extent of the apostasy and how should Catholics deal with this clear incoherence?**
It's certainly a sign that some Catholics have decided that the agenda of the sexual revolution is more important than the

religious doctrine they were taught as Catholics growing up, and which they seemingly continue to believe in, as Speaker Pelosi and President Biden continue to proclaim themselves Catholic and are proud of that fact. Yet, they treat religion as just another political aspect of their life, and they will say whatever they need to to obtain or maintain their power, their elected office. They will try to minimize or distort any teaching of the Church that is in conflict with the agenda of the secular Left. This is truly regrettable because it's obvious to anyone who knows the minimum about Catholicism that you can't *as a Catholic* first say, "I believe abortion is evil and wrong and a sin," and then *as a politician* say, "I consider abortion to be an essential woman's right that should be financed by the government because there is nothing wrong with it." You can't say those two things logically and maintain that you are a serious person. You obviously believe one or the other, and I think we know which one they believe.

**There's been some debate over whether Joe Biden is actually Catholic. Is he, given his many un-Catholic political positions? What does canon law say about this?**
He is a Catholic who doesn't follow the teaching of the Church. Once you're baptized a Catholic, you're always a Catholic. That is a canonical teaching based on sacramental reality. Baptism is an incorporation into the Mystical Body of Christ. It is an act of God administered by a human agent—usually a priest, but a lay person can baptize in a case of emergency. The question is, are Catholics always faithful to their obligations as Catholics? They aren't. If they embrace heresy, they become a heretic, but they are always called back to full Catholic unity and still

have an obligation before God to embrace those truths once again and reject their errors. Christianity does not consist of a self-defined, do-it-yourself set of doctrines. That's not the way Christianity was founded. It's sad to say, but after the Protestant Reformation, a significant part of Christianity embraced that position, and that's why you have thousands and thousands of Protestant churches where each one has a different set of doctrines from the next. The Catholic Church rejects that idea.

**Doesn't the fault in these cases primarily rest with the bishops and their failure to properly confront, catechize, and discipline such political leaders?**
Catholics who support legal abortion have to be rebuked and instructed to abandon this position because it's a contradiction of their obligation as Catholics to embrace the truth. If they refuse to do that, they should be treated according to what canon law sets forth in the provisions regulating those who are manifest public sinners—meaning that they are not qualified to be given the sacraments nor can they hold Church office, though that's not usually a problem here. The question of excommunication is a more complicated one. The bishop who has authority over the person would have to determine if the grounds existed for declaring that person excommunicated according to canon 1329 as an accomplice to an abortion, which crime carries an automatic excommunication according to canon 1398. That involves establishing a direct causal link to an abortion that took place such that "without their assistance, the crime would not have been committed" (canon 1329).

**Why are the bishops continually failing to take necessary action for the sake of the common good in the public square?**
The bishops are divided. We know that, and it was manifested in those who criticized Archbishop Gomez when he issued a statement on Inauguration Day calling President Biden to task for his position on abortion. Two bishops—Cardinals Tobin and Cupich—publicly disagreed with the wisdom of doing that. And we already know that the Cardinal Archbishop of Washington, DC, Wilton Gregory, has said he will allow Biden to receive Holy Communion if he attends Mass in his archdiocese. This is a very big problem that we have such division. And I have to say that the canonical case for not giving him Communion is airtight. There's no doubt that he shouldn't be receiving Communion. But canon law is not always treated as an obligatory category by bishops, and not only in the United States but elsewhere.

**Why is that?**
When they think it's to their advantage, they'll use it, and when they think it's going to cause them problems, they'll ignore it. And that's a big problem. We saw what happened in the child sex-abuse crisis. The claim they made was that the canonical provisions for dealing with sex abuse were inadequate until recent changes. That's simply not true. They were simply not used. They were not invoked, and that's a big problem. The recent changes are good because they make it easier to proceed against sexual abuser clerics, but the existing laws were adequate, just not invoked in many cases.

***Why was it so easy for them to ignore canon law through all of that and to still ignore canon law today?***
Because there are no independent prosecutors in the Church. In the civil society, the executive is subject to an independent judiciary, and within the executive branch you have the attorney general who is also tasked with monitoring people in the executive branch, so he has a certain amount of independence. He doesn't prosecute at the discretion of the president, so the president could, in principle, be prosecuted by the attorney general if he committed a crime. In a diocese, if a bishop did something against canon law, there's no provision in canon law for an independent prosecution of him by a diocesan authority. What can be done, though, is an appeal to the higher authority.

Basically, bishops enjoy total authority in their diocese subject to canon law and supervision by the pope. Many of them ignore canon law, and oftentimes the pope is unaware of, or doesn't choose to intervene, when problems occur.

***What is the role of Catholics in the public square, and how do we restore the influence of Christianity in civil and public life?***
The role of lay Catholics is to guide the social order according to the possibilities that are afforded them, in paths that are in harmony with God's revelation and natural law. We should work to establish the kind of justice, equality, freedom, and opportunity that are inherent in a Godly society ordered according to God's revelation, and this will take different forms.

We're not talking about a theocracy where the pope rules over the civil order in every country, but we *are* talking about Catholic citizens bringing Catholic teaching to bear on the laws and customs of a society. Because the plain fact of the matter is that one of the reasons why we enjoy such a wonderful society in the United States is that most of our laws and customs have their origin in the Christian social order, as it existed in England over the history of the English nation. English history is marked by the influence of Catholicism over all aspects of social and political life. The foundation of our American legal system, then, is marked and formed by the presence of a Christian spirit, teachings, and customs in the life of the citizenry, and we want to support and encourage that.

**One serious and persistent problem that faithful Catholic politicians face is the unpalatability of their positions in today's culture. How can they ever be elected when the predominant culture is so anti-Catholic and considers Church teaching "hateful"?**

As a legislator, you can't check your faith at the door when you enter the halls of Congress, as St. Josemaría Escrivá said in his book *The Way*.[21] Faith is the most important thing in your life, and the Faith ought to guide the way you act. We must witness to the truth and not tailor political convictions to please anti-Catholic prejudice. Otherwise, we are just playing a game of musical chairs or "king of the hill," jockeying to occupy roles of importance. There is nothing in the Faith that would cause harm to other people who are not of the Faith. They might

---

[21] St. Josemaría states, "Have you ever stopped to think how absurd it is to leave one's Catholicism aside on entering a university, a professional association, a cultural society, or Parliament, like a man leaving his hat at the door?" Josemaría Escrivá, *The Way* (New York: Image, 2009) no. 353. https://www.escrivaworks.org/book/the_way-point-353.htm.

object to things that are proposed for laws based on a religious principle. For instance, they might say Christian societies outlawed incest because it goes against the Bible, and argue that because they don't believe in the Bible, they think incest should be legal. The response is, the Bible teaches the same thing that the natural moral law teaches. Incest is a taboo in primitive societies that have no knowledge of Christianity but nonetheless see the bad results that come from pregnancies that result from incest; and you also see the devastating effect on close family ties when they are sexualized.

**The same would be true for abortion, wouldn't it?**
Yes, it is not only a religious issue but also a natural law issue. It is a human rights issue with a religious motivation among the vast majority of those who want to uphold the rights of the unborn, to speak on behalf of those with no voice. Most abolitionists in England who were against slavery had no personal contact with the African slaves being transported to North America but said, "This is wrong." Just so, people who say that unborn children, as a class, deserve the same protection as born children, even though they don't personally know them, are upholding justice and truth. Both groups, motivated by religious principles, appealed for social justice based on the natural law principle that every human being enjoys the right to live, without the threat of enslavement for Africans in centuries past or minus the threat today of being killed by abortion for our unborn brothers and sisters.

***Are LGBT issues essentially a natural law issue as well?***
Everyone enjoys natural rights and is bound by natural duties simply by virtue of being a member of the human race. There are various legal classifications of human activity or personal status—e.g., being legally married, a minor or someone habitually deprived of the use of reason, a member of the military, or member of the clergy—that result in specifications of rights and duties. Those rights granted in law should not contradict our natural rights and duties. There is no natural right to unnatural sexual activity, and two people of the same sex who engage in such behavior have no natural right to be granted recognition by the State as persons married to each other. There is no natural right for a man—nowadays we need to add the adjective *biological* to specify that we are speaking about someone whose DNA is male—to claim to be a woman, as this is an impossibility. Nature teaches us what things are in themselves, and all the laws of nature, physical and metaphysical, guide us into the right use of creation.

***Returning to the question of the role of Catholics in civil society...***
The influence of Christianity is present in our laws and customs in the United States, so we have to vigorously defend those laws and customs which come under assault or are cast aside or misunderstood. We also have to encourage Catholics to get involved in public life, in the world of academia, politics, media, and culture, where they can have influence not simply based on their Catholic Faith but because they are good at what they do, i.e., people with professional competence who are striving always to improve their knowledge and job performance.

Those involved in political life should be knowledgeable in defending positions in accord with natural law. Academics should be able to respond to new challenges as they come up and do so intelligently. Those involved in the world of publishing and other media have tremendous influence, actually or potentially. Through the world of the internet and other modern communications, if you're good at what you do and put in the time and effort, you can, for instance, start a YouTube channel and gain a lot of influence over people in a way that could never have happened in the past because you would've needed an agent and a break to get on a national television network. In May 2021 for instance, Ben Shapiro's *The Daily Wire* news website generated more Facebook engagement on its articles than *The New York Times*, *The Washington Post*, NBC News, and CNN combined.[22]

But in order to really have influence for the good, you have to be knowledgeable and holy, not self-interested and not doing it simply to become a celebrity.

**Some Catholics are worried about tyrannical tendencies in governments worldwide. What is the healthy way to respond to that with a Christlike spirit?**
Human affairs have a legitimate sphere of independence for people to develop different fields of knowledge and activity without necessary reference to the hierarchy of the Catholic Church. But what happens in civil society has a definite impact

---

[22] Miles Parks, "Outrage as a Business Model: How Ben Shapiro Is Using Facebook to Build an Empire," National Public Radio, July 19, 2021, https://www.npr.org/2021/07/19/1013793067/outrage-as-a-business-model-how-ben-shapiro-is-using-facebook-to-build-an-empire.

on the life of the Church, and therefore on the life of the faithful. We should try to do something for the good, but we should do so knowledgeably, understanding the way the world works. There are some political fights that cannot be won overnight, and they are going to require a long-haul approach. Whatever you can do to develop your knowledge and ability and to develop talent in other people, that's a way to counter destructive practices and theories. But we may not live to see the victory.

The better you know the principles of Christian social teaching and the duty to put a Christian spirit into all that we do, even when it's hidden in the manner of just being a devout Catholic who's an excellent building engineer, for example, that's the way to live. In other fields with public influence, you're going to have to be up-front about the Faith. In theology, philosophy, political theory, and academic life in general, if you're going to defend your faith and defend the common good, then necessarily you're going to have to oppose atheistic, Socialist, Communist forces that would grant no legitimacy to a Catholic set of arguments, or propositions, or examples from history, but would just dismiss them as illegitimate. This is where the liberal Western world is corrupt, because rather than even engage in the question "Is there a God, and what does he expect of man?," they basically rule that out as bigotry and superstition that is holding people back and is an instrument of power in the hands of primarily white men in the Church to oppress everybody else. We should never give into that and think that it's actually the case. No. Jesus Christ is the one who sends us out, and he is God, and therefore his message is the truth of God, and he has said that he is with us until the end of the ages (Matt 28:18–20), so he's with us in the fight, and we have to be ready for it.

*So, Catholics need to fortify themselves with the Church's teaching and her history to better prepare for the battles to come?*

You have to analyze how Catholics have lived in different political orders historically, and how they lived with their neighbors, and how they inspired and enacted laws and customs that upheld the common good, social justice, human dignity, prosperity, education, medical advances, and technical progress. All of these things come from living in a society in which we believe in the Ten Commandments, the rule of law, the sanctity of contracts, the duty to help those who can't help themselves, which are all Christian principles. Those are attractive to people of goodwill, and they tend to diffuse power and authority over a broad range of communities and social groups within the political community.

The American social order in my opinion, and this is a subject of lots of debate, does reflect a Catholic understanding of both original sin and the capabilities for human comity and progress which, if undertaken in a moral way, is fertile territory for promoting religion in society.

*The late Francis Cardinal George (1937–2015) famously said, "I expect to die in bed, my successor will die in prison and his successor will die a martyr in the public square."[23] Do you think we might come to a point in the not-too-distant future*

---

[23] Tim Drake, "Cardinal George: The Myth and Reality of 'I'll Die in My Bed'—What Cardinal Francis George Really Said," *National Catholic Register*, April 17, 2015, https://www.ncregister.com/blog/cardinal-george-the-myth-and-reality-of-ill-die-in-my-bed.

*when not only the clergy but the laity, too, might see imprisonment, persecution, and possible martyrdom?*

The history of the twentieth century is that leftist, coercive collectivist societies always arrest the clergy and terrorize the people to try to make them not practice their faith. The same is going on now in Communist China. To say that Communism is a modern manifestation of historical Chinese culture is an absolute lie. Communism is a fraudulent social vision introduced by Europeans throughout the world, and it is a great means by which some people use their power to aggrandize themselves and eliminate their enemies under the guise of being a friend of the people. If it happens in Western European societies and those influenced by their thinking, it could certainly happen in the United States and Canada.

The Lord told us that "a disciple is not above his teacher" (Matt 10:24), and every Catholic priest knows this when he is ordained. Innumerable priests have gone the way of the martyrs and suffered at the hands of unjust governments, but that is just a confirmation of the Faith. Because people gave their lives for what is true and took literally what the Lord said, namely, "take up your cross" (Matt 16:24)—in this case, the cross of your own crucifixion. But that truly conforms us to Christ and is eternally fruitful.

*In his letter to the Ephesians (6:10–17), St. Paul writes,*

> *Finally, be strong in the Lord and in the strength of his might. Put on the whole armor of God, that you may be able to stand against the wiles of the devil. For we are not contending against flesh and blood,*

> but against the principalities, against the powers, against the world rulers of this present darkness, against the spiritual hosts of wickedness in the heavenly places. Therefore take the whole armor of God, that you may be able to withstand in the evil day, and having done all, to stand. Stand therefore, having fastened the belt of truth around your waist, and having put on the breastplate of righteousness, and having shod your feet with the equipment of the gospel of peace; besides all these, taking the shield of faith, with which you can quench all the flaming darts of the Evil One. And take the helmet of salvation, and the sword of the Spirit, which is the word of God.

*How are we to understand St. Paul's words? What weapons of attack and defense does the Christian need in these times to quench the darts of the evil one and stand against the principalities and "the world rulers of this present darkness"?*

We need to promote and encourage Catholic intellectual formation, beginning with basic catechesis. The *Catechism of the Catholic Church* should be read and studied by every Catholic over the age of sixteen. The faithful need to educate themselves by using all the resources available from the many authentically Catholic publishing houses, media outlets, educational apostolates and the like. The Thomistic Institute of the Dominican Fathers is a great example of an effort to counter the darkness of ignorance and error by teaching the truths of theology and philosophy on college campuses and through the internet. EWTN, the Augustine Institute, Scott Hahn's St. Paul Center for Biblical Theology, Catholic Answers, the Catholic Productions app featuring Brant Pitre and John Bergsma—these are just a few of the places where you can find solid Catholic teaching offered in an appealing and understandable format.

**Which great saints of the past are an example to us today in standing up for truth in a hostile culture?**
There are so many. My list includes St. Irenaeus, St. Athanasius, St. Augustine, St. Thomas Aquinas, St. Robert Bellarmine, St. Catherine of Siena, St. Francis de Sales, St. John Bosco, St. John Henry Newman, St. Edith Stein, St. Pius X, and St. Josemaría Escrivá. All of them taught the truths of the Faith with courage and wisdom. None of them considered that their role was to pretend that the world is not hostile to the Church. No, they faced that hostility with utter conviction in the truth of the Gospel, and taught others to have confidence in God's providence amidst the trials of this world. Get to know these saints and you will find strength for the battles ahead.

*Chapter 6*

# TRUST AMID THE TUMULT

"He rose and rebuked the winds and the sea."
(Matt 8:26)

*Throughout the history of the Church, in the writings of St. Catherine of Siena, but even as early as* The Shepherd of Hermas,[1] *the Church is depicted as both resplendent and humiliated, and even ragged. St. Catherine of the Siena in particular was painfully aware of the scandal of the clergy and the harm that it did to the Church. Fr. Murray, infighting has been a reality over the course of the Church's history, but it seems particularly acrimonious and widespread throughout the Church in our times. How much should such disputes, even among the hierarchy, be tolerated?*

---

[1] *The Shepherd of Hermas* records a reported private revelation received by a Roman Christian in (probably) the early second century which contains symbolic teachings about the nature of the Church and of penance. Some of the Fathers considered it canonical.

Infighting means that there are disagreements between Churchmen or people in positions of authority, such as academics or lay people, who are attentive to what's going on in the Church. In other words, people involved in the life of the Church don't always agree and end up criticizing each other. That is *not* a problem in and of itself because legitimate criticism is an absolute duty of a Christian in order to defend the Faith and guide souls in sure paths and away from erroneous ways.

What is *not desirable* is the *use of argumentation to promote heresy and immorality in the life of the Church.* Specifically, by claiming that those who are defending tradition and the Faith are casting aspersions on the motives and intentions of people promoting the wrong things, and therefore these defenders must remain silent. It is claimed that we have to presume that everyone is acting in good faith and just let them go where they want. If someone is promoting error and immorality and is, in fact, acting in good faith, that's *irrelevant* to the fact that they're promoting error and immorality. They have to be stopped because Christ did not found the Church to mislead people. Therefore, those who represent Christ among the hierarchs and those who are trying to explain the Faith to others, whatever their role in the Church, have an obligation to be faithful to Christ's message. If their convictions are such that they can't accept that message, they have to recognize that the problem is with them, and that it is they who need to change. And if they can't make that change, then they have to at least be honest enough to say, "This is my opinion of what Christ taught and meant, but it is not what Catholicism teaches."

***And if a high-ranking prelate is unwilling to say this? Then what?***

Then you refute their arguments in making the truth clear. For instance, for those advocating the ordination of women to the priesthood, the Church has made quite clear through her teaching and practice that this is impossible. Therefore, *to agitate for it is to agitate for something that is not part of the Deposit of Faith* and can never become part of the Church's practice because it is not the intention of Christ. *The Church alone* has the right and ability to teach authoritatively what the intention of Christ is as regards the nature of the sacraments. The Church teaches that only baptized males are capable of receiving priestly ordination. That is a definitive teaching, a doctrine of the Church that is unassailable and which cannot be overthrown or modified or changed in any way.

***A woman is not the proper matter for the sacrament.***

Exactly. A woman can go through a ceremony, and the correct form of words can be used by a bishop attempting to ordain her, but *nothing* will happen. Therefore, people who keep promoting this idea need to be told to stop it because the true cause of disunity and infighting is their promotion of something that is contrary to the Faith, not the fact that people oppose them, even with vehemence, in the public square.

***The lack of unity in the Church is no new phenomenon. St. Paul, in 1 Corinthians 1:12, spoke of quarreling and factions: some followed him, some Apollos, and some Peter. Is the lack of unity in the modern Church different from the early Church,***

***and if so, how? How do we understand the Church's position in light of this history?***

The lack of unity—meaning the disputes between bishops, between the pope and bishops, between priests, lay people and theologians—shares many similarities with the arguments manifested in the New Testament. For instance, Peter and Paul arguing about how to incorporate non-Jews into the life of the Church and what responsibilities there were to the Old Covenant law. Then you had the great Christological and Trinitarian heresies confronted by the Fathers of the Church and the early ecumenical councils. There have always been disputes in the life of the Church.

What is new in our own age, of course, is that communications media makes possible the instantaneous sharing of divergent points of view. The media, which in many cases is anti-Catholic, likes to highlight disputes as a sign that the Church lacks confidence in her teaching or that her leadership is contemplating changing that teaching. The secular leftist media, which dominates American and European media by and large—there are some alternative media—is hostile to Catholic truth claims, to traditional ways of life, and particularly to Catholic sexual moral teaching. The angle they approach it with is, "When will the Church catch up with enlightened modern society and stop stigmatizing and prohibiting behaviors that the Church has always taught are sinful?" And now the world is saying that the Church's promotion of her teaching is an immoral form of shaming and bullying.

The response of the Church's magisterium, and of those who are faithful to her perennial doctrine, is: to teach the truth is only viewed as a shameful act by those who deny it or misunderstand it. It's the duty of those who are ashamed of the

Church's teaching, yet who remain in the Church, to change their thinking—not for the Church to accommodate herself to their ideas. The reason, of course, is because the Church is not the owner or creator of her doctrine. She is the guardian of doctrine and the ambassador of Christ. The magisterium of the Church exists to defend and promote knowledge of the truth against both ignorance and error—and we have a large amount of both in the modern scene.

*During World Youth Day in Denver, Colorado, in 1993, Mother Angelica was very critical of a liberal interpretation of the living Stations of the Cross—a famous moment that marked the beginning of a fight-back against progressive novelties being introduced into the Church. Mother Angelica looked straight into the camera and said, "I'm tired of you, liberal church. I have yet to hear anyone contradict you or distress you. Well, I'm saying it, as an individual who has a right before God to be Catholic, and I resent you pushing your ways, your anti-Catholic, ungodly ways on the masses in this country." How has this battle against heterodoxy changed since then?*

Mother Angelica's impassioned reaction was prompted by a theatrical production that included actors depicting different personages in Christ's Passion and Death, and they chose a woman to represent Christ. This was a *provocative act of defiance of reality* and was obviously meant to promote the ordination of women to the priesthood. The movement to pressure the Church to adapt Catholic doctrine and practice to the norms of Western liberalism in the modern age is still with us, and it was very much present during the pontificate of Pope John Paul II. One of the reasons he issued so many documents reaffirming different points of Catholic teaching, including on the ordination of women and the inherent immorality of abortion, was because a good number of people in the Church were stridently challenging those teachings.

Those people are still around, and one of the differences is that they have been emboldened during the pontificate of Pope Francis to make their protest movement more forceful, public, and unabashed. The hierarchy in Germany is actively promoting an agenda—regarding different issues of morality and sacramental practice—that was specifically rejected by both Pope John Paul II and Pope Benedict XVI.

Pope Francis is much more tolerant of what we'd call "liberal approaches" to Christianity being proposed and even implemented in the Church in ways that were unimaginable in the previous pontificates. For instance, the Pontifical Academy for Life and the Pontifical Academy of Social Sciences are conducting activities that were never thought of as even being possible in the last two pontificates, by inviting proponents of abortion, birth control, and population control to speak at Church conferences, with the notable absence of contrary voices to defend the teaching of the Church. The John Paul II Institute in Rome was abolished and refounded, and very fine professors were let go. The oath to uphold Catholic teaching that was taken by the members of the Pontifical Academy for Life—which was composed by Dr. Jerome Lejeune,[2] whose cause for canonization has been introduced—has been removed. And Fr. James Martin, S.J., who is a proponent of liberalizing Church practice and teaching regarding homosexuality, is now an advisor to the

---

[2] A famed French geneticist and saintly Catholic.

Vatican Secretariat of Communications. This was all unimaginable in the previous pontificates.

So the infighting, which always existed and always will, takes on a new drama and disturbing aspect when people are put into positions of authority who teach things that are harmful to the practice of the Faith—and the people defending the Faith are marginalized and caricatured as regards both their ideas and their motives. The papal advisor, Fr. Antonio Spadaro, S.J., has shown a great willingness to criticize, in unfair and inaccurate ways, the actions and even the motives of traditional and conservative Catholics in the United States and elsewhere. It's very disturbing. He also mischaracterizes evangelical Protestants in the US, and what they're up to.

We know that the Apostles had disagreements. St. Peter and St. Paul had a fight or disagreement about what to do in the early Church. Bishops historically have fought at ecumenical councils.

**It's said that St. Nicholas punched out the heretic Arias at the Council of Nicaea (325) for denying the divinity of Christ.**
Yes. We want to avoid fisticuffs and assault and battery, but *we do not want to avoid the necessary unpleasantness* that comes when the defense of Catholic teaching is met by derision on the part of innovators, who would produce great harm in the life of the Church if their proposals were accepted.

**In the broadcast referred to above, Mother Angelica went on to criticize the "liberal church," saying: "You call me a conservative Catholic. I'm not conservative. I'm just Catholic."**

***Are categories like heterodox and orthodox, conservative, liberal or progressive Catholics valid?***

Well, you can have baptized Catholics who end up promoting progressive religious ideas. I think that when we refer to someone as a progressive Catholic or a liberal Catholic, it's shorthand for a person who is baptized and professes to hold the Faith, but who nonetheless want to change doctrine and practice. The women's ordination lobby is one example, or those who want the Church to endorse contraception, abortion, and divorce and remarriage—all of which are innovations that would go against the Church's teaching.

There is a temptation to say that labels are not useful, but if you went to the supermarket and the cans had no labels, you wouldn't know what you were buying. What Cardinal Newman said is correct: Catholicism by its nature is conservative. That doesn't mean that all Catholics have to agree with the Republican political program or with whatever the particular conservative government in their country is doing. But in the Church it will mean conserving what has been handed on, and not altering it or changing it. That has to be seen as an essential obligation for all Catholics.

***What do you say to those who believe EWTN, other people in Catholic media, and wealthy American benefactors are involved in an "ultra-conservative" conspiracy to oppose, or even oust, Pope Francis?***

The adoption of language equivalent to Hillary Clinton's criticism of radio host Rush Limbaugh and others who criticized her and husband, President Bill Clinton—calling it all a "vast right-wing conspiracy" in 1998—is a put-down and a disreputable way of referring to fellow Catholics. Hopefully, those who make these claims would admit that those they are criticizing have the same goal as they do, which is the promotion of the mission of the Church. To reduce them to an unacceptable group who conspires, i.e., meets together for evil purposes—that's the implication—is a very weak and, in fact, untrue argument on their part. It's as if they are trying to say, "We're unassailable because we're not right-wing or a conspiracy."

Catholicism, as Cardinal Newman said, is by its nature conservative because we defend what has been handed on to us. We don't change it. In the realm of religion, to say of someone, "He's a conservative Catholic," should be seen as a compliment because it means that person takes what is received and safeguards it with fidelity. Meanwhile, the liberal project in general is quite clear: it is to change teachings and practices.

**Pope Paul VI famously said in 1972, just seven years after the end of the Second Vatican Council, that the "smoke of Satan" had entered the temple of God, leading to "confusion and sometimes absurd contradictions."[3] How much are differing interpretations of Vatican II the cause of conflicts between conservatives and progressives?**

I think the efforts of progressive Catholics nowadays are a continuation of what Pope Paul VI was so concerned about. We are seeing a concerted effort to change Catholic doctrine and practice in ways that are completely contradictory to the Faith of the

---

[3] Pope Paul VI, Homily on the Ninth Anniversary of His Coronation as Pope, June 29, 1972, https://www.vatican.va/content/paul-vi/it/homilies/1972/documents/hf_p-vi_hom_19720629.html.

Church. Satan's efforts to drag souls to Hell by leading them into sin, error, and unbelief are always a threat to the Church. How unbelievably tragic when members of the Church embrace teachings and practices that lead people precisely into sin, error, and even unbelief.

*In the same homily, delivered in St. Peter's Basilica on the Solemnity of SS. Peter and Paul, Pope Paul VI spoke of a "state of uncertainty" reigning in the Church. He said, "It was believed that after the Council a sunny day would come for the history of the Church. Instead, it has been a day of clouds, of storms, of darkness, of searching, of uncertainty."[4] Joseph Cardinal Ratzinger, the future Pope Benedict XVI, famously predicted that the final outcome of this upheaval would be a smaller but purer Church. Are the conflicts of the present time the necessary birth pangs of the long-delayed "new Pentecost?"*

God in his providence has allowed us to experience this time of upheaval. His grace is not lacking. Our correspondence to grace is what is required. When we are faithful to God and his Church, then the mission of the Church advances in ways that are visible and invisible. If we want to learn how to live the Faith and to promote the mission of the Church, we should look to what the saints did who lived in times of similar upheaval, such as the Arian crisis or the Protestant Reformation.

---

[4] Pope Paul VI, Homily on the Ninth Anniversary of His Coronation as Pope.

*In an address delivered during a visit to the US in 1976, then-Cardinal Karol Wojtyła[5] said, "We are now standing in the face of the greatest historical confrontation humanity has gone through. I do not think that wide circles of American society or wide circles of the Christian community realize this fully. We are now facing the final confrontation between the Church and the anti-Church, of the Gospel versus the anti-Gospel."[6] What do you believe Cardinal Wojtyła meant by the "anti-Church"?*

The anti-Church are those forces that promote a vision of human life that excludes God and the Church, that seek to obliterate any presence of the Church in both society as a whole and in the life of each believer. The anti-Church was plainly at work in Communism and National Socialism. It is also present in the attempts to radically redefine Catholic teaching and to remake the Church in the image of permissive Western liberalism. The Church must resist this relentless enemy of God's truth.

*In the light of Cardinal Wojtyła's comments in 1976, it is almost chilling to think of Sr. Lucia's message to Carlo Cardinal*

---

[5] Cardinal Wojtyła of Krakow, Poland, became Pope John II in October 1978.

[6] Fr. C. John McCloskey, III, "The Final Confrontation," *The Catholic Thing*, June 1, 2014, https://www.thecatholicthing.org/2014/06/01/the-final-confrontation/. In his American Bicentennial talk given in the United States, Cardinal Wojtyła also said,

> We must be prepared to undergo great trials in the not-too-distant future; trials that will require us to be ready to give up even our lives, and a total gift of self to Christ and for Christ. Through your prayers and mine, it is possible to alleviate this tribulation, but it is no longer possible to avert it. . . . How many times has the renewal of the Church been brought about in blood! It will not be different this time.

*Caffarra, when he asked for her prayers for the founding of the John Paul II Institute in Rome. She told the cardinal that "a time will come when the decisive battle between the kingdom of Christ and Satan will be over marriage and the family." Indeed, Cardinal Caffarra confirmed shortly before his death in 2017 that Sr. Lucia was referring to this time.[7] Should we read this as a call to arms?*

We must defend any teaching that is attacked, and in our day the sanctity of marriage and family are under plain assault in the Western world. Marriage and family are at the heart of human life and flourishing. The Christian understanding of human sexuality is the source of personal and social fulfillment and peace. When sex is divorced from marriage and parenthood, it becomes an all-consuming force that destroys social harmony and creates personal misery and hopelessness. The relentless and unbridled search for physical pleasure with no concern for God's plan is self-destructive behavior. It leads souls to damnation, which is what Satan wants.

*But some might ask how can we fight when, since the Council, the Church has effectively laid down her arms?*

I do not agree that the Church herself has laid down her arms in the fight to uphold God's truth, although some Churchmen have sadly done so. God is good and favors those who are faithful to him. He will never abandon us. At the same time, he calls us to fidelity and to a courageous defense of his truth. There are many in the Church who are doing just that.

---

[7] Diane Montagna, "Cardinal Caffarra: 'What Sr. Lucia Wrote to Me Is Being Fulfilled Today,'" Aleteia, May 19, 2017, https://aleteia.org/2017/05/19/exclusive-cardinal-caffarra-what-sr-lucia-wrote-to-me-is-being-fulfilled-today/.

***What are the reasons behind the liturgy wars? Why are the old and new forms of the Mass a cause of such friction in the Church?***

The reform of the Mass and the other liturgical rites following the Second Vatican Council resulted in a loss of a sense of the sacred and the eternal through the elimination of words and gestures that promoted a supernatural understanding of worship. The revised liturgy was intentionally reworked to be more akin to Protestant worship in style and didacticism, less mystical and Heaven-directed. While the Tridentine Mass shares many similarities in style and emphasis with the Divine Liturgy of our Eastern Orthodox brethren, that cannot be said of the post-Conciliar Mass. The fight in the Church is thus a confrontation between those who want to keep past practices in the past, and those who want to recover the sense of the sacred which is so ably fostered by the traditional worship of the Latin Church.

***Why is the Traditional Latin Mass such a threat to some?***

The dynamic of the Second Vatican Council, and the liturgical reforms enacted subsequently, was in the direction of updating, modernizing, and reforming in response to so-called "current needs and expectations." The question, however, is whose needs and whose expectations? There are many needs and expectations out there, and what matters is who gets to decide which ones are taken seriously and which ones are disregarded. The liturgical movement in the twentieth century had evolved from an effort to study the history of the liturgy—and to promote a greater knowledge and appreciation of that sacred heritage—into an effort to rework and modify the liturgy, often manifesting a rationalistic spirit hostile to anything not immediately understandable. The many Catholics who were and are dissatisfied by what resulted defended the Church's liturgical heritage by seeking to maintain the older rites. In doing so they gave witness to a resistance to the principles and goals of the liturgical reformers. Rather than engage in a principled debate, most defenders of the reformed liturgy caricature the ideas and motives of the defenders of traditional liturgical rites, calling them nostalgic or worse. That response often indicates a refusal to engage their critics and to explain and defend their reforming ideas.

*A key figure in the counter reform that many would say was begun under Archbishop Marcel Lefebvre, the founder of the Society of St. Pius X (SSPX), was the British Catholic writer Michael Davies. Shortly after his death in 2004, Cardinal Ratzinger praised Davies, saying,*

> *I had the good fortune to meet him several times and I found him as a man of deep faith and ready to embrace suffering. Ever since the Council, he put all his energy into the service of the Faith and left us important publications, especially about the sacred liturgy. Even though he suffered from the Church in many ways in his time, he always truly remained a man of the Church. He knew that the Lord founded his Church on the rock of St. Peter and that the Faith will find its fulness and maturity only in union with the Successor of St. Peter."[8]*

[8] "Mr. Michael Davies, Former President of the International Una Voce Federation:

*Michael Davies has been a marginal figure for many because traditionalists for many years have been marginalized. Have you read his writings, and do you think it's time to give him greater prominence? How might his legacy help bring healing and peace to the Church?*

I was privileged to meet Michael Davies through the kindness of Roger McCaffrey. I had been reading his books for years and found his writings to be courageous and informative. He was a true gentleman and fearless seeker of truth. He was a convert to the Faith who loved the Church and her teachings and practices and was distressed to see a Protestant spirit entering into the Church. I read his book *The Order of Melchizedek* before I entered the seminary, and it helped me to understand the meaning of the priesthood. He collected important sermons by John Henry Newman in his book *Newman Against the Liberals*, which helped me to understand that a non-dogmatic form of Christianity was not true Christianity. Davies worked hard to defend the Faith, and his writings will stand as a testament to a truly Catholic response to the upheavals that shook the Church after the Second Vatican Council.

*Some of the most acrimonious and unfortunate infighting takes place within conservative or traditional groups, so much so that the circular firing squad seems to apply only to*

---

An Appreciation," International Una Voce Federation, http://www.fiuv.org/p/michael-treharne-davies-appreciation.html. Taken from Leo Darroch's foreword to the 2009 edition of Davies's book *Pope Paul's New Mass*. Darroch is a former president of the International Una Voce Federation.

***them. Why do you think this is? And how damaging is it to the Church's mission?***
People only fight with those whom they consider to be threats, and in any movement defending a set of ideas and principles, there will be differences of opinion on what to emphasize, what to tolerate, how to do so, and how not to do so. That is inevitable and can be a source of mutual improvement if the differing sides acknowledge that adjustments in tactics are normal and beneficial where there is unity in seeking the same goal. Uncharitable, reckless, and dishonest criticisms are poisonous and unchristian. Anyone who wants to promote the mission of the Church amidst her current difficulties needs to remember that the daily pursuit of holiness is not an optional add-on to the defense of the truth, but rather a necessary aspect of that defense.

***The Left seems to stick together more. Is it because they are united in their goal and so indifferent to the truth that they're willing to sacrifice it?***
When various groups of armed revolutionaries are trying to take over the seat of government, they do not really care who is firing the artillery shells into the presidential palace. They are just glad that the building is being reduced to rubble, and the government is being destroyed. Only when the fighting is over will score settling occur, and one group will emerge with all the power. The others will either submit or face extinction.

***Even on the most fundamental questions about "binding and loosing"(Matt 18:15–18) and the stewardship of the sacred mysteries (Matt 24:46), the shepherds of the faithful seem to be at complete loggerheads with each other. For example,***

**the United States Conference of Catholic Bishops (USCCB) had an acrimonious dispute in June 2021 about whether to conduct a report into Eucharistic coherence, that is, to ensure that the faithful only receive Communion when they are seeking to conform their lives to the teaching of the Church. Although the USCCB voted to commission this report, a considerable number of bishops voted not to do so. This seems very serious when even the idea of thinking about ensuring that the faithful are not "eating and drinking condemnation" on themselves provokes such substantial opposition. How do we find ourselves in this position?**

For years most bishops have refused to enforce canon 915, which says that those "obstinately persevering in manifest grave sin are not to be admitted to holy communion." Cardinal Burke did so when he was Archbishop of St. Louis, but he was one of the few. Now that we have a Catholic president who supports and promotes legalized abortion, the majority of the bishops understand that they must act. Otherwise it will appear that one can be a Catholic in good standing and at the same time reject her nonnegotiable teaching that abortion is gravely immoral. The president needs to understand that his promotion of abortion is harmful to his soul and that receiving Holy Communion is only spiritually beneficial if one conforms his life to the Gospel and is in the state of grace. Denying him Holy Communion will undoubtedly be the occasion for him to examine his conscience and come, by God's grace, to the only truthful conclusion, which is that promoting the killing of unborn children is a grave sin that must be repented of.

*Various measures have been suggested by various bishops in order to deal with the problem of Eucharistic incoherence, such as increases in evangelization and catechesis and the holding of various Eucharistic rallies. What has happened, do you think, to the old-fashioned method of excommunicating notorious public sinners and heretics, or encouraging the faithful to attend the sacrament of Confession on a weekly or biweekly basis and even perhaps to consider that sometimes they might be free, but not well prepared, to receive Communion?*

There is an alarming and documented loss of faith in the Real Presence of Our Lord in the Holy Eucharist among Catholics. Given that, the reception of Holy Communion becomes a routine with no meaning beyond participating in a ritual with everyone else at Mass. The notion that the reception of Holy Communion in a consciously unworthy manner could contribute to one's eternal damnation is widely unknown. A public defense of the holiness of the Eucharist as provided for in canons 915 and 916 would do a great deal to remedy that ignorance, and also prompt Catholics to reexamine their understanding of what the Holy Eucharist is: the true Body and Blood of the Incarnate Son of God, Jesus Christ.

*Is the infighting actually a good thing in that it's a sign that somebody cares about the truths of the Faith?*

Absolutely. Passivity in the face of evil and disorder is a sure sign of weak faith and a lack of the courage needed to be a good shepherd when wolves threaten the flock.

***If, as we believe, the Church is guided by the Holy Spirit and the gates of Hell will not prevail against her, and that she cannot be led into error, why the need to resist or fight at all?***
Because "your adversary the devil prowls around like a roaring lion, seeking someone to devour" (1 Pet 5:8), and because we are called to "fight the good fight of the faith" (1 Tim 6:12). The Good Lord calls us to take up our cross, which will include resisting anything that would corrupt or destroy our fidelity or lead others to abandon God and his truth (see Matt 16:24–26).

***The Church previously had mechanisms for addressing heresy in a more public manner whereas now, it seems to be privatized or almost eliminated. What do you think of the present mode of addressing errors and heresies committed by baptized Catholics? Is a return to stigmatization a good option?***
In the past, there was more zeal to publicly call out Catholic authors who wrote books that contradicted Catholic teaching, and warnings were given publicly, and privately, to these authors. Fr. Tony Flannery of Ireland was disciplined by Pope Francis.[9] Under Pope John Paul II it certainly happened, as in the case of the Sri Lankan priest and theologian Fr. Tissa Balasuriya. There was in the past a regular expectation that books containing heresies would be identified and called out by the Holy See.

---

[9] Patsy McGarry, "Fr Tony Flannery Questions Suspension over Views Senior Clerics Share," *The Irish Times*, January 4, 2021, https://www.irishtimes.com/news/social-affairs/religion-and-beliefs/fr-tony-flannery-questions-suspension-over-views-senior-clerics-share-1.4449708.

***This was the case with liberation theology.***

Yes, with the Holy See's two instructions on liberation theology.[10] The Congregation for the Doctrine of the Faith's documents were largely in response to either pastoral practices that were in violation of Catholic norms or writings of theologians that cast doubt upon or contradicted Catholic teaching. We're not getting much of that lately.

***In fact, we're getting a bit of the opposite with the rehabilitation of controversial figures, such as Fr. Eugenio Melandri, who was incardinated into the Archdiocese of Bologna, Italy, by Matteo Cardinal Zuppi,*[11] *Fr. Ernesto Cardenal, who got a***

---

[10] Both instructions were issued by the Congregation for the Doctrine of the Faith: *Instruction on Certain Aspects of the Theology of Liberation* (1984), https://www.vatican.va/roman_curia/congregations/cfaith/documents/rc_con_cfaith_doc_19840806_theology-liberation_en.html; and *Instruction on Christian Freedom and Liberation* (1986), https://www.vatican.va/roman_curia/congregations/cfaith/documents/rc_con_cfaith_doc_19860322_freedom-liberation_en.html.

[11] As cited in Edward Pentin, *The Next Pope: The Leading Cardinal Candidates* (Manchester, NH: Sophia Institute Press, 2020), 640:

> In September 2019, Cardinal Zuppi, with the permission of the Congregation for Clergy, incardinated into the Archdiocese of Bologna Fr. Eugenio Melandri, the "red priest" who was suspended *a divinis* for twenty-eight years after running in the 1989 European elections as a member of the Proletarian Democracy party, a far-left Italian political party. In 1992, Fr. Melandri was elected to the Italian parliament for the Communist Reform party. He was also the co-founder of *Senzaconfine* (Borderless), an association that works to promote the rights of immigrants and refugees and integrate them into Italian society. On October 20, 2019, Fr. Melandri celebrated Mass for the first time since his suspension, but he died one week later, at the age of 71, after a long illness. One year earlier, he was received in Casa Santa Marta in Vatican City by Pope Francis, who had him serve his Mass. There are no reports of his renouncing his Communist affiliations before he died.

famous dressing down on the tarmac in Managua, Nicaragua in 1983 by Pope John Paul II,[12] or Brazilian theologian and former Franciscan Fr. Leonardo Boff, who even contributed to Pope Francis's 2015 encyclical *Laudato Si'*.[13]

The reform and subsequent reconciliation of rebel priests and theologians is always the goal of disciplinary measures. When reconciliations are announced without any public evidence of repentance on the part of the offending parties, we are left wondering if such repentance has, in fact, occurred. Public offenses against the Faith of the Church ordinarily require public repentance to repair the scandal given.

*Do you see any signs of hope?*

The last document of the Congregation for the Doctrine of the Faith saying "no" to blessings for homosexual unions is a welcome example of what's needed.[14] I hope it will be followed by more such documents because that's not the only contested area in Catholic life. We sorely need a document to reaffirm that there's no such thing as a "transsexual" or "transgender" person, that God's creation is inviolable and is not subject to any human change. You are born a man or a woman, and you will die the same—and nothing can change that.

---

[12] Robin Gomes, "Pope Lifts Suspension on Nicaraguan Priest Fr. Ernesto Cardenal," Vatican News, February 19, 2019, https://www.vaticannews.va/en/pope/news/2019-02/pope-francis-lifts-sanctions-ernesto-cardenal.html.

[13] Julio Loredo, "Leonardo Boff: The Pope's Radical 'Ecotheologian,'" *National Catholic Register*, December 18, 2020, https://www.ncregister.com/blog/leonardo-boff-the-pope-s-radical-ecotheologian.

[14] Again, see CDF, "*Responsum* of the Congregation for the Doctrine of the Faith to a *Dubium* regarding the Blessing of the Unions of Persons of the Same Sex," Holy See Press Office, March 15, 2021, https://press.vatican.va/content/salastampa/it/bollettino/pubblico/2021/03/15/0157/00330.html#ing.

**The Scripture passage on the calming of the storm says that Jesus "rose and rebuked the winds and the sea" (Matt 8:26). Are you saying that most of the infighting and disunity is caused by people diverging from the Catholic Faith, and that what's needed today is a "rebuking of the winds" of doctrinal confusion and a reassertion of Christ's teaching?**

Yes. The history of heresy in the Church is that the Catholic faithful believe with a serene and tranquil spirit what is taught to them, and they live by that Faith. Then an innovator comes along and tells you, "What they told you about this matter, you must no longer believe that." That's what happened throughout the history of the early Church, then with Martin Luther, John Calvin, and the rest.

**But now it seems that it is Pope Francis himself who is saying this.**

The Pope is clearly saying some new things, and it's demonstrable that he's aware that what he's doing is in fact changing things from the past. The case of the death penalty is quite clear. He said we can no longer teach what the Catechism taught, the same Catechism that existed when he assumed the throne of Peter. I disagree with him, and I think he's made a mistake in this regard.

The same thing happened with *Amoris Laetitia*, Pope Francis's 2016 post-synodal apostolic exhortation. The previous teachings under John Paul II and Benedict XVI are quite clear regarding the inability of divorced-and-remarried Catholics to be given Holy Communion. They have no right to ask for it or be given it due to their situation until they change and remedy that situation. The Pope doesn't agree with that. That's quite clear.

The 2019 Abu Dhabi document—which states that "the pluralism and the diversity of religions, color, sex, race, and language are willed by God in his wisdom"—is not really a papal teaching in the formal sense of proposing it for the belief of Catholics.[15] It is an agreement between certain parties, but the Pope agrees to something *not* because he is Jorge Bergoglio and happens to like it. He was in Abu Dhabi as the pope of the Catholic Church. Therefore, in a certain way, he is committing the Church to this statement and promoting it as something that needs to guide our thinking. It is quite clear to me that this document's controversial statement on the diversity of religions is incompatible with the Church's teaching. God does not positively will that other religions exist. In other words, he did not give multiple revelations or cause the foundation of multiple churches or religions. God did not will the diversity of religions as he willed the sexes, male and female.

It is true that the Pope himself said privately that the diversity of religions is the permissive will of God.[16] The permissive will of God refers to the things that God allows to happen,

---

[15] Pope Francis co-signed the "Document on Human Fraternity for World Peace and Living Together" with Sheik Ahmad Al-Tayyeb, Grand Imam of Cairo's Al-Azhar Mosque, during an interreligious meeting in Abu Dhabi on February 4, 2019. Diane Montagna, "Pope Francis under Fire for Claiming 'Diversity of Religions' Is 'Willed by God,'" LifeSiteNews, February 5, 2019, https://www.lifesitenews.com/news/pope-francis-under-fire-for-claiming-diversity-of-religions-is-willed-by-go.

See the Abu Dhabi document itself at https://www.vatican.va/content/francesco/en/travels/2019/outside/documents/papa-francesco_20190204_documento-fratellanza-umana.html.

[16] Diane Montagna, "Exclusive: Bishop Schneider Says Vatican Is Betraying 'Jesus Christ as the Only Savior of Mankind,'" LifeSiteNews, August 26, 2019, https://www.lifesitenews.com/news/bishop-schneider-vatican-is-betraying-jesus-christ-as-the-only-savior-of-mankind.

but he does not will them to happen. If someone murders his neighbor, we say that doesn't happen outside the ambit of divine providence because God is the ruler of all creation, but he doesn't intend the murder. The author of the crime is responsible for the act, and a murderer is acting against God's will, whether he knows it or not. Therefore, it cannot be attributed to the divine will.

When God allows something to happen that is *contrary* to his positive will, we don't attribute that as being part of God's plan. God's plan was that there be male and female; that is the active will of God, not the permissive will. But the existence of Islam, Buddhism, and other religions is not part of God's plan—absolutely not. What we know to be God's plan, because Christ taught it, cannot be contradicted. And Christ never told the Apostles, "Go out and teach everything I taught you," adding "when you encounter these other religions, leave them alone because it's part of God's will that they be out there." No. Jesus commissioned us to "make disciples of *all* nations" (Matt 28:19, emphasis added). That's our irrevocable mission.

### *Do you think there can be a heretical pope?*

There has been a discussion and debate about this over the centuries. People don't want to believe that a good God could ever allow there to be a heretical pope. So if a pope becomes a heretic, he's therefore not really the pope anymore. Maybe, maybe not. The problem is this: Who can verify that the pope has truly fallen into formal heresy? There is no God-given human authority with the power to pass binding legal judgment on the pope. It is certainly possible, God forbid, for a pope, like any other Catholic, to lose the Faith by his own embrace of heretical teaching or even to become an atheist, although these are highly unlikely outcomes. But they are possible. You can't limit the possibilities of how God may let humanity err and wander.

**Especially because we do believe the Church will live through the mysteries of her Divine Bridegroom. In the hour of Christ's Passion, the Apostles seemed to think that such suffering and sacrilege could not possibly happen to their Lord. If the Church today is indeed living through her passion, then it would be wrong of us to believe, "This can't happen."**
Exactly. The supernatural perspective is clear. It's a mystery to accept that it is possible for someone in a position of authority to betray his mission and do something contrary to the role he accepted. The guarantee of infallibility, meaning that the pope will not teach anything against the Faith, is circumscribed to moments when he actually exercises his teaching authority in a clear, binding and obligatory way. For example, *de fide* definitions are distinct from and do not include statements that the Pope makes at a Wednesday audience, or on an airplane, or to a journalist.

**Our Lord says in the Sermon on the Mount that the Church is "a city set on a hill" that "cannot be hidden" (Matt 5:14), and yet people often despair of demonstrating the truths of the Faith at this time, when the attributes of the Church seem so clouded: her unity, her sanctity, and her unbroken Apostolic Tradition. How can we learn to see the true Church amid the storm of infighting?**
The Church's unity, sanctity, and apostolicity remain untouched even when the actions of men cause those attributes to seem to

be absent. Christ's Mystical Body, which is the Church, perdures indefectibly amidst crises. God will never abandon his Church, just as he did not abandon his Son on the Cross or in the grave. The witness of the martyrs over the centuries teaches us that their deaths, which look like defeats for the Church, are, in fact, victories that point to the ultimate fulfillment of all hope in Heaven.

**How can we convince a non-Catholic that the Church is holy, in light of the terrible scandals and the suspicion that the hierarchy is complicit in them?**
The Church is holy even when Christ's representatives on earth are unholy. One should not expect the Church to be led only by men incapable of betraying Christ, given that Our Lord himself chose Judas Iscariot as one of his Twelve Apostles. What God allowed to happen by creating man with free will, i.e., sinful disobedience to God and his law, is something we will always encounter in this world. It's a serious mistake to be scandalized to the point that you would claim that the Catholic Church cannot be God's Church because men like Theodore McCarrick have been members of the College of Cardinals. Christ warned us that scandals will occur, and woe to them who cause scandal (Matt 18:7).

**Often Catholics raised in the last fifty years, when they open the writings of St. Augustine or St. Thomas, if they took a page at random, they'd find it quite difficult to sympathize or agree with the teaching they find there because of the homiletic experiences they've had in the Church. How can we maintain to a Protestant, for example, that we stand in the**

***presence of unbroken Apostolic Tradition when the Fathers and Doctors seem so alien to contemporary Catholics?***

Our current educational decline is a sad reflection not of anything lacking in the unbroken teaching of the Church but rather of the failure of our culture to appreciate the true, the good and the beautiful. We live in an age of skepticism, and many Catholics have adopted the attitude, "I only believe in what you can prove to me." The Faith is under judgment from the start, and thus various teachings of the Church are rejected as "not proven to my satisfaction." Rather than believing in Christ and his Church as a total-package deal, people pick and choose, which usually means rejecting hard teachings that require personal self-abnegation and sacrifice. Self-serve Catholicism is a caricature of the Faith, but many Catholics have fallen into this pattern.

***The doctrine and the practice of Catholics in Poland or Uganda would likewise seem quite different to Catholics in parts of the United States or other wealthy Western countries. How is a Church of this nature truly Catholic?***

It all comes back to Our Lord Jesus Christ. We need to put on "the mind of Christ" (1 Cor 2:16). The Lord works through his Church wherever it is present in the world. It can be jarring to Americans and Western Europeans to see how people from different parts of the world practice their faith, but that is a salutary shock. When the Faith is the most important thing in our lives, then we are not shocked to see how other people who share that conviction live their lives. However, when the Faith is just one more aspect of our lives, then we can be bothered by seeing people who reject that approach. We should ask ourselves, "Whose approach reminds me of what Jesus said and did?"

*How important is a rediscovery of the Four Last Things to our reconnecting ourselves to reality?*

Death, Judgment, Heaven and Hell: the first two are inevitable for everyone. One or the other of the last two is where we will end up forever because of our own choices in life. We need to be reminded of this regularly. We tend to avoid thinking of our death, and we too often dismiss the idea that we could lose our souls for all eternity. But we are called to live holy lives and to be prepared each day to die well, which means to die in the state of grace. God is all-loving, which means that he provides us the grace to attain heavenly life with him. It is up to us to do his will and thus grow in his grace and love. But through our own sins we can lose our souls. To sin is to misuse our free will by choosing what is evil. That is what the Faith teaches us.

*According to opinion polls, perhaps less than half of Catholics believe in the Real Presence of the Lord in the Eucharist. Combined with the many other points on which Catholics dissent from the teachings of the Church on essential matters, it would seem statistically unlikely that more than a very small minority of Catholics on a given Sunday are making non-sacrilegious Communions. This would seem to suggest that the structures of the Church as currently established are procuring and worsening the damnation of the flock, rather than their salvation. This seems a serious threat to the Church's identity, as the "sacrament of salvation" or "the one fold of the Redeemer." How are we to address this?*

The documented lack of faith of many Catholics in the Real Presence is a disaster and an indictment of the failed catechesis of the past fifty years. The remedy is renewed preaching on this most wondrous Blessed Sacrament in which God himself comes to us under the humble appearances of bread and wine that conceal his true Body and Blood. The question of who receives Holy Communion unworthily or sacrilegiously depends upon the knowledge that each communicant has of his obligations as a Catholic. Those obligations include belief in the Real Presence, freedom from mortal sin, freedom from canonical sanctions, not living in a public state of serious sin, and fasting for one hour before receiving Holy Communion. The pastors of the Church need to remind Catholics of these obligations. One can be subjectively unaware that one's objective failure to fulfill any of these obligations requires that one not receive Holy Communion. Sadly, many people have been misled to believe that anyone can receive Holy Communion without even considering that there are any prior obligations on their part.

**Elizabeth Anscombe, the famous British Catholic philosopher of the twentieth century, is said to have remarked that if we truly believed in what the Eucharist is, we would never rise from our knees in the course of Mass. But today the posture, demeanor, and general behavior of many priests and people seem to communicate precisely the opposite. How are we to restore the sense of the supernatural among the faithful?**
Anscombe was right. External bodily movements and posture, such as genuflecting, kneeling, bowing, observing silence at the times requiring silence, dressing properly for church, avoiding socializing in church before and after Mass, are ways to show God that we recognize his sovereignty and majesty, and are grateful to be in his house going about his business. The Mass is a foretaste and preview of heavenly glory. We should approach

with awe and trembling the altar of God, so we can receive well the graces he will give us each time we come to worship and adore him. Casualness and bonhomie are for the gathering after Mass on the sidewalk or plaza in front of the church. Once refreshed by the Lord, we go forth and live out our experience of God's love by showing that love to our neighbors and friends. But first we need to focus precisely on being refreshed by the Lord, avoiding all distractions. That is one of the main reasons why so many young Catholics are stunned and overjoyed when they first come into contact with the Latin Tridentine Mass, the Extraordinary Form. Worship and reverence are unmistakably inculcated from the moment the priest says, "*Introibo ad altare Dei*,"[17] to the end of the Last Gospel.

---

[17] Latin for "I will go unto the altar of God," the prayer that begins the Extraordinary Form of the Mass.

*Chapter 7*

# AWAKENING CHRIST

"Even the winds and sea obey him." (Matt 8:27)

**St. John Henry Cardinal Newman, when writing about the role the laity played during the Arian crisis, said that even though it was the time of great Doctors of the Church—SS. Athanasius, Hilary, the two Gregories, Basil, Chrysostom, Ambrose, Jerome, and Augustine (all bishops except for one)—it was nevertheless during that time that the lay faithful "proclaimed and maintained" the divine Faith entrusted to the Church far more than the bishops. Are we living in a similar time, absent the Doctors?**

If I were to seek true and certain witnesses to the Faith of the Catholic Church in Germany today, I would do better to speak with Mass-going lay men and women, especially parents of devout families who attend the Extraordinary Form of the Mass, than to speak with a large percentage of the German bishops. The German Synodal Way is plainly a revolutionary movement sponsored by the bishops. They are actively and consciously undermining the Faith handed down to us from the Apostles. They refuse to listen to criticisms by those who are shocked and dismayed by their revolutionary ways. This episcopal betrayal of their sworn duty to uphold and promote the Catholic Faith is a scandal with consequences reaching beyond Germany. The laity who oppose the heretical innovations of the Synodal Way are true witnesses to the unchanging Faith of the Church.

*As St. Peter Chrysologus said in his homily on the Calming of the Storm (Matt 8:23–27), "Christ does not need the vessel, . . . but the vessel needs Christ. Without the heavenly helmsman the vessel of the Church is unable to sail over the sea of the world and, against critical odds, arrive at the heavenly harbor." St. Louis de Montfort points out that God does not even need the Blessed Virgin but has freely elected to save the world through her. Could it be that in these times he will choose to save his Church through the laity?*

Christ remains always with his Church and will raise up new servants of her renewal as he has done repeatedly throughout history. Think of the great saints of the Catholic Counter-Reformation who defended Catholic truth against errors. Lay people throughout the world are in the forefront today of efforts to promote the mission of the Church through means new and old. Many commentators said that the era following the Second Vatican Council would be the age of the laity in the Church. They were correct but not in the sense many had thought, which was that the laity would "help" the Church to change her ways and even doctrines. The most influential lay men and women in the Church today are those calling us back to fidelity to the doctrine of the Faith.

# AWAKENING CHRIST

*In his 1988 apostolic exhortation on the vocation and mission of the lay faithful in the Church and the world,* Christifideles Laici, Pope St. John Paul II quotes St. Augustine, who says, "We are the Body of Christ because we are all 'anointed' and in him are 'christs,' that is, 'anointed ones,' as well as Christ himself, 'The Anointed One.'"[1] *The anointed offices of the Old Testament were priest, prophet, and king. Obviously, in the Church, the function of sanctifying, teaching, and governing are performed actively by the clergy, but surely the laity participate in them, too, in some way?*

The laity are anointed by the gift of the Holy Spirit at Baptism, and that gift is renewed and strengthened at Confirmation. They are called to offer their lives as a living sacrifice to God, which means fulfilling God's will in all things, especially by offering up to him their difficulties and trials. This is the active participation of the priestly people of God in the offering of worship in spirit and in truth. It is not, however, a participation in the ministerial priesthood of Christ, which is conferred only upon those who are sacramentally ordained to the priesthood, becoming priests of the New Covenant. Those consecrated as bishops enjoy the fullness of the priesthood and exercise the threefold charge of sanctifying, teaching, and governing the flock of Christ. The gift of the Holy Spirit received by bishops and priests is meant for the spiritual welfare of those committed to their charge. The living faith and holiness of the faithful are the blessed fruit of the pastoral charity of

---

[1] St. Augustine, Ennar. in Ps. XXVI, II, 2: CCL 38, 154ff. As cited in John Paul II, *Christifideles Laici* (1988), § 14, https://www.vatican.va/content/john-paul-ii/en/apost_exhortations/documents/hf_jp-ii_exh_30121988_christifideles-laici.html#_ftn19.

good shepherds who lead the flock of Christ into green pastures of sound teaching and active sacramental life.

*In* **The Dialogue** *of St. Catherine of Siena, specifically in her "Treatise of Discretion," the Lord says to St. Catherine that the face of his bride the Church will be washed by the tears, sweat, and prayers of his "other christs"; that is, of the baptized who have conformed their will to his, and whose tears are mingled with the Blood of Christ, i.e., with divine charity. How is this union of our sufferings with the Lord's for the sake of the Church best accomplished?*

The surest path to grow in holiness and faith is to fulfill with great love our ordinary duties in life, especially those which are onerous, or distasteful, or demanding upon our time. Patience, forbearance, and generosity of spirit when bearing our burdens will help us to truly know Christ Jesus and become one with him in intention and desire. I recommend frequent prayer to God the Holy Spirit for light and strength to know what our duties are and how to best fulfill them. Glances at the crucifix help us to remind ourselves of Christ's supreme act of love for mankind. St. Josemaría Escrivá recommended that we carry a small crucifix in our pocket or purse. It is a great suggestion.

*In her various apparitions in the nineteenth and twentieth centuries, Our Lady constantly emphasized penance, most dramatically when the angel with the flaming sword in the Third Secret of Fatima points at the earth and shouts three times, "Penance! Penance! Penance!"*[2] *Would you say that the most urgent call upon the faithful is to make reparation for so much sin in the Church and the world today, including a general turning away from God?*

We should make reparation for the sins and offenses of mankind against God and his law. Our prayers, sacrifices, and good works will gain many graces for ourselves and others, and will also serve to demonstrate to those around us that there is a better way to live than that proposed so enticingly by the world. Selfishness, the reckless pursuit of pleasure, money, and self-aggrandizement, and all the other ugly vices so visible in Western society need to be countered and rebuked by the heroic witness of dedicated Catholics who live and love the Faith. We should offer up our sacrifices and penances in reparation for the sins mankind has committed against the Good God who loves us so much.

*J. R. R. Tolkien once famously wrote to his son, "Out of the darkness of my life, so much frustrated, I put before you the one great thing to love on earth: the Blessed Sacrament. . . . There you will find romance, glory, honor, fidelity, and the true way of all your loves on earth." This intense devotion to Our Lord in the Blessed Sacrament by so many of the lay faithful is wounded and obstructed by the banal fashion in which so many of their pastors elect to celebrate the sacred mysteries. In fact, Bishop Athanasius Schneider has said that the deepest*

---

[2] Congregation for the Doctrine of the Faith, The Message of Fatima (2000), https://www.vatican.va/roman_curia/congregations/cfaith/documents/rc_con_cfaith_doc_20000626_message-fatima_en.html.

*wound in the Church today is the loss of reverence for Our Eucharistic Lord. What can the laity concretely do to heal this wound in the Church?*

The first thing is to pray for our priests and seminarians, asking God to give them a deep love for Christ in the Holy Eucharist. Pray especially that priests will renew at every Mass they celebrate the fervor with which they celebrated their first Mass. We must encourage priests we know to give themselves completely to God in the reverent celebration of the Mass, observing the spirit and the letter of the liturgical norms and the rubrics in the Roman Missal. When a layman attends a Mass celebrated poorly, or worse, celebrated with complete disregard for the rubrics, he should offer many prayers and sacrifices for that priest. If fraternal correction seems likely to be well-received, speak with the priest with Christlike charity. In the case of rebel priests who take pride in their destructive behavior, pray for them and, when possible, avoid their Masses. Sadly, writing to the bishop to raise objections to irreverence and disobedience, while it should be a welcome means of trying to help remedy liturgical chaos, is often not well-received and results in no episcopal action that effectively remedies a problem.

*In the Acts of the Apostles, St. Paul says that one day wolves would arise out of the episcopate and prey upon the flock (Acts 20:29–30). The Church teaches us that "the whole body of the faithful cannot err in matters of belief" (CCC 92). We saw how this* sensus fidei *at work in the Arian crisis created a rupture between clergy and laity, when the laity identified many of their shepherds as wolves in disguise. Today there also seems to be a collapse in confidence among the laity*

*in the moral integrity and actual belief of the clergy. How should the faithful express the* sensus fidei *in the face of this contemporary betrayal by our shepherds?*
Stay strong in faith, constant in prayer, and trust in God's providence. God will raise up more good shepherds to guide the flock. I firmly believe that most priests and bishops are faithful to Christ, his Church, and his doctrine. But some bishops want to change that doctrine and, in fact, endorse "strange teachings" (Heb 13:9). What we need today are strong shepherds who will actively defend the Faith of the Church against all enemies, especially those who misuse their authority in the Church to advance errors and immorality. Reminding our shepherds to be on the lookout for wolves, from wherever they may appear, is an act of charity because our love of God requires that we not sit by passively when spiritual harm is visited upon the flock of Christ. The vast majority of bishops and priests are heartened and strengthened by faithful lay men and women who reject the revolutionary ideas being trumpeted these days by reckless innovators.

*St. Catherine of Siena once said, "We've had enough exhortations to be silent. Cry out with a thousand tongues—I see the world is rotten because of silence." How can the lay faithful best rise up, overcome their fears, and make their voices heard in the face of often vitriolic opposition from dissenters?*
We must remind ourselves that the Faith we learned as children in catechism class—presuming it was true Catholic teaching—was true then and is true now. Anything that plainly contradicts the Faith handed down from the Apostles is to be rejected and scorned. Modern notions of progress do not apply to the doctrine of the Faith. "New and improved" teaching,

meaning anything that contradicts the perennial teaching of the Church, is not to be accepted. The modern dynamic of change and improvement in technical and material things does not apply to revealed truth. The truth does not change. The only improvement desired is that the truth be better enunciated and explained by the shepherds and better understood and believed in by all the faithful. St. Catherine's words remind us that we should always be firm and courageous in stating the truth of Christ, no matter how many times we are contradicted or accused of being mistaken. Vitriolic or untrue accusations should be noted and then ignored.

**Are the laity sometimes too tempted into activism, into the need to "do" something when, if they only became saints, they would achieve far more for the Church? Would you say the neglect of the interior life by the laity does far more harm to the Church than not taking practical action, however noble that might seem?**

Everyone in the Church is called to holiness. We all need to grow in interior life, meaning the union of our heart, mind, and will with God. This growth necessarily includes a serious life of prayer. The more we truly pray, the closer we come to God, who draws us by his grace. Lay men and women who strive for holiness *by that very striving* promote the mission of the Church. Each person has to decide what practical actions he wishes to take to respond to the crisis in the Church. But an activist spirit must be avoided, by which I mean a frenzied attempt to achieve visible results in this or that area of concern. This inevitably leads to disappointment, bitterness, and frustration when God's providence does not bend to our usually well-intentioned aims. We need to pray and act, and then leave the rest in the hands of God.

**In the old days, people used to refer to the Church on earth as the "Church Militant," but then after the Council we were told that this was too strident and un-ecumenical. Have we lost something by dropping this term?**

There is nothing wrong with the traditional descriptions of the Church on earth, in Purgatory, and in Heaven as being the Church Militant, the Church Suffering, and the Church Triumphant (*Ecclesia militans, dolens et triumphans*). On earth, the baptized are called to "fight the good fight of the faith" (1 Tim 6:12), ever watchful to resist "the devil [who] prowls around like a roaring lion, seeking someone to devour" (1 Pet 5:8). We are all soldiers of Christ. If we somehow believe that there will be no struggle in this world to remain faithful to Christ, then we are truly mistaken. The devil will try to influence us to reject Christ and ignore his doctrine. To live a life of faith and virtue requires a spirit of holy resistance to anything that would drag us down into unbelief and sin. We pray to St. Michael the Archangel to assist the Church in her struggle against the evil one.

**How can the clergy foster Church militancy among the laity and what form should that take?**

A young man volunteers to serve his country in the military because he loves his country. The same motive should prompt us to have the spirit of standing guard for the Church and defending her against those who attack her teaching and way of life. To do that, we need an educated laity. Again, I recommend that everyone over the age of sixteen should carefully read the entire *Catechism of the Catholic Church*. That is the best place to start. We should all be lifelong learners who constantly improve our knowledge and understanding of the teachings of Christ and his Church. Online instructional videos are very useful means of deepening our knowledge and love of the Faith. The *Aquinas 101* series of the Thomistic Institute is just one example of the many educational materials that are available and understandable.

***Many of the faithful today are highly demoralized and feel that the structures of government in the hierarchy have been captured by non-believers and wicked men addicted to unnatural vice. They don't know whom to trust or what to do about those who've shown themselves to be untrustworthy and are leading souls astray. Then there are priests and lay faithful who are a threat to the Faith and to the Church. Should we go to war against these figures—metaphorically speaking—to defeat them?***

The revelations of the criminal sexual immorality and abuse of sacred authority by Theodore McCarrick, the former cardinal who assaulted minors and seminarians, teach us an important lesson: there are Judases present among the successors of the Apostles. These men accept the sacred office of bishop and then use it to satisfy their unnatural lustful desires with victims they took criminal advantage of because of their authority as a priest or bishop. The popular outcry against McCarrick and other morally reprobate bishops helped prompt the Holy See to finally take action. The pervasive cover-ups and lies about criminal priests and bishops reveal that a false notion of what was best for the Church, the victims, and even the perpetrators themselves, caused—in fact—tremendous harm. The Holy See needs to do much more to root out clerical immorality and episcopal protection schemes. The case of the Argentine Bishop Gustavo Zanchetta, under criminal investigation for the sexual abuse of two seminarians, yet given a job in the Holy See while that investigation was underway, remains a stunning example of how the Holy See still fails to do what needs to be done to confront evil and regain the trust of the faithful. Thankfully, there are reliable reports that Zanchetta is no longer working at the Holy See. And he will soon face trial in Argentina.

***The Prussian general and military theorist Carl von Clausewitz famously wrote, "In tactics, the means are the fighting forces . . . the end is victory." Should the faithful have more of a "fight to win" attitude—of course I mean in the spiritual sense—in which the faithful combatants are willing to make any sacrifice to obtain a complete victory with the help of the Holy Spirit?***

In the life of the Church, the only real victory is the victory over sin and death, meaning the salvation of souls, which is known in Heaven but concealed, apart from canonized saints, from our eyes. We must do all we can to promote our own salvation and that of everyone else. Our fight is "against the principalities, against the powers" (Eph 6:12). We need to become accustomed to making many sacrifices to promote the salvation of souls. But we need to be mindful that while we work, we must not have the expectation that God will reveal to us all the good we have done for souls in this life. That will come in the next world for those who hear the saving invitation: "Come, O blessed of my

Father, inherit the kingdom prepared for you from the foundation of the world" (Matt 25:34).

**What would you say to those faithful who see this almost like a David and Goliath moment, where the laity seem so insignificant in the face of the array of forces lined up against the Church?**

We are all servants of the Lord who make a difference by simply being who we are. Fr. John Hardon, S.J., once said that we should not underestimate the good we do simply by living as practicing Catholics. The nature and extent of each person's influence will depend on the circumstances in which divine providence places him. Msgr. Fernando Felices of the Archdiocese of San Juan, Puerto Rico, once told me that we are all instruments in the hand of the Lord, but some instruments are more useful than others. We make ourselves more useful by cooperating with God's grace and living according to his law—day in, day out. Our faithful witness to Christ and his Church is truly powerful.

**In these times, it would seem as if the Church's influence over the world, her credibility in the eyes of the world, and the conformity of the world to the natural moral law have reached levels lower than any time since the last of the great Roman persecutions (303–313). Over a century and a half ago, Cardinal Newman said: "Commonly the Church has nothing more to do than to go on in her own proper duties, in confidence and peace; to stand still and to see the salvation of God." Is his confidence justified in the current crisis?**

Cardinal Newman's observation retains its force in our own day even when some Churchmen neglect or even rebel against fulfilling their proper duties. Our confidence has its source in the hope we place in God's goodness and love. Our peace is found in our union with God, which is not a form of escapism from problems but rather the height of realism, recognizing that this world and its troubles are passing while "the Lord is my rock, and my fortress, and my deliverer" (Ps 18:2).

**Do you believe the Church will become smaller in the coming years?**
Yes and no. The decline in belief and practice among Catholics in the Western world will undoubtedly continue as it has for my entire lifetime. This is an immense sadness and cause for lamentation. It is also an indictment of the failed effort to make Christianity more acceptable to that mythical creature called "modern man." Men of every age, now or in the past, are not inspired by a religion that makes few demands and seems to be always in the process of changing and adapting to the expectations of a world that has no interest in seeing Christianity survive, let alone prosper. Yet the growth of the Church in Africa and Asia, its continued strength in places such as Mexico and the Philippines, are signs of hope. Wealth is a blessing, but it poses serious perils if not subordinated to God's purposes. The love of wealth is spiritually blinding. We all need to be reminded that when we die, we will all be held accountable by God for how we lived our lives and what we did with the blessings he bestowed upon us.

***If you had one piece of advice for mothers and fathers in raising their children in these troubled times, what would it be?***
Show your children that you love each other and that you love God above all things. Children learn first by seeing what adults do and then later connect that with what they say. It is easier to believe that God is good if children have an experience of goodness from those who say they believe in God and follow his law.

***Many young people today ironically seem to be the main harbingers of tradition, in contrast to the older generations, many of whom seem stuck in the failed progressive ideologies of the 1960s, 1970s, and 1980s. How can young people best mobilize themselves and their peers to resist the widespread apostasy and turning away from God?***
Young people today have an especially stark choice: to immerse themselves in an anti-Christian culture that treats life as one big game of "king of the hill," in which everyone competes to have the most stuff and be the most envied, or to take life seriously and connect with God the Creator and Redeemer in pursuit of the joy that comes from knowing the living God. It is a choice between a worldly life of selfish preoccupation and a godly life of self-giving to God and our fellow man.

***To whom should the laity look for guidance and hope? Who are our mentors today? Where are the G. K. Chestertons, Cardinal Newmans, Ronald Knoxes, Malcolm Muggeridges, Mother Angelicas, Dorothy Days, Flannery O'Connors, Archbishop Sheens, St. Thomas Mores, Blessed Pier Giorgio Frassatis, and Gianna Beretta Mollas?***

The internet has made it fairly easy to find a galaxy of Catholic writers, speakers, teachers, journalists, priests, bishops, men and women religious, dedicated lay men and women who are actively promoting the mission of the Church in fidelity to the doctrine of the Faith and her rich heritage of prayer, asceticism and works of charity. I will name just a few of the figures who I find most informative and inspiring: Cardinal Sarah, Cardinal Raymond Burke, Cardinal Müller, Archbishop Charles Chaput, Bishop Athanasius Schneider, Roberto de Mattei, Scott Hahn, John Bergsma, Brant Pitre, Edward Feser, Mary Ann Glendon, Janet Smith, Fr. Roger Landry, Alice von Hildebrand, Sandro Magister, Robert Royal, Raymond Arroyo, Bill Donohue, R. R. Reno, and George Weigel. The new and old religious orders of women who engage in Catholic education and works of charity are very inspiring. And so are the many dedicated diocesan and religious priests I know who faithfully carry out their assignments with love and dedication.

*Of course, true hope rests with Christ. Father, you've spoken in our discussion about the loss of faith in the Real Presence among the laity. It is said that St. Philip Neri once noticed a woman leaving Church immediately after receiving Communion and dispatched two acolytes to accompany her for ten minutes while the Real Presence persisted. The Church Fathers saw the miracle of the calming of the storm as an allegory of the presence of Christ within the soul. How much of a difference do you think it would make if priests taught and reminded the faithful of Whom it is they bear within them spiritually at all times, please God, but even physically in those precious moments after Communion?*

I remember being taught as a child that it takes about ten minutes for the Sacred Host to be fully digested. During those minutes those who have received Holy Communion are truly living tabernacles. What a wondrous truth! We who carry Christ's Body within ourselves should strive to live as worthy vessels of God's gift of himself, both for those ten minutes and for the rest of the day. I highly recommend the practice of making a thanksgiving after Mass. Speaking to Jesus who has come into us reminds us of how blessed we are to be nourished by the Bread of eternal life, Christ's Body sacramentally present in the Holy Eucharist. The loss of belief in the Real Presence of Christ in the Holy Eucharist is a tragic fruit of worldliness and doctrinal confusion. The remedy will come through a combination of prayer, good preaching and teaching by priests and bishops, penance, the reverent celebration of the Holy Mass, and above all a revival of true love for Our Lord who remains with us and has not left us orphans. God is with us in the Mass and in the tabernacle. Do we take that fact seriously? We should.

**How can the hearts of men be awakened so that they can seek solace only and always in the Heart of Christ?**
A glance at the crucifix reminds us that the God who made man suffered death at the hands of men, yet that death was his freely offered gift of love, which was revealed as his triumph over sin and death when Christ Our God rose gloriously from the tomb on the third day. Love means death and life: death to sin and life with God. Love is our vocation and the only worthy action plan for our journey through this world towards the next. The Sacred Heart of Jesus, pierced for love of mankind, invites us to be united to him in the absolute certainty that he will lead

us through the sorrows and joys of this life into the green pastures of eternal beatitude, where the storms of this world have forever ceased.

St. Augustine is the theologian whose writings are a sure guide to understanding the unfolding of God's plan of salvation for our world through his Church. Though she be wracked by the storms of sin and error, Christ is there to save us when we fear that we may perish. He calms the storm in our hearts when we cry out to him, and blesses us with God's peace, here and hereafter. He does not abandon us: "I am with you always, to the close of the age" (Matt 28:20).

☙

## "Awaken Christ in your Heart"[3]
### Sermon 13 on Matthew 8:23–27
### St. Augustine

Were not Jesus asleep within you, you would not be exposed to all these storms; but interior peace and perfect calm would be your happy lot, through Jesus watching with you. For what is the meaning of Jesus asleep? Your faith in Jesus has fallen asleep. The tempests of the sea arise; you see evil men flourishing, good and just men in trouble and misery; your faith is shaken and tossed about as by furious waves. And in this temptation your soul says, "Is this thy justice, O God, that the wicked should flourish, whilst the just are in trouble and misery?" You say to God, "Is this thy justice?" And God says to you, "Is this your

---

[3] D. G. Hubert (ed), *Sundays and Festivals with the Fathers of the Church* (R & T Washbourne: London, 1901), 71–72.

faith? Have I promised you the perishable things of the world? Have I called you to be My followers, i.e., Christians, that you should flourish in this life? Are you grieving because you see the wicked enjoying all earthly pleasures, who shall hereafter be tormented with the devil?" But why all these complaints? Why are you disturbed by the waves of the sea and the storm? Because Jesus is asleep; i.e., because your faith in Jesus has been laid asleep in your hearts. How will you be delivered from this great danger? Awaken Jesus, and say to him, "Lord, save us, we perish; the waves of temptation rise against us and threaten our souls with impending death." And Jesus will awake, that is, your faith will return to you. And with his help you will recognize that the happiness the wicked enjoy will not abide with them. For, either it will be taken from them while they live, or they will be forced to leave it when they die. But the happiness promised to you will abide for ever and ever. What is granted to the wicked for a time, will soon be taken away; for they flourish like the flower of the grass: "All flesh is as grass; the grass is withered, and the flower thereof is fallen away; but the word of the Lord endureth for ever" (1 Pet 1:24–25).

Turn, therefore, your back upon that which falls and is perishable, and your face to that which abides to the end. Now that Jesus is awake, the storm shall no more shake your hearts, the waves shall not fill your barque. Your faith commands the winds and the waves, and the danger shall pass away, when a great calm will follow the storm.